FORTY-SIX SELECT SCRIPTURE NARRATIVES FROM THE OLD TESTAMENT

By Johann Hübner

PART 1

translated into Delaware Indian by Abraham Luckenbach,

Edited with an English word-for-word translation
by Raymond Whritenour

Copyright © 2020 by Raymond Whritenour

All rights reserved. No part of this book may be used or reproduced in any manner whatsoever including Internet usage, without written permission of the author.

Book design by gopublished.com

ISBN: 978-0-9990100-9-9

[iii] **NEWINACHKE WOAK GUTTASCH PIPINASIKI GISCHEKHASIKI ELEKPANNI WENDENASIKI UNTSCHI MECHOWEKI NACHGUNDO-WOAGANI BAMBIL.**

FORTY AND SIX SELECTED SCRIPTURAL THINGS-WHICH-WERE-SO WHICH-ARE-TAKEN-FROM FROM THAT-WHICH-IS-OLD OF-THE-COVENANT THE-BOOK.

GISCHITASIK ELLENIECHSINK UNTSCHI

A. LUCKENBACH

THAT-WHICH-IS-MADE DELAWARE BY A. LUCKENBACH

"Weuhokeyit, tacu wundauchsii achpoan schuk, wulahah wtelli wundauchsin endchink aptonaganall Gettanettowit wtonink wuntschi ktschihillak."—Mat. 4: 4.

"An-embodied-one not he-does-not-live-by bread only, better he-thus lives-by as-many-as-there-are words the-Great-Spirit from-His-mouth from they-flow-out."—Matthew 4: 4.

PREFACE

The Moravian missionary, Abraham Luckenbach, began the bulk of his translations into the Delaware Indian language after retiring from active service in 1833. This particular work was printed and published in 1838. There is, so far as I know, no manuscript of this work now in existence; thus, my transcription of the text herein has been copied directly from the printed pages of the book, a copy of which I procured on the rare book market. Photocopied pages of it were also provided to me by Todd Thompson and Jim Rementer.

This work is a Delaware translation of forty-six, out of the fifty-two Old Testament narratives in Johann Hübner's <u>Zweymal zwey und fünfzig auserlesene Biblische Historien aus dem Alten und Neuen Testamente</u> ("Twice two and fifty select Biblical Histories from the Old and New Testaments"), published at Leipzig in 1714. An American edition, in German, was published at Harrisburg, Pennsylvania in 1826. It is this latter edition from which I transcribed the German text for this book; and, it seems probable that this is the edition from which Luckenbach made his translations. The 1826 publication is profusely illustrated with Biblical scenes and may have been where Luckenbach got the idea to illustrate his Delaware book; though he used a set of woodcuts which are not the same as the illustrations in the 1826 book. Hübner's original book is not illustrated and I have decided not to use any pictures in this edition either, since it would unnecessarily increase the physical size and, thereby, the costs associated with printing and pricing. In any case, the illustrations I've seen appear quite anachronistic for the time periods of the events depicted.

For my primary market (such as it is), it would have been desirable to use an English translation of Hübner's German; however, although there was an English edition published at Philadelphia in 1838, it often did not translate Hübner's "Practical Application" and "Pious Reflection" commentarial sections, but employed its own new versions. Luckenbach clearly translated Hübner's German text, so using the English was out of the question. English readers will have to be satisfied with my word-for-word English translation of the Delaware text.

Each chapter of Hübner's text is divided into four parts: "Biblical Narrative," "Distinct Questions," Practical Application," and "Pious Reflection." Luckenbach translates into Delaware all of these except "Distinct Questions"—a kind of running catechism on every page of Hübner's histories.

This is the first volume of three planned to complete this title. It consists of the first twenty chapters of the forty-six included in Luckenbach's book. As with other translations of the United Brethren into Delaware, paraphrase of the original German text is employed throughout. In places, the translator inserts more detail—sometimes, of great length--into the narratives than is found in the corresponding German. For all chapters recounting stories from the Pentateuch (as in this volume), the majority of these deviations from Hübner's work are direct copies of Denke's Delaware translations of Risler's Old Testament excerpts. In some cases, he changes Denke's wording a very little bit, but it's clear that he had Denke's manuscript in front of him during the writing of his own translation of the Pentateuch stories. Occasionally, short digressions from the German text are Luckenbach's own. Of course, the Practical Application and Pious Reflection sections always adhere to Hübner's work; however, the latter section, which is wriitten in rhyming verse by the German author, is rendered in prose by the Delaware translator.

The narrative texts herein are arranged, top to bottom, in German, Delaware and English, in italics, bold type and plain type, respectively. Ideally, each section of the Delaware is no less than three lines and no

PREFACE

more than five lines of text. In rare instances, two lines or six lines must be used. Exceeding these limits would make it very difficult for the reader to match the Delaware words with the corresponding English words. The Delaware text indicates each page of Luckenbach's 1838 book inside brackets, preceding the first word on every page, like this: [84]. The corresponding place in the English section is shown inside brackets, like this: **[84]**, just to help the reader keep his or her place in the narrative.

English word-for-word translations found inside braces, like this: {they-wrestle-with-each-other}, are renderings of Delaware words not found anywhere else in the Moravian corpus of Delaware vocabularies or printed books, to date. Many are not found in any other Delaware works, either—whether Southern Unami or Munsee. However, their meanings are relatively simple to ascertain by their semantic elements, and/or by their German equivalents when those are present. When a translation inside braces is preceded by a question mark, like this: {?do-not-let-him-exasperate-you), that translation is nothing more than guesswork. (There are very few of these, thankfully.)

A Delaware word followed by another word in brackets, like this: **hokey** [?**hokeyall**], almost always indicates that I think Luckenbach's word is incorrect and the bracketed word is correct. If I'm fairly sure this is the case, then I place Luckenbach's word inside the brackets and my replacement in the text, like this: **gotta [L., gatta]**. In both cases, I often bracket only that part of a word I think is incorrect or am fairly sure it is incorrect, like this: **genachgiechgussin [?-gussit]** and this: **endalauchsitschil [L., enda lauch-]**.

A list of "new" words can be found in the Appendix.

As always, throughout my translation work, I frequently consult the huge database of Mission Delaware dictionaries, vocabularies, grammars and narrative texts, as well as the Southern Unami online Lenape Talking Dictionary (www.talk-lenape.org) put together by Jim

FORTY-SIX SELECT SCRIPTURE NARRATIVES FROM THE OLD TESTAMENT

Rementer; the Munsee <u>Delaware-English / English-Delaware Dictionary</u> compiled by John O'Meara; <u>Delaware Verbal Morphology</u>, by Ives Goddard; and, to a lesser extent other works by these experts and a few others.

Luckenbach also translated all fifty-two of Hübner's New Testament histories. He planned to have that printed and published as a companion volume to this one, but it was never done. The manuscript is housed at the Moravian Archives, Bethlehem, Pennsylvania. I have made a transcription and rough draft English translation of it and plan to publish it, too, in book form, someday, God willing.

Ray Whritenour
Butler, NJ 1/15/20

CONTENTS

Address to the Delaware Christian Indians. 1

A PRAYER BEFORE READING THE SCRIPTURE.. 13
Papatamoewoagan eweget auwen geta achkindank Patamawos wtaptonagan.
A-prayer that-which-one-uses who wants-to one-(who-wants-to)-read-it God His-word.

A PRAYER AFTER READING THE SCRIPTURE.. 17
Papatamoewoagan ewegenk gischachkindasike Patamawos wtaptonagan.
A-prayer that-which-someone-uses when-it-is-finished-being-read God His-word.

OF THE CREATION OF HEAVEN AND EARTH. 21
1. ELEGUP.—Patamawos enda gischelendank wemi elgigunk Pemhagamikgek woak Pemapanek. 1. Mos. 1 Cap.
1. THAT-WHICH-WAS-SO.—God when He-creates-them-by-thought all as-wide-as the-world-round-about and the-sky. Genesis 1st Chapter.

CREATION OF MAN AND WOMAN. 27
2. ELEGUP.—Patamawos enda gischihatup Lennowall woak Ochquewall. 1 Mos. 1 & 2 Cap.
2. THAT-WHICH-WAS-SO.—God when He-made-them man and woman. Genesis 1st & 2nd Chapters.

GARDEN OF EDEN 33
3. ELEGUP.—Netami Gischelemindpanik elsichtitup sekachpichtitup talli Paradiesink. 1 Mos. 2 & 3 Cap.
3. THAT-WHICH-WAS-SO.—First those-who-were-(first)-created what-they-did so-long-as-they-were-there in in-Paradise. Genesis 2nd & 3rd Chapters.

MAN'S FALL 41
4. ELEGUP.—Enda hakink lihillachtitup netami Gegeyjumenaninkachge. 1 Mos. 2 & 3 Cap.
4. THAT-WHICH-WAS-SO.—When to-Earth they-fell first our-late-(first)-elders. Genesis 2nd & 3rd Chapters.

CAIN AND ABEL 55
5. ELEGUP.—Kaina enda nhillat Chessemusall Abellal. 1 Mos. 4 Cap.
5. THAT-WHICH-WAS-SO.—The-late-Cain when he-kills-him his-younger-sibling Abel. Genesis 4th Chapter.

OF THE FLOOD 63
6. ELEGUP.—Enda psindpek Haki. 1 Mos. 6, 7, 8 & 9 Cap.
6. THAT-WHICH-WAS-SO.—When it-floods-the-Earth. Genesis 6th, 7th, 8th & 9th Chapters.

TOWER OF BABEL 73
7. ELEGUP.—Enda hokunk likhechtit Quenaqua talli enda luwundasik Babel. 1 Mos. 11 Cap.
7. THAT-WHICH-WAS-SO.—When on-high they-built-it-so a-tower there where it-is-called Babel. Genesis 11th Chapter.

ABRAHAM AND SARAH 79
8. ELEGUP.—Abrahama woak wikimatschil Sarah enda lauchsichtitup. 1 Mos. 18 Cap.
8. THAT-WHICH-WAS-SO.—The-late-Abraham and his-spouse Sarah when they-lived. Genesis 18th Chapter.

CONTENTS

SODOM AND GOMORRAH. 87
9. ELEGUP.—Sodomink woak Gomorrahink talli. 1 Mos. 19 Cap.
9. THAT-WHICH-WAS-SO.—In-Sodom and in-Gomorrah in. Genesis 19th Chapter.

ABRAHAM OFFERETH ISAAC. 97
10. ELEGUP.—Isaac enda gachta wihundinke. 1 Mos. 22 Cap.
10. THAT-WHICH-WAS-SO.—Isaac when wants-to when-someone-(wants-to)-sacrifice. Genesis 22nd Chapter.

MARRIAGE OF ISAAC. 105
11. ELEGUP.—Isaac enda wikingetup. 1 Mos. 24 Cap.
11. THAT-WHICH-WAS-SO.—Isaac when he-married. Genesis 24th Chapter.

[vi] *ISAAC BLESSETH JACOB*. 113
12. ELEGUP.—Isaac enda mamtschitsch wulapensohalat wunitschanall. 1 Mos. 27 Cap.
12. THAT-WHICH-WAS-SO.—Isaac when lastly he-blesses-him his-child. Genesis 27th Chapter.

JACOB'S VISION. 125
13. ELEGUP.—Jacob enda lonquongup. 1 Mos. 27 & 28 Cap.
13. THAT-WHICH-WAS-SO.—Jacob when he-dreamed-about-something. Genesis 27th & 28th Chapters.

JACOB'S MARRIAGE. 133
14. ELEGUP.—Jacob enda wikingete. 1 Mos. 29 Cap.
14. THAT-WHICH-WAS-SO.—Jacob when he-marries. Genesis 29th Chapter.

JACOB WRESTLETH WITH GOD. 143
15. ELEGUP.—Enda achquepenalguk Patamawossall. 1 Mos. 32 & 33 Cap.
15. THAT-WHICH-WAS-SO.—When {he-wrestles-Him} God. Genesis 32nd & 33rd Chapters.

JOSEPH'S BRETHREN SELL HIM 153
16. ELEGUP.—Joseph wimachtall enda mhallamundup Chessemusall Josephall. 1 Mos. 35 & 37 Cap.
16. THAT-WHICH-WAS-SO.—Joseph his-brothers when he-is-bought their-younger-sibling Joseph. Genesis 35th & 37th Chapters.

JOSEPH'S CHASTITY AND IMPRISONMENT. 165
17. ELEGUP.—Joseph enda wachtschangussitup woak kpahasitup talli Egyptenink. 1 Mos. 39 Cap.
17. THAT-WHICH-WAS-SO.—Joseph when he-was-enslaved and he-was-imprisoned in in-Egypt. Genesis 39th Chapter.

JOSEPH DELIVERED FROM IMPRISONMENT 175
18. ELEGUP.—Joseph enda ktinnind untschi enda kpahasitup talli enda kpahotink. 1 Mos. 40 Cap.
18. THAT-WHICH-WAS-SO.—Joseph when he-is-taken-out from where he-was-imprisoned there where people-are-imprisoned. Genesis 40th Chapter.

JOSEPH'S BRETHREN GO TO EGYPT TO BUY CORN 191
19. ELEGUP.—Joseph wimachtall enda peltichtit Egyptenink eli mawottaganik. 1 Mos. 42 & 43 Cap.
19. THAT-WHICH-WAS-SO.—Joseph his-brothers when all-of-them-come to-Egypt because there-is-a-famine. Genesis 42nd & 43rd Chapters.

JOSEPH MAKETH HIMSELF KNOWN TO HIS BRETHREN 207
20. ELEGUP.—Joseph enda woatelat hokey [?hokeyall] necama majawi wtelli wimachtin. 1 Mos. 44 & 45 Cap.
20. THAT-WHICH-WAS-SO.—Joseph when he-makes-it-known-to-them himself he rightly that-he is-a-brother. Genesis 44th & 45th Chapters.

[ix]

Address to the Delaware Christian Indians.

My beloved Indians,

[xii] **Ehoalek welsittamek weimachtumellek Elenapewijek!**

You-whom-I-love you-who-believe you-who-are-my-brethren you-who-are-Delaware-Indians!

I herewith present to all of you who are desirous of acquiring a more thorough knowledge of, and acquaintance with, the sacred Oracles of God,

Wemi endchijek eli gachtatamek allowi achgegimgussijek untschi Patamawos eluwilek geschiechek wtaptonaganink, woak gachta allowi nostamek woak pendamek nel neckachtingil Patamawos wtaptonaganall, jun sche, gelelendelelenewo,

All as-many-as-you-are because you-desire-it more you-are-taught concerning God that-which-is-most-true that-which-is-holy of-His-word, and want-to more you-(want-to)-understand-them and you-(want-to)-hear-them those those-things-which-are-left-behind God His-words, here look-here!, {I-present-it-to-you},

a translation into your own language, of a number of Scripture Narratives, selected from the sacred volumes of the Old and New Testaments.

eli gischekhigeja kiluwa eliechsijek, kitschi cheltol kitschijeyjuwiki pipinasiki elekhasikil elekpanni, untschi mechoweki woak weskingi eluwi geschiechek Bambilink elewundasik Bible.

as I-am-done-writing-it you how-you-speak, truly they-are-many great-things those-which-are-chosen those-which-are-written those-which-were-so, from of-the-old and of-the-new most holy books-from that-which-is-called the-Bible.

I flatter myself with the thought, that the possession of such a treasure will be an encouragement to you and your children hereafter, to apply yourselves more ardently to the exercise of reading and meditating upon

Bischi nuwingi woak nhageuchsuwi ktitehalelohumo, untschi eli wulitolekup jun Bambil, ktellitsch untschi liechgussinewo nahelii ktamemensemowawak ahanhuqui gischigitschik, wentschitsch wingi achkinsijek woak penauwelendamek

To-be-sure I-gladly and hopefully I-cause-you-to-think, of how I-made-it-for-you this book, that-you-will by you-(will)-be-done-to-thusly together-with your-children over-and-over-again those-who-are-born, so-that-will gladly you-read and you-consider,

those great truths and events, which, from the beginning of the world, have been exhibited and revealed by the great Ruler of the Universe to the children of men.

wemi nel elekpanni eki nutschi hattekup Pemhagamigek woak wemi nel ganschilewall [L., ganschi lewall], Patamawos na eluwilissit Gegeyjumhet hokunk epit, eli penundelat woak weit-schiechtauwatup nel wtamemensemall ju endalauchsitschil [L., enda lauch-].

all those things-which-were-so beginning in-the-beginning those-things-which-were-here the-world-round-about and all those wonders, God That Holy-One the-Ruler on-high where-He-is, as He-shows-them and He-demonstrated-it-to-them those His-children here those-who-live-here.

This book will give you a summary historical account of the creation of the world, the fall of man,

Untschi jul neckachtingil elekhasikil ktelli kschiechi woatelukgenewo

nel elekpanni elekhasikup enda gischelendasikup Pemhagamigek, woak nek netami gischihendpanik elinamichtitup enda machtechinhittit mattauchsowoaganink;

From these things-which-are-left-behind those-which-are-written you-thus clearly you-are-made-aware-of-them those as-they-were those-things-which-were-written when it-was-created-by-thought the-world-round-about, and those first those-who-were-(first)-made how-they-were-treated when they-drop into-sin;

the flood, the lives of the Patriarchs, God's particular dealings with the children of Israel, as his covenant people,

woak wtenk untschi elekup enda psindpekup haki, woak [xiii] ikalissi wtenk untschi elsichtitup nek pipinundtschik welsittankpaninkachge Abrahama, Isaaca woak Jacoba, nahelii nekik untschi hokewawunk ahanhoqui gischigitschik, eluwihillendtschik, Israelii Amemensak, Patamawos elgiqui natschihat woak sachgagunatup ne talli.

and after wards how-it-was when it-flooded the-Earth, and **[xiii]** further after wards what-they-did those those-who-are-chosen those-late-deceased-believers the-late-Abraham, the-late-Isaac and the-late-Jacob, together-with those from from-themselves over-and-over-again those-who-are-born, those-who-are-named, of-Israel the-children, God like-as He-tends-them and He-led-them that in.

including an era of 4,000 years before Christ.

Wemi elekhasikil elekpanni eki nutschiechingup Pemhagamigek, tek ika petschi enda pat, petschi wtachquonk Jesus Christ, nane achkindasik newen tellen tchapachki tchi gachtinewi.

All those-things-which-are-written as-they-were beginning that-which-began the-world-round-about, {there} there until when he-comes, hither he-visits-us Jesus Christ, that it-is-counted four-times ten so-many-hundred so-many of-years.

When you peruse the contents of the New Testament, you will perceive, that all what is recorded there, is an exact fulfillment of that, which God had spoken and promised in the [x] Old Testament dispensation.

Nane petachkinsijeke enda luwundasik weskink nachgundowoaganii Bambil, schitta New Testament, nane talli kmochgamenewo kitschii wemi pachgantschi leep, endchi mechoweki Bambilink elekhasikup, Patamawos nigani woatelatup wtamemensumall, junitsch leu.

That when-you-read-here where it-is-called that-which-is-new of-the-covenant the-book, or New Testament, that in you-find-it truly all wholly it-was-so, as-much-as of-the-old book-of that-which-was-written, God beforehand He-made-them-aware-of-it His-children, this-will it-be-so.

You will find there, that God did send his Son to be the propitiation for our sins, "that he is the Lamb of God which taketh away the sins of the world,"

Nane ktenda nemenewo wulamoewoagan kitschi leu, Patamawos metschi wtelli gintschtschinan ehoalatschi Quisall, jun talli Pemhagamigek, wentschitsch wuliechtaquonk kmattauchsowoaganena, nan eluwihillind Tegauwontowit eli nejundankup wemi elgigunk Pemhagamigek mattauchsowoaganall.

Then when-you you-see-it the-truth truly it-is-so, God already that-He dispatches-him him-whom-He-loves His-son, here in the-world-round-about, so-that-will he-amend-it-for-us our-sin, that-one who-is-named the-Gentle-Spirit because he-carried-them-on-his-back all as-wide-as the-world-round-about the-sins.

and that "the grace of God which bringeth salvation, hath appeared unto all men,

Ktenda nemeneen kitschii leu Patamawos ogoktomagelowoagan wentapensohalgejank woak petenumaquonk kikemhalgussowoagan weitschiechtund wemi ju endalauchsitschil [L., enda lauchsitschil],

Then-we we-see-it truly it-is-so God His-grace we-are-made-useful-by and it-brings-it-unto-us salvation he-is-made-clear every here one-who-lives-here,

teaching us, that denying ungodliness, and worldly lusts,

nane guntschi wulamoechgeneen, wentschitsch wingi ponelendamank wemi pallistamuwi machtapei lauchsowoagan, woak wemi pemwingelendamuwi mattauchsowoagan Pemhaga-migek wentschijeyik;

that we-thereby we-are-convinced-of-the-truth, so-that-will gladly we-(will)-give-it-up every disbelieving impious way-of-life, and all {wicked-pleasurable} sin the-world-round-about that-which-is-of;

we should live soberly, righteously and godly in this present world,"

woak ktelliechgeneen wentschitsch pilsuwi, schachachgapei woak patamoei lauchsijank ta segauchsijank Pemhagamigek talli.

and we-are-done-to so-that-will purely, righteously and godly we-(will)-live-so definitely so-long-as-we-live the-world-round-about in.

"and that these things were written, that we might believe that Jesus is the Christ, the Son of God, and that believing we might have life through his name." John, 20, 31.

Woak ikalissi guntschi penundelukgeneen leu, wemi "jul elekhasikil nane untschi kiluna gischekhasowall, [xiv] **wentschitsch kepena woak witschi wulistamank Jesus wtelli Christin Wequisemukuk Getanittowitschi, woak ktelli nhagalaneen, wentschitsch meschinemank hallemi pomauchsowoagan wtellewunsowoaganink." John, 20: 31.**

And further we-thereby we-are-shown it-is-so, all "these things-which-are-written that for us they-are-finished-being-written, **[xiv]** so-that-will we-likewise also with we-believe-(with)-it Jesus that-he is-the-Christ him-whom-He-has-for-a-Son the-Great-Spirit, and that-we we-trust-(in)-him, so-that-will we-receive-it eternal life by-his-name." John 20: 31.

The Bible is not only true, but is expressly declared, that "all Scripture is given by inspiration of God." 2 Tim. 3, 16. "Holy men of god spake as they were moved by the Holy Ghost." 2 Pet. 1: 21.

Matta schuk wulamoewoaganall wemendchekhasikil talli Bibleink, ulaha kitschi laptonewak, ktelguna Patamawos wtallogaganak, wemi miltinall Patamawos wtaptonaganall, untschi Welsitschi Mtschitschangunk. 2 Tim. 3: 16. Nekik geschiechauchsitpanik aptonepanik eli penundelukhittit Welsitschi Mtschitschanquall. 2 Pet. 1: 21.

Not only the-truths all-as-many-as-those-which-are-written in in-the-Bible, better truly they-speak-thusly, they-tell-us God His-servants, all they-are-given God His-words, by-the-Holy Spirit-by. 2 Timothy 3: 16. Those those-who-lived-holy they-spoke as He-shows-them the-Holy Spirit. 2 Peter 1: 21.

The Bible, with the help of the Holy Spirit, affords a sure direction to God, to heaven, to everlasting bliss; from its contents we are made acquainted with its divine author.

Welsit Mtschitschanquall nhagalat, auwen pendank schitta achkindank elekhasik talli Bibleink, nan kitschii lohumauwan elhagechink Patamawosink, awossagamewunk, woak hallemi Pomauchsowoaganink. Jun aptonagan elekhasik talli Bibleink, guntschi nauwaneen Wetaptonaganit Patamawos.

The-Holy Spirit one-who-trusts-(in)-Him, someone who-hears or who-reads that-which-is-written in in-the-Bible, That-One truly He-shows-it-to-him how-lies-the-way to-God, to-Heaven, and eternal life-to. This word that-which-is-written in in-the-Bible, we-thereby we-recognize-Him He-Who-is-the-Word God.

But in order to dispose you to the making of a sanctified use of this inestimable gift, which you will consider as an addition to those privileges already conferred upon you, as members of the Christian community—

Schuk Ehoalachgik wentschi a witahemellek ktelli lapendamenewo jun juke eli meschinemek eluwilek geschiechek Bambil, bischi metschi wulelemuxinewo enda witapensohalgussijek Patamawos wtamemensemall enda lapendamichtit wtaptonaganall, woak juke eliechgejek allowi gulutagenewo ne welhik miltowoagan;

But beloved-ones so-that could I-help-you that-you you-find-it-useful this now as you-receive-it the-most-true holy book, to-be-sure already you-are-wonderful when you-are-made-to-have-a-benefit- with God His-children when they-find-it-useful His-words, and now as-you-are-done-to-thusly more {?you-use-it-well} that good gift;

give me leave to entreat you to be cautious in letting it lay idle in your possession, or to "bury the talent in the earth"

ihiabtschi lelemik wentschitsch gihimellek, ktelli a wingi achkinsinewo woak penauwelendamenewo, wemi endchaptonachgattol elekhasikil ika talli. Katschi schuk nutschque ktakolsiwunewo, elsitup milindup talli "ngutti pund elawachtik welhik nane mauwi wtagolsinep talli hakink."

still allow-me so-that-will I-exhort-you, that-you should gladly you-(should)-read and you-(should)-consider-it, all as-much-as-they-mean those-things-which-are-written there in. Don't only for-nothing do-not-put-them-away-for-safe-keeping, as-he-did who-was-given-it there "one pound that-which-is-worth that-which-is-good then went- and he-(went-and)-stored-it in in-the-ground."

without reaping that benefit therefrom, for which it was put into your hands; for this would certainly increase your accountability and enhance your misery at the day of retribution.

Jun a lissite auwen untschi jun eluwelendasik Patamawos [xv]

wtaptonaganink eli juke latschessowet unachgink, woak schuk machtauwegete, schachachgitsch allowi guschaptonalgussutsch talli mekeniechink ntutemawachtowoaganii gischquike, eli nutschque mescheninkup gantschi [?ganschi] welhik Patamawos wentschijeyik.

This would if-he-(would)-do-so a-person concerning this that-which-is-called God **[xv]** His-word-concerning as now he-possesses in-his-hands, and only if-he-misuses-it, surely-will more he-will-be-chastised in that-which-is-the-end of-examination when-it-is-the-day, because for-nothing he-received-it amazingly that-which-is-good God that-which-is-from.

Permit me, therefore herewith to urge you to a diligent reading, studying, and meditating upon the contents of this book, with a single eye to the glory of God, and the salvation of your immortal souls.

Nane wentschi lelemik ikalissi guntschitamellek Ehoalachgik: papatamoei achkinsik woak penauwelendamook gachta wemi aptonaganall nekachtingil elekhasikil, wentschitsch m'chelemind woak nhagalind Patamawos woak pommauchsichtit ktemaki ktschitschanguwawak.

That therefore let-me further I-admonish-you beloved-ones: prayerfully read and consider you-want-to all words those-which-are-left-behind those-which-are-written, so-that-will He-be-honored and He-(will)-be-trusted God and they-(will)-live poor your-(poor)-souls.

I would recommend you to do this under the special and continual guidance of the Holy Spirit, by whose divine teaching alone, you can be taught to understand its true **[xi]** *meaning and cherish its purport.*

Jun gutschi lissik Welsit Mtschitschank elitsch alouchsohalquek woak sachgagunukquek wentschitsch tepi lissijek ngemewi; necama gintsch achgegimqueque natsch guli nostamenewo woak wingelendamenewo wemi elaptonachgagil.

This you-thereby do-so the-Holy Spirit as-will He-empower-you and He-(will)-lead-you so-that-will enough you-do-so constantly; he a-little-while when-He-teaches-you then-will you-well you-(will)-understand-it and you-(will)-delight-in-it all that-which-they-mean.

When you pray for this divine aid, think of the Savior's words: "If ye being evil, know how to give good gifts unto your children, how much more shall your heavenly Father give his Holy Spirit to them that ask him?"

Nundamhemajeque [?Nundahemajeque] wentschitsch nostamek woak lapendamek ktehuwawunk, nane meschatamook [L., meschandamook] Patamawos wtaptonaganall elaptonalatup Gegegimatpannil, eluetup: "Bischik matta welilissihumo knita milanewo knitschanowawak welhik miltowoaganall, allowi miqui Gochuwa milawalltsch winuwamgukil, Welsitschi Mtschitschanquall."

{When-you-are-in-want-of-something} so-that-will you-understand-it and you-(will)-find-it-useful in-your-hearts, then think-of-them God His-words those-which-He-spoke-to-them his-disciples, as-he-said: "To-be-sure not you-do-not-act-good you-can you-give-them-to-them your-children good gifts, more by-far your-Father He-will-give-Him-to-them those-who-beseech-Him, the-Holy Spirit."

"Ask and ye shall receive, seek and ye shall find, knock and it shall be opened unto you." Whenever you open this book, forget not to pray, that the Holy Spirit may open your understanding.

"Winuwek wentschitsch milgussijek, ndonamook wentschitsch mochgamek, popohamook wentschitsch tauwunemagejek." Endchen natenummek woak tauwunemek jun Bambil wentschitsch ika achkinsijek, nane woak papatamook Welsit Mtschitschank wentschitsch woak tauwunemauwat ktehuwawall wentschitsch nostamek.

Ask so-that-will you-be-given-something, seek so-that-will you-find-it, knock so-that-will {you-be-opened-to-it}." As-often-as you-take-it and you-open-it this Book so-that-will there you-read, then also pray the-Holy Spirit so-that-will also He-open-them-for-you your-hearts so-that-will you-understand.

I hope you will ever feel grateful to your Christian friends and benefactors who have contributed towards the publication of this work, and who, under God, have been the means of putting the same into your hands.

Ehoalachgik ta eet ihaschi kwonsowalawunewo nekik Elango- mquekquik Welsittankik, eli milquek jun Bambil nek [xvi] **Patamawos eli wulelendank litaquekquik wentschitsch latschessowejek jun Mamalekhican.**

Beloved-ones not perhaps ever you-do-not-forget-them those those-who-are-your-friends the-believers, how they-give-it-to-you this Book those **[xvi]** God as He-is-glad-about-it those-who-establish-you so-that-will you-possess-it this writing.

May you ever remember them in your prayers, and ask the Lord to bless them for bestowing such a blessing upon you and your posterity, which is calculated to be "a lamp unto your feet, and a light unto your path."

Abtschi wingi papatamoelchanewotsch ehendchen papatamajek, Patamawos wtellitsch wulapensohalan nel milquekquil jun Bambil, nan litasik, taat linasik schigalek nendawek woaselenican li ksitowawink elochwejek woak woaselenican gelenasik elemagechink anink elhagechink pomsgajek hallemi Pommauchsowoaganink.

Always gladly you-will-pray-for-them habitually-as-often-as you-pray, God that-He-will bless-them those those-who-give-it-to-you this Book, that {it-is-established-thusly}, as-if it-is-observed-(as-if) it-is-thin you-carry-a-lamp a-lamp to to-your-feet as-you-walk and a-lamp which-is-held {as-the-way-goes-through} in-the-road as-the-road-lies you-walk eternal to-(eternal)-life.

May this book ever prove to be "a savor of life unto life to your souls, that you thereby may be enabled to receive a clearer knowledge of yourselves and your blessed Savior,

Gulah untschi jun Bambilink tepi alouchsohalind ktemaki ktehuwa woak ktschitschanguwa wentschitsch kikechtit woak pomauchsichtit petschi hallamagamik Patamawossink talli,

Oh-that from this Book-from enough it-(anim.)-is-empowered poor your-(poor)-heart(s) and your-souls so-that-will they-mend-in-health and they-(will)-live unto forever in-God in,

for the strengthening of your faith in, and increasing of, your love towards him, who has loved you and gave himself for you.

woak nane untschi ajalowi kulamoechgunewo [L. wula-], wentschitsch nenamek ktemakhak elek ktehuwawink, woak eliechink gischiechinkup kikemhalgussowoaganowa talli Jesus Christink woak tschitanissohalgejek wentschitsch nhagalek woak ahoalek necama aptahoalquek woak mekup hokey untschi kiluwa.

and that for more-and-more it-(will)-convince-you-of-the-truth, so-that-will you-recognize-it {that-which-is-pitiful} as-it-is in-your-hearts, and as-it-lies it-was-finished your-salvation in Jesus Christ-in and you-are-strengthened so-that-will you-trust-(in)-him and you-(will)-love-him he who-loves-you-to-death and he-gave-it his-body for you.

I am your brother,
  Abraham Luckenbach,
New Fairfield, River Thames, U. C. April 8th, 1836.

Kimachtowa
  Abraham Luckenbach
New Fairfield, River Thames, U. C. April 8th, 1836.

Your-brother
  Abraham Luckenbach
New Fairfield, River Thames, U. C. April 8th, 1836.

Gebet eines Kindes wenn es eine biblische Historie lernen will.

[1] PAPATAMOEWOAGAN EWEGET AUWEN GETA ACHKINDANK PATAMAWOS WTAPTONAGAN.

A-prayer one-who-uses who wants-to who-(wants-to)-read-it God His-word.

Herr Gott himmlischer Vater, ich dein liebes Kind will anjetzo dein Wort zur Hand nehmen, und aus demselben lernen, wie ich recht glauben, christlich leben und endlich selig sterben soll.

Wo ki nihillalian NPatamawos epijan talli awossagame! Ni ktemaki ktamemensum nhakey, juke ngatta achkinsin geschiechek eluwiwulik ktaptonagan, nane untschi achgegimil, wentschitsch majawi hitta wulistama woak schachachgapewi lauchsija, woak wulistamuwi equauchsija.

O You my-Lord my-God where-You-are in Heaven! I poor Your-(poor)-child (is) myself, now I-want-to read that-which-is-holy that-which-is-most-good Your-word, that for teach-me, so-that-will rightly skillfully I-believe and righteously I-live, and believingly {I-depart-this-life}.

Ach sende doch deine Weisheit aus deiner heiligen Höhe, und aus dem Throne deiner Herrlichkeit, daß sie mit mir sey, und mit mir arbeite, auf daß ich erkennen möge, was vor dir gefällig ist!

Milil weuchsowoagan untschi hokunk, enda geschiechek epijan talli awossagame, enda lemattachpijan ktallewussowoaganink, wentschitsch allouchsohalink woak witahemink, ntelli nennamenall woak wingelendamenall nel welhikil ki eli wulelendaman.

Give-it-to-me knowledge from on-high, where it-is-holy where-You-are in Heaven, where you-sit in-Your-power, so-that-will there-bestrengthening and there-(will)-be-helping, that-I recognize-them and delight-in-them those good-things You as You-are-glad-about-them.

Schärfe doch mein Gedächtniß, daß ich dein Wort recht fassen und begreifen könne!

Litauwil ndehenk wentschitsch wingelendama ktaptonaganall, woak tepi nostamenall woak gelelendamenall [?gul-].

{Establish-it-for-me} in-my-heart so-that-will I-delight-in-them Your-words, and enough I-understand-them and {You-are-glad-about-it}.

Erleuchte doch meinen Verstand, daß ich dich, Gott Vater, und den du gesandt hast, Jesum Christum daraus erkenne!

Gischachsummauwil npenauwelendamoagan woak nostamoewoagan, wentschitsch a tepi woahelan ki [2] NPatamawos Wetochemellan, woak won eli petalogalatup NJesus Christ.

Enlighten-it-for-me my-consideration and my-understanding, so-that-in-the-future could enough I-(could)-know-You You **[2]** my-God You-Who-are-my-Father, and this-one as You-sent-him-hither Jesus Christ.

Heilige doch endlich auch meinen Willen, daß ich das Böse verwerfen, und das Gute erwählen, und also nicht nu rein Hörer, sondern auch ein Thäter deines Worts sey!

Pilsohata wemi ntitehewoaganall woak ndajandamoewoaganall, wentschitsch a tepi matschinama medhik woak wingelendama welhik. Woh litauwil NPatamawos wentschitsch matta schuk pendamowa ktaptonagan alod ntellitsch nosogamen woak lauchsin.

Purify-them all my-thoughts and my-wishes, so-that-in-the-future should enough I-(should)-be-displeased-with-it evil and I-(will)-delight-in-it that-which-is-good. O {establish-it-for-me-thusly} my-God so-that-will not only I-(will)-not-(only)-hear-it Your-word yet that-I-will follow-it and live-so.

A PRAYER BEFORE READING THE SCRIPTURE

Das bitte ich dich um deines lieben Sohnes Jesu Christi meines Herrn und Heilandes willen.

Wemi jul guwinuwamellen untschi ehoalatt quisis NJesus Christink eli nihillalid woak Pechpomauchsohalid.

All these I-ask-You by him-whom-You-love Your-son Jesus Christ-by as he-is-my-Lord and he-is-my-savior.

Göttliche Antwort. Ich will dich unterweisen, und dir den Weg zeigen, den du wandeln sollst, ich will dich mit meinen Augen leiten. Ps. 32, 8.

Patamawos eli nachgutink nitsch ktachgegimellen woak ktalohumolen tomagan elochwejan neschginquall untschi ksachgaguneltsch. Ps. 32: 8.

God as He-answers I-will I-(will)-teach-you and I-(will)-show-you the-way how-you-walk my-eyes by I-will-lead-you. Psalm 32: 8.

Gebet eines Kindes, wenn es eine biblische Historie gelernet hat.

PAPATAMOEWOAGAN EWEGENK AUWEN METSCHI GISCHACHKINDANK PATAMAWOS WTAPTONAGAN.

A-prayer someone-uses who already one-who-finishes-reading-it God His-word.

Ich danke dir mein lieber himmlischer Vater, durch Jesum Christum deinem lieben Sohn, daß du mich anjetzo aus deinem heiligen Worte hast in der wahren Weisheit unterrichten lassen.

Genamellen ehoalan Wetochemellan, epijan talli awossagame, untschi NJesus Christink ehoalatt Quisis, eli achgegimijanup untschi geschiechek [3] ktaptonaganink, woak woatelinep ika untschi, ne majawi wulamoejuwiki achgegingewoaganall.

I-thank-You You-whom-I-love You-Who-are-my-Father, where-you-are in Heaven, by Jesus Christ-by him-whom-You-love Your-son, as You-taught-me by that-which-is-holy **[3]** Your-word-by, and You-made-me-aware there by, that rightly they-convince-one-of-the-truth the-teachings.

Ach gieb doch nun auch von oben herab deinen göttlichen Segen dazu! Und wehre dem Satan, daß er nicht Unkraut unter den Waizen streuen, oder das Wort gar wieder von meinem Herzen nehmen möge;

Woh NPatamawos! Wulapensohata, untschi hokunk epijan, nel aptonaganall ekindamanni, woak katschi lelemahan metsit wentschitsch senehiket alsque talli ndehenk, schitta lappi ntschigenukgun nel welhiki aptonaganall,

O my-God! Bless-them, from on-high where-You-are, those words those-which-are-read, and don't do-not-let-him he-who-is-evil so-that-will he-sow weeds in in-my-heart, or again he-takes-them-away-from-me those good words,

sondern laße es die zu ehren, und mir zu meiner zeitlichen und ewigen Wohlfahrt hundertfältige Früchte bringen,

schuk gulah jun a leke, ki nane untschitsch gemechelemuxin, alod ni ntellapendamentsch nhakenk woak ntschitschankunk petschi hallamagamik, woaktsch neichquo wentschigink gischigenamia nguttapachki tchinkgi,

but oh-that this would if-it-(would)-be-so, You that by-will You-be-honored, yet I I-will-find-it-useful in-my-body and in-my-soul unto forever, and-will it-be-seen that-which-grows-from I-(will)-raise-them one-hundred so-many-of-them,

damit ich nach dem Exempel deines lieben Kindes Jesu Christi, täglich zunehmen möge, nicht nur an Alter und Jahren, sondern auch an Weisheit und an Gnade bey dir und den Menschen, Amen.

wentschitsch a tepi lek ntelli allemikin eheschi gischquik, ehoalat Quisis N'Jesus Christ elgiqui allumigitup endalauchsite Pemhagamikgek, ntellitsch matta schuk allowi cheli gachtinamiwon, alod ntegauwussitage untschi Gettanittowitink woak ju endalauchsitink. Amen.

so-that-in-the-future could enough it-(could)-be-so that-I grow every day, him-whom-You-love Your-son Jesus Christ like-as he-grew when-he-lives-in the-world, I-thus-will not only more many I-(will)-be-(many)-(more)-years-old, yet if-he-shows-me-favor from from-the-Great-Spirit and here from from-those-who-live-here. Amen.

Göttliche Antwort. Gehe hin mit Frieden, der Gott Israel wird dir geben deine Bitte, die du von ihm gebeten hast. 1 Sam. 1, 17.

Patamawos eli nachgutink, nalauwi alumsgal, nachpochwel Patamawos olangundowoagan, necama ktelliechguntsch wemi koecu li eli winuwamattup. 1 Sam. 1: 17.

A PRAYER AFTER READING THE SCRIPTURE

God how He-answers, "Safely go-away, go-with God His-peace, He He-will-do-it-for-you every thing toward what you-asked-Him. 1 Samuel 1: 17.

Die 1.

[4] 1 ELEGUP.

---

1 AS-IT-WAS.

Von dem Werke der Schöpfung. 1. Mose, 1ste und 2te Capitel.

Patamawos enda gischelendank wemi elgigunk Pemhagamigek woak Pemapanek. 1 Mos. 1.

God when He-creates-them-by-thought all as-wide-as the-world and the-sky. Genesis 1.

Am Anfange schuf Gott Himmel und Erden. Und die Erde war wüste und leer, und es war finster auf der Tiefe,

Eki nutschiechinkup Patamawos wtelli gischelendamenep awossagame woak Pemhagamigek, nane leep jun haki nhittami niskinaquot woak alachat, ulahah pisgapamukquot ika talli enda mchitquek.

In-the-beginning He-began God that-He created-them-by-thought heaven and the-world-round-about, then it-was-so this Earth at-first it-looks-nasty and it-is-empty, moreover it-is-dusky there in where there-is-great-depth.

und der Geist Gottes schwebete auf dem Wasser.

Nane talli Patamawos Welsit Mtschitschank achquispe pommihilleu wentschitsch ktschukpekgihhillak enda mchitquek.

That in God the-Holy Spirit [comes-over-the-water] he-flies so-that-will it-move-the-water where there-is-great-depth.

Ueber dem ganzen Werke der Schöpfung brachte Gott sechs Tage zu. Am ersten Tage ward das Licht erschaffen. Am andern die Feste des Himmels, oder das Firmament.

Guttasch endchi gischquike Patamawos gischelendamenep [5] wemi koecu. Nane netami gischquike Patamawos gischelendamen elewundasik wochejek. Nane wentachquichink gischgu Patamawos gischelendamen Pemapanek, schitta enda tschitanigachink awossagame.

Six as-many as-there-are-days God He-created-it-by-thought **[5]** every thing. That first when-it-is-the-(first)-day God He-created-it that-which-is-called light. That second day God He-creates-it-by-thought the-sky, or where it-is-firm heaven.

Am dritten Tage das Erdreich mit seinen Gewächsen. Am vierten Tage Sonne, Mond und Sterne.

Nane nacha gischquike Patamawos gischelendamen haki, nachpi wemi wentschiginki, wemi endchelenawachgi linakhoki skikquall woak egihenki. Nane newo gischquike Patamawos gieschelemawall gischgunii gischochwall woak nipaii gischochwall woak nel alanquewall.

That three when-it-is-day-(three) God He-creates-it-by-thought earth, with all those-things-which-grow-from-(it), all as-many-kinds-as they-look-like grasses and plants. That four when-it-is-day-(four) God He-creates-them-by-thought of-the-day the-luminary and of-the-night the-luminary and those stars.

Am fünften Tage die Fische und die Vögel.

Nane palenach endchi gischquike, Patamawos gischelemapani wemi mbink talli epitschil, endcheleneyachgissitschil namesall, woak pemapanek talli wemi endchagewichtit tscholensak.

OF THE CREATION OF HEAVEN AND EARTH.

Then five as-many as-it-is-day-(five), God He-created-them-by-thought all in-the-water in those-which-are-there, {as-many-kinds-as-they-are} fishes, and the-sky in all {as-many-tribes-as-they-are} birds.

Am sechsten die Thiere und die Menschen.

Nane guttasch tchi endchi gischquike, Patamawos gischelemapanil wemi endchelenawachgissitschil neuchgatatschil awessissall, woak wtenk untschi ihiabtschi nane gischquike wtelli gischelemanep Wetschitschanquitschil.

That six so-many as-many as-it-is-the-day, God He-created-them-by-thought all {as-many-kinds-kinds-as-they-are} those-which-are-four-legged beasts, and after wards still that when-it-is-(that)-day He-thus created-them-by-thought human-beings.

Und Gott sahe an alles, was er gemacht hatte, und siehe da, es war alles sehr gut. Am siebenten Tage darauf ruhete Gott der Herr von allen seinen Werken, die er gemacht hatte.

Nane Patamawos elhoquete penanke wemi koecu endchi gischelendank, nane wunemen li husca wulinaquot, nane nischasch endchi gischquike Patamawos Nihillalquonk wtelli liwiechin untschi wemi koecu endchi gischelendank woak mikindank.

That God as-He-looks-at-it when-He-beholds-it every thing as-much-as He-creates-by-thought, then He-sees here exceedingly it-looks-good, then seven as-many as-it-is-the-day God our-Lord He-thus rests from every thing as-much-as He-creates-by-thought and that-which-He-works.

Nüzliche Lehren.
WELAPEMQUO ACHGEGINGEWOAGAN.
PRACTICAL APPLICATION.

1. Gott der Herr hat Himmel und Erde, und alles was darinnen ist, aus nichts erschaffen: Was hat man daraus zu lernen? Man kan die große Allmacht Gottes daraus erkennen lernen?

1. Patamawos nihillalquonk gischelendamenep awossagame woak Pemhagamigek untschi matta koecuniwi. Jun guntschi nemeneen Patamawos guntschi wtallouchsowoagan.

1. God our-Lord He-created-them-by-thought heaven and the-world-round-about from not it-is-not-real. This from-we we-see-it God we-from His-power.

2. Alles was Gott in sechs Tagen gemachet hatte, das war sehr gut: Was hat man daraus zu lernen? Man kann die große Weisheit des Schöpffers daraus erkennen lernen.

2. Wemi koecu Patamawos gischelendangup nel guttasch endchi gischquike shaki, nane wunemen li [6] husca wulinaquot. Nane guntschi woatelukgeneen. Gischiechquonk Patamawos elgiqui ganschi wewoatank woak weuchsit.

2. Every thing God that-which-He-created-by-thought those six as-many as-there-are-days so-long-as, then He-sees-it here [6] exceedingly it-looks-good. That from-us it-is-made-known-to-us. He-Who-makes-us-holy God like-as amazingly He-is-wise and He-knows-what's-going-on.

3. Gott hat das andere alles um des Menschen willen erschaffen:

3. Wemi gischelemendtschik awessissak woak wemi pili gischelendasiki Patamawos wtelli gischelendamen wentschitsch lapendamichtit wetschitschanquitschik.

3. All those-who-are-created-by-thought the-beasts and all other things-created-by-thought God He-thus creates-by-thought so-that-will they-find-them-useful the-human-beings.

Was hat man daraus zu lernen? Man kan die große Güte Gottes daraus erkennen lernen.

Ta koecu eet jun guntschi woatelukgeneen? Jun wuntschi kschiechi penundelukgeneen, Patamawos elgiqui achgettemagelik woak welilissit.

(Is) not a-thing perhaps here from-us is-it-(not)-made-known-to-us? This from we-clearly we-are-shown, God like-as He-is-merciful and He-acts-good.

Gottselige Gedanken.
WELAPENDASIK PENAUWELENDAMOAGAN.
PIOUS REFLECTION.

Im Anfang schuf der Herr den Himmel und die Erde, Das alles ward aus nichts durch Gottes Wort allein:

Patamawos Nihillalquonk nhittami gischelendamen Awossagame woak Pemhagamigek. Jun wemi gischelendasikgup untschi Patamawos gantschi allouchsowik wtaptonaganink.

God our-Lord first He-created-them-by-thought heaven and the-world-round-about. This all this-which-was-created-by-thought by God amazingly it-is-strong by-His-word.

So oft ich diesen Bau forthin betrachten werde, So ofte wird dabey diß mein Gedanke seyn: Der dieses alles hat aus nichts erschaffen können, Der ist ja wohl mit Recht ein großer Herr zu nennen.

Juke untschi abtschi eheschi penamane jul wemi gischelendasikil nanitsch schawi nemigomgussi wentschi litehaja: Na auwen elsit

ju wemi hitta gischelendank untschi matta koecuniwi, won wtellgixin wentschitsch wilchgussit eluwelemuxit Patamawos Nihillalquonk.

Now therefore always every-(time) when-I-look-at-them these all these-which-were-created-by-thought then-will immediately I-(will)-be-reminded so-that I-think: That Person what-He-does here all skillfully He-creates-them-by-thought from not it-is-nothing, This-One He-is-worthy so-that-will He-be-named {He-Who-is-thought-greatest} God our-Lord.

Die 2te Historie.

[7] 2 ELEGUP.

2 AS-IT-WAS.

Von der Schöpfung des Menschen 1 Mose, 1ste und 2te Capitel.

Patamawos enda gischihatup Lennowall woak ochquewall. 1 Mos. 1: 10-27. 2: 7-28.

God when He-made-them man and woman. Genesis 1: 10-27 & 2: 7-28.

Wie Gott mit denen andern Geschöpfen fertig war, so sprach er: Latzt uns Menschen machen, ein Bild das uns gleich sey.

Nane Patamawos metschi gischelemapannil wemi takquokil awessissall, nane laptonep wtellowen: Gischelematamook wetschitschanquitschik, linaxichtitetsch kiluna elinaxijank.

Then God already He-created-them-by-thought all other beasts, then He-spoke-thusly He-says: "Let-us-create-them-by-thought human-beings, let-them-look-like us what-we-look-like.

Hierauf machte Gott zwey Menschen, ein Männlein und ein Fräulein: Der Mann bekam von Gott den Namen Adam; die Frau aber ward von ihrem Manne Eva genennet.

Nane Patamawos gischelemapanil nischowall wetschitschanquitschil, ngutti lennowall woak ngutti ochquewall. Na lenno Patamawos wteluwihhillan Adam; na ochque, lennowall wtelluwilchgun, Eva.

Then God He-created-them-by-thought they-are-two human-beings, one man and one woman. That man God He-names-him Adam; that woman, the-man he-names-her, Eva.

Erstlich schuf Gott den Mann aus einem Erden=Kloße, und blieβ ihm einen lebendigen Athem in seine Nase.

Patamawos nhittami [8] gischihapanil lennowall untschi phakei haki ulehellechemhallapanil eli putalat wikiwonink pemauchsowik lechewon.

God first [8] He-made-him a-man from a-piece-of earth He-gave-him-life as he-blows-at-him in-his-nose that-which-is-living breath.

Wie Adam fertig war, so sagte Gott: Es ist nicht gut daβ der Mensch allein sey, ich will ihm eine Gehülfin machen, die um ihn sey.

Metschi gischelemende Adam, nane Patamawos luep: Tacu wuliechenowi, wtelli nechohalenin lenno, witahemguk woak abtschitsch witauchsomguk ngischeleman.

Already when-he-is-created-by-thought Adam, then God He-said: Not it-is-not-good, that-he is-alone the-man, one-who-helps-him and always-will she-live-with-him I-(will)-create-her.

Hierauf nahm er dem Mann eine Ribbe ans dem Leibe heraus, wie er schlief, und schloβ die Stätte zu mit Fleisch. Aus dieser Ribbe bauete Gott der Herr ein Weib, und brachte sie zu ihm.

Nane Patamawos ika wendenummen lenno hopochquanink untschi, ngutti hopigekan neli tschitani gauwilid, woak enda ktinasik hopochquanink, wtelli lappi wsamuiton wujoos ika hatteu. Na ju untschi ngutti hopigekan Patamawos wuntschi gischihan na ochquewall woak petawan lennowall.

Then God there He-takes-it-from the-man from-his-side from, one rib while strongly he-sleeps, and where it-is-taken-out from-his-side, he-shuts-it the-flesh there it-is-there. Then this from one rib God from-He made-her that woman and He-brings-her-to-him the-man.

Da sagte Adam: Das ist doch Bein von meinen Beinen, und Fleisch von meinem Fleisch. Darauf setzte Gott den heiligen Ehestand ein, und

CREATION OF MAN AND WOMAN.

segnete das erste Paar mit diesen Worten:

Nane Adam newote wtelli luen: necama wochganim ni newochganim, necama wujoosum ni nojusum. Nane Patamawos kwischiechtauwan geschiechek tachquapohaltowoagan wikingewoagan wulapensohalapanil nel niganiechinkgi tequachpohalendtschi woak wtellawall:

Then Adam when-he-sees-her he-thus says: she (is) bone (of) my my-bone, she (is) flesh (of) my my-flesh. Then God He-made-it-for-them that-which-is-holy marriage (matrimony) He-blessed-them those {first-ones} those-who-are-married and He-says-to-them:

Seyd fruchtbar und mehret euch, und füllet die Erde und machet sie euch unterthan, und herrschet über die Fische im Meer, und über die Vögel unter dem Himmel, und über alles Thier das auf Erden kreucht.

Achsegik woak allemigik, wachtschuwiechinook ju haki, woak nihillatamook wemi koecu. Quigeyjumhauwanewotsch namesak epitschik talli mbink kitahicanink, woak nek tscholensak epitschik talli pemapanik woak awessissak pomochxitschik woak pepamsgatschik jun talli hakink.

Scatter and grow, fill-it this Earth, and own-it every thing. You-will-rule-them fish where-they-are in in-the-water in-the-ocean, and those birds those-who-are-there in the-sky and beasts those-who-creep and those-who-walk-about here in in-the-Earth.

Nüzliche Lehren.
WELAPEMQUO ACHGEGINGEWOAGAN.
PRACTICAL APPLICATION.

1. Der erste Menscch ist aus dem Erden=Kloß erschaffen worden: Was folget daraus? Das folget daraus, daß der Ehestand ein Gott gefälliger Stand, und Kinder ein Segen Gottes seyen.

1. **Netami wetschitschanquit wtelli gischelemuxin untschi pakei haki. Nane untschi tepi migomgussin woak penundelan ju endalauchsit wentschitsch abtschi tangelensochwet.**

1. The-first human-being he-thus is-created-by-thought from a-piece-of earth. That by enough he-is-reminded and He-shows-him-how here he-who-lives-here so-that-will always he-(will)-walk-humbly.

2. *Gott hat den Ehestand im Paradies eingesezet, und einen schönen Segen darüber gesprochen: Was folget daraus? Das folget daraus, daß der Ehestand ein Gott gefälliger Stand, und Kinder ein Segen Gottes seyen.*

2. **Patamawos wtelli gischiechtonep geschiechek wikingewoagan talli Paradiesink, schitta welhik [9] menenachkhasikink, woak wtelli wulapensohatamenep. Jun wuntschi Patamawos wtelli woadhiken elgiqui mchelendank wikingewoagan, woak wtelli gattatamen wemi auwen nosogamen nachpi kschiechauchsowoaganink.**

2. God He-thus established-it holy marriage in in-Paradise, or that-which-is-good [9] the-garden-in, and He-thus blessed-it. This from God He-thus witnesses-it like-as He-thinks-highly-of-it marriage, and that-He desires-it every person to-follow-it with with-clean-living.

3. *Gott hat im Anfang, nur ein Paar Menschen erschaffen: Was folget daraus? Das folget daraus, daß ein Mann nicht mehr als eine Frau; und eine Frau nicht mehr als einen Mann auf einmal nehmen soll.*

3. **Patamawos eki nutschi gischihapanil nischowall wetschitschanquitschil schuk. Nane guntschi Patamawos penundelukguna wtelli gottatamen, lenno wulahellantsch mauchsilowall ochquewall schuk; woak ochque wulahellantsch mauchsilowall lennowall schuk.**

3. God beginning in-the-beginning He-made-them two human-beings only. That us-by God He-shows-us-how He-thus desires-it, a-man he-will-have-her she-is-one woman only; and a-woman she-will-have-him he-is-one man only.

CREATION OF MAN AND WOMAN.

Göttselige Gedanken.
WELAPENDASIK PENAUWELENDAMOAGAN.
PIOUS REFLECTION.

Aus Erde ward von Gott der erste Mensch erschaffen Dem Gott sein Ebenbild aus Gnaden hat geschenkt;

Untschi phakei haki Patamawos gischihapanil netami wetschitschanquitschil, woak necama Patamawos wtellinaxowoaganink wtelli gischelemuxin.

From a-piece-of earth God He-made-him first a-human-being, and he God in-His-likeness he-thus is-created-by-thought.

wie kan doch nun ein Mensch sich in sich selbst vergessen, wenn er dann und wann an seinen Ursprung denkt? Mir soll der Erden=Kloß allzeit vor Augen schweben, so oft mein Herze will nach hohen Dingen streben.

Kaski eet haschi kmechelensin ki ju endalauchsijan kechitti a schuk penauwelendamanne ta wentschijeyian? M'chelensowoagan gatta pejewike talli ktehenk, kmeschandamentsch phakei haki wendenasik kakey elek.

Able-to perhaps ever are-you-(able-to)-be-proud you here you-who-live-here a-little would only if-you-(would)-consider-it where you-are-from? Pride wants-to if-it-(wants-to)-come in in-your-heart, you-will-remember-it a-piece-of earth that-which-is-taken-from yourself (is) what-it-is.

Die 3te Historie

[10] 3 ELEGUP.

---

3 AS-IT-WAS.

Von dem Stande der Unschuld im Paradies. 1 Mos. 2te und 3te Capitel.

Netami Gischelemendpaninga elsichtitup sekachpichtitup enda palachpichtitup talli Paradiesink schitta welhik hakihagan elewundasik. 1 Mos. 1, 2, 3.

First those-late-ones-who-were-created-(first) what-they-did so-long-as-they-were-there when they-were-innocent in in-Paradise or that-which-is-good the-garden that-which-is-called. Genesis 1, 2 & 3.

Adam und Eva lebten anfangs im Stande der Unschuld. In diesem Stande hatten sie das Ebenbild Gottes an sich.

Naga Adama woak Evasa nhittami wtellauchsinewo palachpuaganink, woak seki nane lissichtit Patamawos wtellinaxowoaganink nachpauchsinewo.

That-late deceased-Adam and deceased-Eve first they-live-thusly in-innocence, and so-long-as that they-do-so God in-His-likeness they-enjoy-it.

Sie waren also ohne Sünde in rechtschaffener Gerechtigkeit und Heiligkeit. Damals war der Tod noch nicht in der Welt, sondern Adam und Eva waren unsterblich.

Nane wtellauchsinewo pallachpuaganink, woak schachachgapewinewo woak kschiechauchsinewo. Nane likhikqui nesquo hattewip angelowoagan; alod Adama woak Ebasa matta angellowi wtelsiwunewo.

Then they-live-thusly in-innocence, and they-are-upright and they-are-holy. Then at-that-time not-yet it-was-not-there death; for the-late-Adam and the-late-Eve not mortally they-do-not-live-so.

Vor den wilden Thieren dursten sie sich nicht fürchten, denn sie mußten den Menschen alle gehorsam seyn. Zur selben Zeit hatten sie auch seine Kleider nothing, sondern im Stand der Unschuld glengen sie nackend.

Matta gochawiwawall awessissall eli wemi [11] awulsittakhittit woak gegeyjumhauwanewo. Nane talli enda pallachpichtit netamiechinkpanik gegeyjumenaninkachge, tacu gachtalquottowi ehachquink wdakquinewo; eli pallachpichtit wtelli sopochwenewop.

Not they-do-not-fear-them the-beasts as all [11] they-obey-them and they-govern-things-for-them. Then there when they-are-innocent those-who-were-first our-(first)-late-elders, not it-is-not-desired clothing they-do-not-put-it-on; because they-are-innocent they-thus they-walked-naked.

Ihre Wohnung war das Paradies. Das war ein schöner Garten, welchen Gott selber angeleget hatte.

Nane wtapinewo woak wikinewo talli Paradiesink, nane luwundasu welhik hagihagan, Patamawos eli nihillatschi gischelendank.

Then they-are-there and they-dwell in in-Paradise, that it-is-called that-which-is-good the-garden, God because Himself He-creates-it.

In demselben standen allerhand schöne Baume, die lustig anzusehen waren. Es begiengen aber die ersten zwey Menschen eine schwere Sünde,

Ika talli nipalawall kecheli wewulsitschil mhitgol, wemi welhigil wentschigingi, wentschitsch wulapendamichtit, nek wetschitschanquitschik. Schuk gantschi pallalogasinewo netamiechinkpana Wetschitschankquitschik, eli pallistawachtit Gischiechquichtitschi Patamawossall.

GARDEN OF EDEN.

There in they-are-stood-up diverse beautiful trees, all those-which-are-good things-which-grow-from, so-that-will they-enjoy-the-benefit-of-them, those human-beings. But amazingly they-transgress those-late-ones-who-are-first the-(first)-human-beings, for they-disbelieved-Him their-Maker God.

darüber ward Gott der Herr zornig, und jagte sie aus dem Paradies. Er setzte auch eine Engel mit einem blosen hauenden Schwerdt vor die Thüre, damit sie nicht wieder hinein konten.

Nane untschi Patamawos ktisgawawall untschi welhik hagihaganink enda wulamallsichtit woak Enschellall ika nipallowall enda esquondeik welhik hakihagan sapelechink tangamican eli glenink wentschi quitelat nel metschi pallalogasitschil wetschitschanquitschi woak matta lelemai lappi ika pachtik.

That for God He-drives-them-out from that-which-is-good the-garden where they-feel-good and an-angel there He-stands-him where there-is-the-gate (of) that-which-is-good the-garden that-which-flashes a-sword as he-holds-it so-that he-forbids-them those already those-who-transgress the-human-beings and not he-does-not-allow-them again there they-do-not-come.

Durch diesen Sünden=Fall haben die Menschen das Ebenbild Gottes verlohren.

Nane wuntschi eli gantschi machtechinhittit machtauchsowoaganink nek netami gischelemendtschik wetschitschankquitschik, nane untschi wtankhittonewo Patamawos wtellinaxowoagan.

That from as amazingly they-fall-hard into-sin those first those-who-are-created-(first) the-human-beings, that from they-lost-it God His-likeness.

An dessen Stelle ist die Sünde in die Welt gekommen, und durch die Sünde der Tod.

Jun metschi ankhittochtite aschitte pejeju mattauchsowoagan, woak untschi machtauchsowoaganink pejeju angelowoagan.

This already when-they-lose-it then it-comes sin, and from from-sin it-comes death.

Adam zeugte darauf Kinder, die seinem Bilde ähnlich waren: Und bis auf diesen Tag werden alle seine Nachkommen in Sünden empfangen und gebohren.

Nane Naga Adama gischigohepanil amemensall, wtelinaxilowall necama elinaxid; woak petschi juke gischquik, nek wemi ahanhuqui hokenk untschi gischigitschik wtelli nachpikinewo machtauchsowoagan.

Then that-late deceased-Adam he-engendered-them children they-looked-like him how-he-looked; and until now (to)day, those all over-and-over-again from-his-body from those-who-are-born they-thus they-are-by-nature sin.

Nützliche Lehren.
[12] **WELAPEMQUO ACHGEGINGEWOAGAN.**
PRACTICAL APPLICATION.

Aus dieser Geschichte kann man den großen Unterschied des menschlichen Geschlechts vor dem Sünden=Fall und nach dem Sünden=Fall erkennen.

Jun untschi eli woatelukquonkquil ktelli nemeneen elsichtitup ju endalauchsitschik nesquo machtechinhittik machtauchsowoaganink, woak elgiqui machtamallessichtit wtenk untschi metenumhittitup machtauchsowoagan.

This from as it-makes-us-aware-of-it we-thus we-see-it as-it-was here they-who-live-here not-yet they-do-not-fall-hard into-sin, and like-as they-feel-bad after from {they-finished-doing-it} sin.

GARDEN OF EDEN.

1. In dem Stand der Unschuld waren die Menschen gerecht und heilig.

1. Wetschitschankquit n'hittami sekachpite enda palachpit, wtelli schachgapewin woak kschiechauchsin.

1. The-human-being first when-he-was-there-so-long-as when he-is-innocent, he-thus is-upright and is-holy.

Nach dem Sünden=Fall aber muß ein jeder singen: Siehe Herr! in Sünden bin ich gebohren, in Sünden empfieng mich meine Mutter.

Ulaha juke seki metschi pallalogasit, wemi auwen schiwelendamowi aski luen: Penna Nihillalian, ntelli gischigin machtauchsowoaganink, woak ngahoes mischenan nhakey enda machtauchsink.

Moreover now so-long-as already he-transgresses, every person sorrowfully must say: Behold my-Lord, that-I am-born in-sin, and my-mother she-receives-him myself when there-is-sinning.

2. In dem Stand der Unschuld waren die Menschen unsterblich. Nach dem Sünden=Fall aber heißt es leider: Ach Herr, lehre uns bedenken wohl, daß wir sind sterblich allzumal.

2. Wetschitschanquit sekachpit enda palachpit, matta a wtelli nachpauchsiwon angelowoagan. *[no more translated]*

2. The-human-being so-long-as-he-is-here where he-is-innocent, not could he-thus (could)-not-possess-it death.

3. In dem Stand der Unschuld wohnten die Menschen in einem Paradies.

3. Seki achpit netami gischihind wetschitschanquit enda pallachpit, talli welhik menenachkhasikink Paradies elewundasik, husca wulatenamo.

3. So-long-as he-is-there first he-who-is-made-(first) the-human-being when he-is-innocent, in that-which-is-good in-the-(good)-garden Paradise that-which-is-called, exceedingly he-is-happy.

Nach dem Sünden=Fall aber müssen wir Menschen ausrufen: Es ist allhier ein Jammerthal, Angst, Roth und Trübsal überall.

Schuk metschi machtauchsite, sasalamu woak lueu? Jun talli Pemhagamikgek techi schuk nsasakquauchsi, ndalemi, macheleneyachi nsacquilissi woak nschiwelendamen nachgowi koecu.

But already when-he-sins, does-he-cry-a-great-deal and does-he-say-so-thusly: Here in the-world-round-about utterly only I-live-troubled-continually, I-am-apprehensive, {manifold-ways} I-act-distressed and I-am-sorrowful-about-it {?every} thing?

Gottselige Gedanken.
[13] **WELHIKIL PENAUWELENDAMOAGANALL.**
GOOD REFLECTIONS.

Wo ist das Paradies mit seinen schönen Bäumen, Darein Gott hat gesezt das allererste Paar?

Tani eet koecu litasu welhik hagihacan nachpi welsitschik mhittgook, Patamawos enda hallatup nelil netami gischelematpannik?

How perhaps a-thing is-it-established that-which-is-good a-garden with those-which-are-good trees, God where He-placed-them those first those-whom-He-created-(first)?

Ach Adam hat es bald mit Eva müssen räumen, Als Gottes Ebenbild einmal verschertzet war: Was ist dann nun zu thun? Ich werde mich bemühen, Ins andere Paradies, wo Christus wohnt, zu ziehen.

Alaqui! Adam nahelii Eva schai untschi ktisgawawak, metschi ankhittochtite Patamawos wtellinaxowoagan. Koecu hatsch juke ndellsin? Ni juke ntellachwelitsch pili Paradiesink wentschi paja Jesus Christ nihillalid epit talli awossagame.

GARDEN OF EDEN.

'Tis-a-pity! Adam together-with Eve immediately from they-are-driven-out, already when-they-lose-it God His-likeness. What it-will-be-asked now do-I-do? I now {I-will-wish-thusly-for} another Paradise-for so-that I-come Jesus Christ my-Lord where-he-is in Heaven.

Die 4te Historie.

[14] 4 ELEGUP.

---

4 AS-IT-WAS.

Von dem Sünden=Fall der ersten Eltern.

Enda hakink lihillachtitup nekachge kikeyjujumenaninkachge. 1 Mos. 3.

When to-Earth they-dropped those-late-ones our-deceased-parents. Genesis 3.

Im Paradies stand der Baum des Erkenntnisses Gutes und Böses.

Nane talli lelai Paradiesink nipawin eluwihhillend wewoatamao-aganii hittguk, welhikink li woak medhikink, wentschi a kaski woatak auwen, welhik schitta medhik.

That in in-the-middle of-Paradise it-(anim.)-stands that-(anim.)-which-is-named of-knowledge the-tree, of-good regarding and of-evil, so-that would able-to he-(would)-be-(able-to)-know-it a-person, good or evil.

Auf demselben wuchsen zwar Früchte, die lieblich anzusehen waren: Aber Adam und Eva dursten nicht davon essen:

Nane ika talli gelitawawall winginaquachtol wentschigingi: schuk matta lelemaiwall Adamall woak Evasall wentschi ika untschi mitschichtit.

That there in they-cling-to-it-(anim.) those-which-are-fine-looking things-which-grow-from: but not they-are-not-allowed Adam and Eva so-that there of they-eat-it.

denn Gott hatte es ausdrücklich verboten und dabey gesagt: Welches Tages du davon iffest, wirst du des Todes sterben.

Patamawos quittelan, wtellawall: Katschi mitschiheek ika wentschigink gischigink eluwihhillind wewoatamoaganii hittuk welhik li woak medhik, ika untschi mitschijeke, schai ktangellohumotsch.

God He-warns-them, he-says-to-them: Don't do-not-eat-it there that-which-grows-from that-which-is-grown that-(anim.)-which-is-named of-knowledge the-tree good regarding and evil, there of if-you-eat-it, immediately you-will-die.

Aber unsere ersten Eltern setzten das Gebot Gottes aus den Augen, und assen von dem verbotenen Baum. Zu dieser Sünde verführte sie der Teufel, welcher sich in eine Schlange verstellet hatte.

[15] **Jun woak pendanke medsit machtando, ninutschi schingalat Patamawossall, eli necama mechi gagelunet woak nanhillowet, nane achgokink laehasop woak achgooko, eli litehat achgook allowi wischixu medhikink li, allowi machtschi luppoe.**

[15] This also when-he-hears-it the-evil-one the-Devil, in-the-beginning he-who-hates-Him God, because he great he-is-a-(great)-liar and a-murderer, then in-a-snake he-acted-thusly and he-is-a-snake, as he-thinks a-snake more he-does-his-best towards-evil towards, more wickedly he-is-clever.

Nane machtando wtachawall Ochquewall, schuk neichgussop achgook, achgookunk linaxop wteliton hokey. Nane ntutemauwan luep: Leu eet Patamawos ktellguwa: katschi mitschiheek ika wentschigink gischigink, wemi juk hittgook, nipaitschik, pemaksitschik hakihacanink?

Then the-Devil he-visits-her the-woman, but he-was-seen a-snake, in-a-snake he-appeared-so he-established-it his-body. That he-asks-it-of-her he-said: Is-it-so perhaps God He-tells-you: Don't do-not-eat-it there the-fruit that-which-is-grown, all these trees, those-(anim.)-which-stand, {those-trees-which-are-round-about} in-the-garden?

Nane Eva nachgomate wtellawall: Gohan nane leu, abtschi nemizihena ika wetschikink gischikink wemi hittgook, jun talli hagihaganink nipaitschik, schuk ngutti hittuk ika wentschikink gischigink Patamawos ntelguna, nquitelukguna:

Then Eve when-she-answers-him she-says-to-him: Yes that it-is-so, always we-eat there the-fruit that-which-is-grown (on) all trees, here in in-the-garden those-(anim.)-which-stand, but one tree there the-fruit that-which-is-grown God He-tells-us, He-warns-us:

Katschi mitschiheek ika wentschikink gischigink won hittuk, katschi nachpene kikeninkheek ika wentschikink gischigink, ktangellohumotsch lissijeque.

Don't do-not-eat there the-fruit that-which-is-grown (on) this tree, don't even do-not-touch-it there the-fruit that-which-is-grown, you-will-die if-you-do-so.

Diese Schlange sprach zum Weibe: Ihr werdet mit nichten des Todes sterben,

Nane achgook apatschi late, wtellowen: Ta hatsch guntschi angellenewo? Tacu techi ne lewi, ktelli angellenewo mitschijeque ika untschi hittgunk, lelai hagihaganink nipaid.

Then the-snake comes-back as-he-says-to-her, he-says: How it-will-be-asked you-thereby (will)-you-die? Not utterly that it-is-not-so, that-you you-die if-you-eat-it there of of-the-tree, in-the-middle of-the-garden that-(anim.)-which-stands.

sondern wenn ihr davon essen werdet, so werdet ihr seyn wie Gott.

Pili liteheu. Patamawos, pili wundachquaptoneu. Wuli woaton eleektsch mitschijeque ika wentschigink gischigink na hittgunk, jun lissijeque ktellitsch mantowinewo, tepitsch lissinewo Gettanittowit elsit,

Otherwise He-thinks. God, otherwise {He-speaks-that-way}. Well-He knows-it how-it-will-be if-you-eat-it there the-fruit that-which-matures that tree-from, this if-you-do-so you-thus-will you-(will)-be-spirit-beings, enough-will you-do-so the-Great-Spirit that-which-He-does,

[Luckenbach only]

woak geschginkguwawall tachgehhellewalltsch [?toch-], wentschitsch witschi woatawek medhik schitta welhik, nane tacu tschitsch knagatamowunewo Patamawos wtaptonagan, wtidehewoagan wentschi nosogamek. Nane wtendchi niski achgelunenep [16] **machtando.**

and your-eyes {they-will-suddenly-awaken}, so-that-will with-(them) you-know-it evil or good, then not once-more you-do-not-rely-on-it God His-word, His-thought so-that-you-follow-it. That as-much-as-he filthily lied **[16]** the-Devil.

Das Weib gedachte von dem Baum müßte nothwendig gut zu essen seyn, weil er klug machte.

Nane Eva medchi pendawate, schai amehhelleu amemensuwi wunagalowewoagan li Patamawosink, woak wtallemi wulipenauwawall nel hittgol, na ika wentschigink gitschigink, husca wulinaquot, woak eli nenk nane liteheu: Gulah leke eluet na achgook ntelli undapendamen mitschiane.

Then Eve as-soon-as as-soon-as-she-hears-him, immediately {it-vanishes} childlike her-(childlike)-trust towards God-towards, and she-begins-to look-well-at-it-(anim.) that tree, that-one there the-fruit that-which-is-grown, exceedingly it-looks-good, and as she-sees-it that she-thinks: Oh-that if-it-be-so as-he-says that snake that-I hear-it-from if-I-eat-it.

Deswegen aß sie nicht allein von der Frucht des Baumes, sondern sie gab ihrem Manne auch davon zu essen.

MAN'S FALL.

Nane wtallemi ajandamen wentschi gutantank na welinaquo, ika wentschigink na hittgunk, eli gattatank woaton wemi koecu, Gettanittowit elgiqui wewoatak; nane untschi pachkenummen woak mitschin, woak milan wechitschil woak necama mitschu.

Then she-begins-to wish-for-it so-that she-tastes-it that which-looks-good, there that-which-grows-from that tree-from, because she-desires-it to-know-it every thing, the-Great-Spirit like-as He-really-knows-things; that for she-breaks-it-off and eats-it, and she-gives-it-to-him her-husband and he he-eats-it.

[Luckenbach only]

Nane metschi pallalogasichtite netami Gischihindpanik, Adama woak Evasa, schai wdamandamenewo woak wuschkinguwawall taat tachgehhellewall, wentschi metschi woatochtit medhik endchi lissichtit.

Then already when-they-transgress first those-who-were-(first)-made, the-late-Adam and the-late-Eve, immediately they-feel-it and their-eyes as-if {they-wake-up}, so-that already they-know-it the-evil as-much-as they-do-so.

Nane nutschi schai aleminewo woak [17] sacquelendamenewo woak wtelinamenewo endchi lindup: Nane gischquik ta elgiqui mitschijan ika untschi na hittgunk, natsch schachachki ktangeltsch.

Then begin-to immediately they-(begin-to)-be-afraid and **[17]** they-are-troubled-in-mind and they-observe-it as-much-as they-were-told: That day definitely like-as you-eat-it there from that tree-from, then-will surely you-will-die.

[Luckenbach only]

Eli matta tschitsch linaxichtik Gettanittowit elinaxit, nane miechanaltinewo ta kaski tschitsch wulelendamowi penauwach-

tiwiwak. Nane untschi pomiechganauenewawall menkipachga menkipachgagi combachquall, wdethuinewo metakhamenewo hokeyjuwawall; eli spamallsichtit [?ts-] eli soopsichtit.

As not once-more they-do-not-look-like the-Great-Spirit how-He-looks, then they-are-ashamed-of-each-other not able-to once-more joyfully they-are-not-(able-to)-look-at-each-other. That for they-weave-them those-which-are-large-leaved of-large-leaved-trees the-leaves, they-make-aprons they-cover-them their-bodies; for they-feel-strange because they-are-naked.

Gegen Abend kam der Schöpfer in den Garten, und rufte: Adam, wo bist du?

Nane giechki wulaquike Patamawos nihillalquichtitschi peu talli welhik gardenink epichtit woak wentschimawal Adamall woak luep: Ta ktappin?

Then nearly when-it-is-evening God their-Lord He-comes in the-good garden-in, where-they-are and He-calls-him Adam and He-said: Where are-you-there?

Es hatte sich aber Adam und Eva unter die Bäume im Garten verstecket, und machten sich Röcke von Feigen=Blättern, denn sie schämten sich nunmehro, daß sie nackend waren.

Na wischasit lenno, nachgomawall Patamawossall woak lueu: Eli amamellan ktelli paan, jun hagihaganink, nane schai newischassi eli sopsija, nane wentschi nemawi gandachpin enda mhittquonsigek.

Then he-is-frightened the-man, he-answers-Him God and he-says: As I-feel-You that-You are-coming, here in-the-garden, then immediately I-am-frightened because I-am-naked, then therefore I-go-and hide where there-are-a-lot-of-bushes.

Wie sie nun Rede und Antwort geben sollten, warum sie Gottes Gebot übertreten hätten?

MAN'S FALL.

Nane Patamawos wtellawall: auwen eet ktellgun ktelli sopsin? Matta ha kmitschii untschi hittgunk ika wentschikink, bischi kwitelellhump: katschi mitschihan? Nane pendamichtite jun, elii Adam woak wikimatschil, nane ta a kaski pachsowewiwak, schuk alaqui!

Then God He-says-to-him: Who perhaps he-tells-you that-you are-naked? Not it-is-asked do-you-eat-it of of-the-tree there that-which-grows-(there)-from, to-be-sure I-warned-you: Don't do-not-eat-it? That when-they-hear-it this, both Adam and his-wife, then not could able-to they-(could)-not-be-(able-to)-deny-it, but 'tis a pity!

so schob immer eines die Schuld auf das andere.

Metschi machtschi luppoewak, metschi owoatonewo elenumhittit, nihillatschi mandundowak nek untschi ahanhoqui gischigitschik, elgiqui nachpikichtit mandundowoagan juke petschi gischquik.

Already wickedly they-are-wise, already they-know-it how-they-act, themselves they-blame-each-other those from over-and-over-again those-who-are-born, so-as they-grow-up-with blame now unto (to)day.

Nämlich, Adam sagte: das Weib hat mich verführet: Und Eva hingegen sprach: die Schlange hat mich betrogen.

Nane Adam wtellawall Patamawossall lueu: Won Ochque petawijannup, npetenumagun untschi hittgunk woak ntelliechgun wentschi mitschija. Schuk Eva aschitte lue: na achgook ngagiwaluk.

Then Adam he-says-to-Him God he-says: This woman she-whom-You-brought-me, she-brings-it-to-me from from-the-tree and she-does-it-to-me so-that I-eat-it. But Eve then she-says: that snake he-deceives-me.

Aber damit war der Schöpfer nicht zu frieden, sondern er jagte sie beyde zum Paradies hinaus. Ja dabey blieb es nicht, sondern ein jedes bekam noch dazu seine besondere Strafe.

Nane Patamawos wdallemi gendeleman,

Then God He-begins-to condemn-them,

[Luckenbach only]

nhittami achgookall, schuk majawi machtandowall, eli achpitawat achgookall [18] wtellawall: Jun elsijann, juke untschi gendelemuxitsch wemi endchelenawachgissichtit awessisak, elinquechinhittit talli, wemitsch auwen gendelemuk, gachteytsch kpomsgeton woaktsch kmitschin haki ta segauchsijan.

at-first the-snake, but rightly the-Devil, as he-abides-in-him the-snake [18] He-says-to-him: This which-you-do, now from you-will-be-condemned all {as-many-kinds-as-they-are} the-beasts, in-their-presence in, in-the-future-every person he-(will)-condemn-you, your-belly-will you-go-on-it and-will you-eat-it earth indeed so-long-as-you-live.

Zur Schlänge aber sagte Gott: Des Weibes Saamen soll dir den Kopf zertreten.

Machtangundowoagan ikatsch ndaton tetauwi li kakenk woak ochquewink; ki kwochganimutsch woak necama owochganimutsch, nantsch kil wdamachgigamen, kitsch aschitte wanquonnink, ktangaman.

Enmity there-will I-place-it between toward toward-yourself and toward-the-woman; your your-seed-in-the-future and her her-seed-in-the-future, then-will your-head he-(will)-tread-it-under-foot, you-will then on-his-heel, you-(will)-prick-him.

Es wird aber durch den versprochenen Weibes Saamen niemand anders verstanden, als Jesus Christus, der in der Fülle der Zeit von einem Weibe sollte gebohren werden.

MAN'S FALL.

Nane schai pendaquot netamiechink pomauchsowaptonamik, pendamenewo nek getemaxitschik wetschitschanquitschik. Won elitsch gischigit untschi ochquewunk, elewunsit Nihillalquonk NJesus Chirst.

Then immediately it-is-heard the-first word-of-life, they-hear-it those those-who-are-poor human-beings. This-one how-will he-be-born of of-a-woman, he-who-is-called our-Lord Jesus Christ.

Zu Eva sprach Gott: du sollt mit Schmerzen Kinder gebähren, und dein Wille soll deinem Manne unterworsen seyn; und er soll dein Herr seyn.

Nane Patamawos aschitte wtellawall Ochquewall: ktellihellentsch enda m'chasktschajann ktellitsch mcheleneyachki awendamen; ktachwitsch linamen [19] enda nunschejane; woak ktelitehewoagan liechtasutsch lennunk welelendank woak necama gegeyjumhaguntsch.

That God then He-says-to-her the-woman: I-will-do-it-to-you when you-are-thick-bellied you-thus-will many-ways suffer; you-will-vehemently be-treated **[19]** when when-you-breed; and your-thinking it-will-be-established by-a-man that-about-which-he-is-glad and he he-will-govern-you.

Zu Adam sprach Gott unter andern:

Nane Adamall wtellawall:

Then Adam He-says-to-him:

[Luckenbach only]

Ki eli glistaman knachauchschum elquon ju lissil, woak ihiabtschi ktelli mitschin untschi hittgunk, bischi quittellen ktellohump katschi ika untschi mitschihan!

You because you-listen-to-her your-old-woman what-she-says-to-you this do-so, and still you-thus eat-it of of-the-tree, to-be-sure I-forbid-you I-said-to-you don't there from do-not-eat-it!

[Luckenbach only]

Nane wentschi gendelendasutsch haki untschi ki, woak sacquauchsowoaganink juke ika untschitsch kmitschin ta segauchsijan. Gawunschall woak alsquewall untschigenoltsch, woaktsch leu ktelli mitschin nel skiekquall ekihenkil talli hagihacanink.

That therefore it-will-be-condemned the-Earth by you, and in-a-troubled-life now there from-will you-eat-things definitely so-long-as-you-live. Briars and weeds they-will-grow-from-(it), and-will it-be-so that-you eat-them those grasses those-which-are-planted in in-cultivated-fields.

Im Schweiß deines Angesichts sollt du dein Brod essen

Gintsch aptiksijanne talli geschginkunk, kmitschintsch ktapoanum, nane luejuju: Ktahitsch mikemossi, wentschi koecu mitschijan; chelitsch kmikemossin ta segauchsijan wentschitsch pomauchsohejan kakey natsch ne ktelsin

A-little-while when-you-sweat in in-your-face, you-will-eat-it your-bread, that it-says: Hard-you-will work, so-that a-thing you-eat-it; much-will you-work definitely so-long-as-you-live so-that-will you-make-live yourself then-will that you-do-so

bis daß du wieder zur Erden weirdest davon du genommen bist, denn du bist Erde, und sollt zur Erden werden.

teek petschi angelanne woak gachtuwepi lappitsch ejeju hakink wendenasikgup. Hakink guntschijeyin woak lappitsch nane ktellinaxintsch.

{there} until when-you-die and your-corporeal-body again-will it-go into-the-earth from-whence-it-was-gotten. From-the-earth you-come-from and again-will that you-will-look-like.

Zulezt machte ihnen Gott noch Röcke von Fellen, und damit mußten sie das Paradies mit dem Rücken ansehen.

Nane Patamawos nihillatschi chessii schakhocquiwanahauwan woak wdakgunahalan. Schuk tacu kaski allowi li achpiwunewo talli Paradiesink,

Then God Himself of-skins He-makes-coats-for-them and He-clothes-them. But not able-to more toward they-are-not-(able-to)-be-there in in-Paradise,

[Luckenbach only]

wentschitsch matta tschitsch pili hittgunk wentschigink, mitschichtik eluwichhillend pemauchsit hittuk, woak nane untschi gunilehellechewiwak jun talli hakink enda schuk sasacquauchsichtit mattauchsowoaganink.

so-that-will not once-more the-other tree-of that-which-grows-from-(it), they-do-not-eat-it the-one-(anim.)-which-is-named he-who-is-living the-tree, and that for they-do-not-live-long here in in-the-Earth where only they-live-continually-troubled in-sin.

[Luckenbach only]

Nane untschi t'gauchsuwi Gischiechquichtitschi tacu wtellelemukguwiwall wentschi allowi shaki achpichtit eli ahoalquichtit, nane wentschi ktisgawanep untschi hagihakanink, elewundasik Eden.

That for gently He-Who-purifies-them not He-does-not-allow-them so-that more so-long they-are-there because He-loves-them, that therefore He-drove-them-out from from-the-garden, that-which-is-called Eden.

[Luckenbach only]

Nane Adam wtelli mikindamen na haki eli wundenasikgup hokey, woak endchen gachta [20] ktukite li Paradiesink, nane

Patamawos wtellihan, Enschel neichgussu glenum sabelechink tangamikan wentschi gebhikamauwat esquandey woak matta tschitsch kaski ika pak.

Then Adam he-thus works-it that earth because it-was-gotten-from his-body, and as-many-times-as wants-to [20] as-he-(wants-to)-turn-back to to-Paradise, that God He-does-it-to-him, an-angel he-is-seen he-holds that-which-is-glittering a-sword so-that he-closes-it-to-him the-door and not once-more able-to there he-is-not-(able-to)-come.

Nützliche Lehren.
WELAPEMQUO ACHGEGINGEWOAGAN.
PRACTICAL APPLICATION.

1. Aus dieser Historie kan man lernen, was der Ungehorsam für eine schwere Sünde sey? Denn um des Ungehorsams willen hat Gott die ersten Eltern aus dem Paradies verstossen.

1. Untschi jul endchi pendamanque [L., -qui] ktelli nemeneen elgiqui gantschi pallalogasit auwen pallistawate Patamawossall. Eli pallistamhittit enda quiteluxichtit netami Gischihendpanik nane untschi Patamawos getschihawall untschi schiki welhik hagihaganink Paradies elewundasik.

1. From these as-many-as as-we-hear-them we-thus see-it like-as terribly he-transgresses a-person if-he-disbelieves-Him God. Because they-disbelieve-it when they-are-warned first those-who-were-(first)-made that from God he-drives-them from the-beautiful good garden-from Paradise that-which-is-called.

2. Man kann ferner daraus lernen, wer die ersten Lügen auf der Welt geredet hat. Nämlich der Teufel, als er zu Eva sagte: Sie würde Gott gleich seyn.

2. Woak ju wuntschi elekgup gowoatelukguneen [L., -geneen] auwen nhittami gechgelunet jun talli Pemhagamigek, [21] woak

auwen wetochemuxit gelunet. Joh. 8: 14. Nane wtellenummenep machtando enda latup Evasall: Kmantowintsch woak tpisqui ktellsintsch Patamawos elsit.

2. And this from as-it-was it-makes-us-aware who first he-who-lies here in the-world-round-about, [21] and who (is) the-father who-lies. [John 8: 14.] That he-did-it the-Devil when he-said-to-her Eve: You-will-be-a-spirit-being and exactly you-will-do-so God as-He-does.

3. Man kan endlich daraus lernen, was man gedenken soll, wenn man in einen Garten kommt. Nämlich man soll an den großen Sünden=Fall gedenken, den die ersten Eltern in dem Paradies Garten gethan haben.

3. Jun elegup kmigomgussineentsch endchen temiki pintschigejanque enda wulinamank welhik gardenink, woak nane ktenda meschtameneen, elgiqui gantschi machtechinhittitup machtauchsowoaganink netami gischihendpanik nelachpichtitup welhik gardenink Paradies elewundasik.

3. Here as-it-was we-will-be-reminded as-many-times-as anything when-we-enter where we-observe-it a-good garden-in, and then when-we we-remember-it like-as terribly they-dropped into-sin first those-who-were-(first)-made while-they-were-there the-good garden-in Paradise that-which-is-called.

Gottselige Gedanken.
WELAPENDASIK PENAUWELENDAMOAGAN.
PIOUS REFLECTION.

Ich höre, daß der Mensch erst nackend ist gegangen, Und daß Gott nach dem Fall erst Kleider hat gemacht,

Juke ntelli pendamen, sopochwenesa netami gischihendpanik, woak nane gintsch elgiqui metschi machtauchsichtitup, nane aschitte achgunahalgussowak.

Now I-thus hear-it, {they-have-walked-naked} first those-who-were-(first)-made, and then a-little-while like-as already they-sinned, that then they-are-clothed.

Wie kan denn nun ein Mensch mit solchen Lumpen prangen?

Kaski eet juke ihiabtschi wuliechen ju endalauchsit [22] wtelli wundelensin elachquitschi wentschi mchelensit untschi nel milgussinall metachquoachemen sopsowoagan? Pallalogasu auwen undachqui li medauweget Patamawos miltowoaganall woak mchelensitak hokey untschi ehachquinkgi.

Able-to perhaps now still is-it-good here one-who-lives-here **[22]** that-he {boasts} how-he-is-clothed so-that he-is-haughty from those-things they-are-given to-cover-it nakedness? He-transgresses who this-way towards he-uses-badly God (His)-gifts and {?it-is-resplendent} his-body by clothes.

Ach Gott, behüte mich vor aller eitlen Pracht! Vom Hochmuth will ich mich zu wahrer Demuth lenken, Und stets an Adams Fall bey meinen Kleidern denken.

Woh N'Patamawos ngenachgihil untschi mchelensowoaganink! Guluppenummauwil [?Guluppenal] Nde li nundajelensowoaganink! Endchen penamane nhakey elachquit; Nemigomgentsch Adama elgiqui pallalogasit.

O my-God guard-me from from-pride! Turn-it-around-for-me my-heart toward toward-humility! As-many-times-as as-I-look-at-him my-body how-he-is-clothed; It-will-remind-me the-late-Adam like-as he-transgressed.

Die 5te Historie.

[23] 5 ELEGUP.

---

5 AS-IT-WAS.

Wie Cain seinen Bruder Abel erschlagen hat. 1 Mos. 4te Capitel.

Kaina enda nhillat chesemussall Abellal. 1 Mos. 4.

The-late-Cain when he-kills-him his-younger-sibling Abel. Genesis 4.

Adam hatte zwey Söhne: Der älteste hieß Cain, und war ein Ackermann: Der jüngste aber hieß Abel, und war ein Schäfer.

Adama nischowak quisopannik, gegeyit luwunsop Cain woak wingi hakihen, nane tenktitit luwunsop Abel woak wingi nutemekschen.

The-late-Adam they-are-two those-who-were-his-sons, the-elder he-was-called Cain and gladly-he farms, then he-who-is-little he-was-called Abel and gladly-he watches-sheep..

Diese beyden Brüder brachten dem Herrn ein Opfer, nämlich Cain von den Früchten seines Feldes, und Abel von den Erstlingen seiner Heerde.

Juk nischowak weimachtintschik wihungewoagan wtelli petauwanewo Patamawossall. Nane Kain petop nel hegihengi gischiginkil untschi wtagihaganink; schuk Abel petawanep Patamawossall nek netami gischigitschik wewulsitschik wtallemunsall.

These they-are-two brothers a-sacrifice they-thus they-bring-it-to-Him God. That Cain he-brought-it those plants those-which-are-grown from from-his-cultivated-fields; but Abel he-brought-it-to-Him

God those first those-(anim.)-which-are-(first)-born those-which-are-very-beautiful his-domestic-animals.

Es gefiel aber dem lieben Gott Abels Opfer besser, als Cains.

Nihillalquonk Patamawos wingelendamen Abellal enda wihungetup, schuk nel Kainall schingi penauwawall [24] **enda wihomguk.**

Our-Lord God He-delights-in-it Abel when he-sacrificed, but that Cain hates-to He-(hates-to)-look-at-him **[24]** when he-sacrifices-to-Him.

Denn Abel war fromm und Cain hingegen war gottlos. Hierüber ergrimmte Cain,

Abela gehella wulilissop, aschitte Cain husca machtapejop, ganquilawall chessemusall Abellal, manatehewoagan machtechen wdehenk, husca manunxop, neichgussop mhittschohai wuschginkunk wtelli ahichgun chessemusall.

The-late-Abel indeed he-did-well, then Cain exceedingly he-was-impious, {he-murmurs-against-him} his-younger-sibling Abel, envy it-lands in-his-heart, exceedingly he-was-angry, it-was-seen bodily in-his-face that-him he-makes-him-angry his-younger-sibling.

[Luckenbach only]

Nane Patamawos quittelawall Kainall woak wtellawall: Katschi manunxitawahan kchessemus, ponelenda, mattatsch ala schingalawachte kchessemus, machtauchsowoaganink kmatechentsch.

Then God he-warns-him Cain and He-says-to-him: Don't do-not-be-angry-with-him your-younger-sibling, let-it-be, not-will cease-to if-you-(will)-not-(cease-to)-hate-him your-younger-sibling, in-sin you-will-land.

[Luckenbach only]

CAIN AND ABEL.

Nane wtellsin Kain, ihiabtschi olhatton talli wdehenk manunxowoagan achtschingiuchsu, quonna ta quitelind, ihiabtschi kimii olhatton talli wdehenk, tacu gotta neichgunamawawun chessemusall, ngemewi witauchsomawall ninutschi elilenitawachtichtitup.

Then he-does-so Cain, still he-has-it in in-his-heart anger he-is-stubborn, even-if definitely he-is-warned, still secretly he-has-it in in-his-heart, not he-wants-to not-have-it-be-seen-by-him his-younger-sibling, constantly he-is-in-fellowship-with-him in-the-beginning as-they-were-accustomed-to-be-with-each-other.

und schlug seinen Bruder Abel todt, als sie beyde auf dem Felde waren.

Nane ngutten ma leep, elii epichtite hagihaganink, nane quihillutawan chessemusall Abellal, nan wtenda luphittehan.

That once in-the-past it-was-so, both when-they-are-there in-the-cultivated-field, then he-attacks-him his-younger-sibling Abel, that-one he-then {beats-him-to-death}.

Wie der Mord geschehen war, so sagte Gott zu Cain: Wo ist dein Bruder Abel? Cain gab troßig zur Antwort: Soll ich meines Bruders Hüter seyn? Aber Gott ließ sich damit nicht abweisen, sondern er sagte ferner; Was hast du gethan?

Metschi nhillowete Kaina, nane Patamawos wtellawall: Ta ha wtappin chessemus Abel, nechgutinke manunkhittaksu lueu: Tacu nowahawi ta epit, tepi hatsch a ni ngenachgiha nchessemus? Patamawos tacu na untschi ponimaiwall, schuk ikalissi wtellawall: koecu ha ktellsihump?

Already when-he-kills-him the-late-Cain, then God He-says-to-him: Where it-is-asked is-he-there the-younger-sibling Abel, when-he-answers he-sounds-angry he-says: Not I-do-not-know-him definitely where-he-is, enough it-will-be-asked should I I-take-care-of-him my-younger-sibling? God not there from He-does-not-leave-him-alone, but further He-says-to-him: What it-is-asked did-you-do?

Die Stimme deines Bruders Blut schreyet zu mir von der Erde. Da nun Cain die That nicht läugnen konnte,

Npendamenep elpehhellak kchessemus omocum, ju hakink untschi petalamo ni elinquechina. Nane quila pachsowe Kain eleningup,

I-heard-it that-which-flows-swiftly your-younger-sibling his-blood, here from-the-earth from it-cries-out-unto Me in-My-presence. That lacks-to when-he-lacks-to-deny Cain that-which-he-did,

so ward er von Gott dem Herrn verflucht, daß er unstät und flüchtig seyn sollte auf Erden.

woak Patamawos schawi wtenda kschaptonalan woak wtellan Kainall: Ki ktellitsch gendelemuxin jun talli hakink, ngemewitsch ktelli misochwen, woak tacu kmochgamowon endatsch nalauwi allachimuijan.

and God immediately He-then upbraids-him and He-says-to-him Cain: You you-thus-will be-condemned here in in-the-Earth, constantly-will you-thus wander, and not you-(will)-not-find-it where-will safely you-rest.

Anstatt nun, daß Cain über seine Sünden hätte sollen Busse thun,

Wuliechenop a Kaina schawi schiwelendamowitehatpanne, eli gantschi pallalogasitup mattauchsowoagan, [25] schuk alaqui nane matta wtellsiwi,

It-(would)-be-good would the-late-Cain immediately if-he-repented, because terribly he-transgressed sin, **[25]** but 'tis-a-pity that not he-does-not-do-so,

so gerieth er vielmehr in Verzweiflung, und sagte: Meine Sünde ist größer, als daß sie mir vergeben werden möge.

CAIN AND ABEL.

ulaha manunxilowall woak logahellelowall wdehall wentschi lat Patamawossall: nosamiechge, allowi samileu nmattauchsowoagan, tacu eet kaski npachkitatamagewon.

moreover he-is-angry and he-is-discouraged his-heart so-that he-says-to-Him God: {It-is-too-much-for-me}, more excessively-it-is-so my-sin, not perhaps able-to I-am-not-(able-to)-be-forgiven.

Dieser Cain hat hernach die erste Stadt auf Erden, mit Namen Hanoch gebauet. Seine Nachkommen sind lauter gottlose Leute gewesen, welche in der Bibel Kinder der Menschen heissen.

Nall na ihiabtschi Kaina wtenk untschi netamiechink uteney wtelli gischiton, wtellewundamenep Hanoch. Wtenk untschi hokenk ahanhucqui gischigitschik wemi machtapewinewo, wilchgussopannik talli mechoweki elekhasikil, ju endalauchsit wentamememensemuxitschik.

That one still the-late-Cain after wards the-first city he-thus made-it, he-called-it Hanoch. After wards from-himself over-and-over-again those-who-are-born all they-are-impious, they-were-named in those-which-are-old scriptures, here one-who-lives-here those-who-are-children-of.

[Luckenbach only]

Guluppatschi Patamawos pili milapannil wequisichtitschi, nek schikquinetschik kikeyak, nan nel wtellowihhellawawall Seth, nek hokenk untschi ahanhocqui, gischigitschik wtelli wulapewinewo, woak wulauchsinewo, woak Patamawos wtaptonaganink talli wilchgussinewo, nek Patamawos wentamemensemuxitschik.

{Also} God others He-gives-them-to-him they-have-sons, those parentless-ones the-elders, that-one those they-name-him Seth, those from-himself from over-and-over-again, those-who-are-born they-thus they-are-upright, and they-live-good, and God in-His-word in they-are-named, those God those-who-are-children-of.

FORTY-SIX SELECT SCRIPTURE NARRATIVES FROM THE OLD TESTAMENT

Die merkwürdigsten unter Seths Nachkommen sind Hanoch und Methusalah. Den Hanoch ist wegen seines frommen Wandels lebendig gen Himmel geholet worden;

Nek nischowak allowi mechelemuxitschik, welsittankpannik Sethink untschi ahanhucqui gischigitschik wilchgussopannik Henocha woak Methusalaha. Henocha eli husca wulauchsitup woak kschiechauchsop, Patamawos wtellihan, ngutten wtelli kikewi matschalan li awossagame.

Those they-are-two more those-who-are-honored-(more), those-who-believed from-Seth from over-and-over-again those-who-are-born they-were-named the-late-Enoch and the-late-Methusalah. The-late-Enoch as exceedingly he-lived-good and he-lived-pure, God He-does-it-to-him, one-time He-thus alive takes-him-home to Heaven.

und Methusalah hat unter allen Menschen am längsten, nämlich neun hundert und neun und sechzig Jahre gelebet.

Naga Methusalaha wemi ju endalauchsitschik allowi gunilehellechepanna. Nane naga peschgonk chapachki woak guttaschchenachge tchi gachtinamopanna woak peschgonk.

That-late-one the-deceased-Methusalah all here they-who-live-here more he-lived-long. Then that-late-one nine hundred and sixty so-many the-late-one-was-(so-many)-years-old and nine.

Nützliche Lehren.
WELAPENDASIK ACHGEGINGEWOAGAN.
PRACTICAL APPLICATION.

1. Adam hatte Anfangs nur zwey Söhne, und dennoch war ein Gottloser darunter. Daraus siehet man, daß es von Anbeginn böse und fromme Leute gegeben hat.

CAIN AND ABEL.

1. Adama nhittami schuk nischilowall quisineyall, ihiabtschi mauchsilowall machtapejuwall. Nane [26] untschi knemeneen eki nutschi schai achpopanik metschilissitschik woak welilissitschik.

1. The-late-Adam at-first only they-are-two his-sons, still he-is-one he-is-impious. That **[26]** from we-see-it beginning in-the-beginning immediately they-were-there evil-doers and those-who-do-good.

2. Kein Mensch hat Cain verführet, und dennoch hat er seinen Bruder ermordet. Daraus siehet man, daß die Boßheit inwendig in dem Herzen des Menschen stecket.

2. Tacu auwen achpiwip eli achquetschihat Kainall wentschi nhillat chessimusall, ihiabtschi n'hillawall. Nane untschi lohumagejank wulamoewoagan eliechink leu. Manunxowoagan wulatagano talli alami ju endalauchsit wdehenk.

2. Not a-person he-is-not-there how he-tempts-him Cain so-that he-kills-him his-younger-sibling, still he-kills-him. That from we-are-shown the-truth as-it-lies it-is-so. Anger {?it-lies-well} there inside here one-who-lives-here in-his-heart.

3. Der liebe Gott mußte wohl, daß Abel todt war, ob es gleich Cain nicht gestehen wollte. Daraus siehet man, daß sich der allwissende Gott nicht betriegen läßt.

3. Quonna Kain pachsowamate Patamawosall wtelli angelelin chessemusall, ihiabtschi Patamawos wuli woatonep li leu. Nane guntschi nemeneen elgiqui wemi koecu wewoatak Patamawos, tacu hittawi achgiwaluxiwi.

3. Even-if Cain if-he-denies-it-to-Him God that-he is-dead his-younger-sibling, still God well he-knew-it here it-is-so. That from-we we-see-it like-as every thing He-really-knows-it God, not skillfully He-is-not-(skillfully)-deceived.

Gottselige Gedanken.
WELAPENDASIK PENAUWELENDAMOAGAN.
PIOUS REFLECTION.

Es hatte Cain kaum den Bruder todt geschlagen, Gleich hörte Gott das Blut des todten Abels schreyn; Hat sich dergleichen nun mit Cain Zugetragen, So wird auch meine Schuld Gott nicht verborgen seyn.

Kain nesquo gachti pachgantschi nhillakgup chessemusall, Patamawos metschi schai opendamen petalamo mocum Abela. Elinankup Kaina enda machtauchsitup, nepitsch woak ndeliechge; nquila litsch ngandhatton endchi koecu machtauchsija.

Cain not-yet nearly entirely he-did-not-kill-him his-younger-sibling, God already immediately He-hears-it it-cries-hither his-blood the-late-Abel. As-he-observed the-late-Cain when he-sinned, I-likewise-will also I-(will)-be-done-to; I-lack-to in-the-future-to I-(will)-(lack-to)-hide-it as-much-as what I-sin.

Ach! darum will ich mich vor allen Sünden scheuen, Daß sie nicht wider mich zu Gott um Rache schreyen.

Nane wuntschi wemi nmattauchsowoaganall nuwingi ponilischimuintsch, wentschitsch matta nguttentsch likhikqui mekeniechink gischquike machtagenimiwonk Gettanittowit elinquechink talli.

That from all my-sins I-gladly {?will-run-away-from}, so-that-will not one-time-will at-that-time that-which-is-the-end when-it-is-the-day you-(will)-not-speak-ill-of-us the-Great-Spirit in-His-presence in.

Die 6te Historie.

[27] 6 ELEGUP.—1656.

---

6 AS-IT-WAS.—2348 B.C.

Von der Sündfluth.

Noaha enda kitalteuhetup woak psindpekup haki. 1 Mos. 6, 7.

The-late-Noah when he-built-a-big-boat and it-was-flooded the-Earth. Genesis 6 & 7.

Die Menschen wollten sich den Geist Gottes nicht mehr strafen lassen.

Nane likhikqui leep ju endalauchsitschik gantschi mamachtauchsinewo, woak matta tschitsch wulilchpiwunewo wentschi quiteluxichtit untschi welsitschi mtschitschankgunk.

Then at-that-time it-was-so here they-who-live-here terribly they-sin-continually, and not once-more they-are-not-willing so-that they-are-warned by-the-Holy Spirit-by.

Gott gab ihnen zwar hundert und zwanzig Jahre Zeit zur Busse: Aber sie bekehrten sich nicht,

Patamawos bischi pehapanil nguttapachki woak nischinachge tchi gachtin shaki, wentschitsch schiwelendamowitehachtit, elgiqui gantschi mamachtauchsichtit.

God to-be-sure He-waited-for-them one-hundred and twenty so-many it-is-years so-long, so-that-will they-repent, like-as terribly they-sin-continually.

sondern sie assen und trunken, sie freyeten und liessen sich freyen.

Schuk techi matta guluppiwunewo, matta koecu litehewiwak; ulaha nalauwi mamizinewo woak mamenachtinewo, wtelli wawikindhattinewo woak mamiltinuwo wikingewoagan.

But utterly not they-do-not-turn-around, not a-thing they-do-not-think; moreover unconcerned they-eat-continually and they-drink-continually, they-thus all-of-them-marry-one-another-continually and they-are-repeatedly-given (in) marriage.

Es war aber noch ein einziger frommer Haus=Vater in der Welt, mit Namen Noah. Demselben befahl Gott, daß er einen großen Kasten oder Arche bauen sollte, drey hundert Ellen lang, fünfzig Ellen breit, und dreysig Ellen hoch.

Ihiabtschi quajaqui mauchsit schachachgapeit lenno achpop jun talli Pemhagamigek elewunsit Noah nan Patamawos wtellapannil: manitol kitaltey, wulitol nachapachki tchaikane segek na amochol, palenachtchinachge gamolachgat, woak nachinachge tchaikane sagolachgat.

Still however he-who-is-one who-is-upright a-man he-was-here here in the-world-round-about he-who-is-called Noah that-one God He-said-to-him: Make-it a-big-boat, make-it well three-hundred so-many-fathoms that-which-is-the-length that boat, fifty {it-is-the-width}, and thirty so-many-fathoms it-is-high.

In diesen Kasten that Noah erstlich allerhand Thiere die nicht im Wasser leben können. Darnach brachte er so viel Speise und Futter zusammen, daß sie ein ganz Jahr davon lebem konnten:

Gischi wulitaque na kitamochol nane pusohalapanil schigantsch endchichtit endcheleneyachgissichtit [L., -ney achg-] awessissak matta lehellechetschik talli mbink; woak ika talli wulatonep michmizink [28] wendauchsichtit ngutti gachtin shaki.

Done when-he-is-(done)-making-it-well that big-boat then he-boarded-them wholly as-many-as-they-are as-many-kinds-as-they-are the-animals not those-who-live in in-the-water; and there in he-stored-it the-food **[28]** they-live-by one it-is-a-year so-long.

Auf die lezt gieng Noah selbst in den Kasten, mit seiner Frau, mit seine drey Söhnen, und mit seinen drey Schwieger=Töchtern, das waren zusammen acht Personen.

Nane metschi wemi gischi leke Noaha wtelli nihillatschi pusin nahelii wunachauchschumall woak nachilowall quisineyall nachpi nachilowall chumall, nane wemi wdentchinewo chasch wetschitschanquitschik.

Then already all done when-it-is-so the-late-Noah he-thus himself boards together-with his-old-woman and they-are-three his-sons with they-are-three his-daughters-in-law, then all they-are-as-many-as eight human-beings.

Und da sie darin waren, so schloß Gott der Herr hinter ihnen zu.

Metschi Noah pusite woak wemi lelemindtschik kitaltejunk achpichtit, nane Patamawos nihillatschi tschitane kpahemen kpahon.

Already Noah when-he-boards and all those-who-are-allowed in-the-ship they-are-there, then God Himself strongly He-shut-it-up the-door.

Darauf thaten sich alle Brunnen der Tiefe und alle Fenster des Himmels auf, und damit regnete es vierzig Tage und vierzig Nächte nach einander. Davon ward das Gewässer so groß, daß es fünfzehn Ellen über die höchsten Berge gieng.

Nane schai achhi gantschi leu, hakink untschi kschi tuppehhelleu m'bi, woak hokunk wuntschi ktschilanop taat sokhasu m'bi, woak jun leu newinachgetchoguni shaki. Nane wuntschi m'chaquichenop, attach pallenach tchaikane tchuppegachtop untschi wemi mengachtingi achquitachtine psindpepannil.

Then immediately very terribly it-is-so, from-the-Earth from swiftly it-flows-out water, and on-high from it-rained-hard as-if it-is-spilled the-water, and this it-is-so forty-so-many-nights so-long. That from there-was-a-high-flood, ten-plus five so-many-fathoms there-was-deep-high-water by all of-the-great-mountains the-mountain-tops they-were-covered-by-water.

Dieses grosse Gewässer blieb hundert und fünfzig Tage stehen; und da mußte alles ersauffen, was einen lebendigen Athem hatte.

Nane nguttapachki palenachtchinachge tchoguni shaki nguttelenawachki tchuppegachtop, nane wuntschi aptupewak wemi enda penkquonk lehellechetschik gischelemendtschik.

Then one-hundred fifty so-many-nights so-long of-one-kind there-was-deep-high-water, that from they-drown all where it-is-dry those-who-live those-who-are-created.

Noah fuhr unterdessen mit seinem Kasten auf dem Wasser herum. Endlich ließ sich der Kasten auf dem Gebürge Ararat nieder.

Schuk Noah kwitaltejum nalai achpamilachtan, woak na leep, eli allemi higahhellak, kitaltey nane talli hakink hatteu, meschakgahhelleu wachtschunk elewundasik Ararat.

But Noah his-big-boat safely it-sails-around, and then it-was-so, as away the-water-abates, the-big-boat then there on-the-land it-is-there, it-goes-to-land on-a-mountain which-is-called Ararat.

Da wollte nun Noah gerne wissen, ob der Erdboden wieder trocken wäre: Deßwegen ließ er zu unterschiedenen Zeiten einen Vogel aus dem Kasten fliegen.

Nane Noah achwi gottatamen weuchsin ta elek talli, metschi penquihhillake haki, nane wuntschi koechen wtellelemawall tschulensall wentschi ktschilid untschi kitaltejunk.

OF THE FLOOD.

That Noah very-much he-desires-it to-know definitely how-it-is there, already if-it-is-dry the-land, that for a-few-times he-let-them birds so-that they-go-out from from-the-big-boat.

Das erste war ein Rabe, und das andere waren drey Tauben. Der Rabe flog hin und wieder her, bis das Gewässer vertrocknet war.

Nhittami wtellelemawall ahasall, wentschi ktschilid, nane wtenk untschi nachowak amimiwak. Nane ahas kotschemunk wdappinep, na shaki abtschi pomihhillan segek kitaltey, gintsch pachgantschi higahhellake.

At-first he-let-it-(anim.) a-crow, so-that it-(anim.)-goes-out, then after wards they-are-three pigeons. That crow outside he-was-there, that-one so-long always he-flies the-length (of) the-ship, until entirely when-the-water-abates.

Die erste Taube kam wieder und brachte nichts mit. Die andere Taube kam wieder, und brachte ein Oel=Blatt in ihrem Schnabel.

Schuk na netamiechink amimi elelemind ktschilin, schai lappi pintschigeu, woak matta koecu nachpochwewon. Nane wtenk [29] wentachquiechink amimi, lappi leleman wentschi allumsgat, nane peton petschi glanndamen ngutti combach pechgeninkgup mhittgunk elewunsit olive.

But that one-who-is-first the-pigeon who-is-allowed to-go-out, immediately again he-comes-in, and not a-thing he-does-not-take-it-along. That after [29] a-second pigeon, again it-(anim.)-is-allowed so-that it-(anim.)-goes-away, then he-brings-it hither he-holds-it one leaf that-which-was-broken-off from-a-tree which-is-called olive.

Die dritte Taube blieb aussen, weil der Erboden nunmehr trocken war. Auf die lezt kam Gott selber, und sagte zu Noah: Gehe aus dem Kasten, du und dein Weib und deine Söhne, und deiner Söhne Weiber.

Nane lappi wtenk untschi amimi allumihilleu wuntschi kitaltejunk, schuk matta lappi pewi, eli metschi juke penkquonk haki. Wtenk untschi Patamawos nihillatschi otchapannil Noahall woak wtellapannil. Ktschil untschi kitaltejunk, ki woak quisak woak chumak.

Then again after wards a-pigeon it-(anim.)-flies-away from from-the-big-boat, but not again he-does-not-come, because already now it-is-dry the-land. After wards God Himself He-came-to-him Noah and He-said-to-him: Go-out from from-the-big-boat, you and your-sons and daughters-in-law.

Als nun Noah den Erdboden zum erstenmal betreten hatte, so bauete er einen Altar, und brachte Gott ein Dank=Opfer.

Nane Noah medchi meschigange jun allasche weskink gischigink haki; nane schai wuliton ehendalipuink, enda lagenk, woak wihomawall Patamawossall nachpi genamoagan.

Then Noah as-soon-as when-it-draws-near this like that-which-is-new which-is-grown-up the-Earth; then immediately he-makes-it-well a-table, where people-perform-ceremonies, and he-sacrifices-to-Him God with thanksgiving.

Das gefiel Gott dem Herrn so wohl, daß er den Noah und seine drey Söhne dafür segnete.

Nane untschi wihundowoagan, wingelendasu elinquechink Patamawos, wentschi wulapensohalat Noahall, nahellii nachilowall Quisineyall.

That from the-sacrifice, it-is-liked in-His-presence God, so-that He-blesses-him Noah, together-with they-are-three his-sons.

Ja er gab ihnen den Regenbogen zu einem Gnaden=Zeichen, daß keine Sündfluth mehr über den Erdboden kommen sollte.

OF THE FLOOD.

Gohan allowi lihan milapannil achgettemageluwi kikenolowoagan, elewundasik manakquon, nane shaki matta ihaschi neichquottowip, wentschitsch abtschi wtenk untschi wtelli woateluxin ju endalauchsit wetschitschanquit, matta ihaschi tschitsch psintpek haki, seki hattek pemhagamigek.

Yes more He-does-it-for-them He-gave-it-to-them a-merciful sign, that-which-is-called a-rainbow, then until not ever it-was-not-seen, so-that-will always afterwards he-thus is-made-aware here one-who-lives-here the-human-being, not ever once-more it-does-not-flood the-Earth, so-long-as it-is-there the-world-round-about.

Nützliche Lehren.
WELAPEMQUO ACHGEGINGEWOAGAN.
PRACTICAL APPLICATION.

1. Um der Sünde willen mußte die ganze erste Welt untergehen: Was kann man daraus lernen? Daß Gott ein eifriger Gott sey, der die Sünden nicht kann unbestraft lassen.

1. Machtauchsowoaganink untschi leep, wentschi psindpegup mesitschewi schigantsch elgigunk pemhagamigek. Nane untschi woatelukguneen Patamawos elgiqui ahi litehenemoalat metauchsitschi woaktsch matta pallihillewi wentschitsch kschaptonalat metauchsitschi ajasgami. [30]

1. From-sin from it-was-so, so-that there-was-a-flood quite entirely as-wide-as the-world-round-about. That from He-makes-us-aware God like-as very-much He-thinks-about-them sinners and-will not He-(will)-not-miss-the-time so-that-will He-chastise-them the-sinners for-good-and-all. **[30]**

2. Gott gab den bösen Leuten vor der Sündfluth hundert und zwanzig Jahren Zeit zur Busse: Was kann man daraus lernen?

2. Patamawos pehapannil ju endalauchsitschi nguttapachki tchi gachtin woak nischinachge, nesquo psindpegup haki, wentschitsch guluppichtit. Koecu eet ju wuntschi gachta penunudeluguna Patamawos?

2. God He-waited-for-them here those-who-live-here one-hundred so-many it-is-years and twenty, not-yet it-did-not-flood the-Earth, so-that-will they-turn-around. What perhaps here from want-to-us does-He-(want-to)-show-us God?

Daß Gott ein langmüthiger Gott sey, der lang auf die Bekehrung wartet.

Sche jun ktelli penundelukguneen, elgiqui wingi pehat metauchsitschil wentschitsch guluppilid woak ponelendamelid omachtauchsowoaganall.

Look-here! This us-thus He-shows-us, like-as gladly He-waits-for-him the-sinner so-that-will he-turn-around and he-(will)-let-go-of-it his-sins.

3. In der ganzen Sündfluth ward dennoch der fromme Noah mit seinem ganzen Hause erhalten.

3. Quonna psindpegup wemi elgigunk pemhagamikgek, ihiabtschi tepi olehelechemhalgussowak welilissit Noaha, nahelii wemi elangomatschik.

3. Even-if it-was-flooded all as-wide-as the-world-round-about, still enough they-are-caused-to-live the-well-behaved-one the-late-Noah, together-with all those-who-are-related-to-him.

Was kann man daraus lernen? Daß Gott ein gerechter Gott sey, der die Frommen nicht zugleich mit den Gottlosen vertilget.

Na ju guntschi nemeneen Patamawos elgiqui schachachgapewit, woak matta wemihawiwall welilissitschil elihat metauchsitschil.

OF THE FLOOD.

Then this from-we we-see-it God like-as He-is-upright, and not He-does-not-destroy-them those-who-do-good as-He-does-it-to-them the-sinners.

Gottselige Gedanken.
WELAPENDASIK PENAUWELENDAMOAGAN.
PIOUS REFLECTION.

Die erste Welt ließ Gott mit Wasser untergehen, Und Noah gieng selbst auch in seinen Kasten ein. Zulezt wird nun die Welt in lauter Feuer stehen,

Netamiechink gischelendasik Pemhagamigek Patamawos wtellelendamen wentschi ktauwihhillak li mbink. Woak Noah (chaasch wtentchinewo) pusinep kitaltejunk. Ajasgamitsch woak leu, mesitsche elgigunk Pemhagamigek tindejunk talli luteutsch medhikteu.

That-which-is-first that-which-is-created the-world-round-about God He-thinks-about-it so-that it-sinks-down thus in-water. And Noah (eight they-are-as-many-as) he-went-aboard in-the-ship. For-good-and-all-will also it-be-so, wholly as-wide-as the-world-round-about in-fire in it-will-burn {?it-(will)-be-a-bad-fire}.

Wo wird zur selben Zeit der Frommen Zuflucht seyn? Ich will, Herr Jesu! mir aus deiner offnen Seiten, Wenn alles wird vergehn, ein Arche zubereiten.

Ta undachqui li eet wtellschimuin welsittank nane likhikqui? Nechgutink: NJesus achpekhok hokenk nitsch ndelschimuin likhikqui endatsch wemi koecu tindejunk talli medtewalltsch.

Where this-way to perhaps does-he-flee-to the-believer then at-that-time? Answer: Jesus the-wound in-his-body I-will I-(will)-flee-to at-that-time when-will every thing in-the-fire in they-will-be-burned-up.

Die 7te Historie.

[31] 7 ELEGUP.—1770.

---

7 AS-IT-WAS.—2234 B.C.

Vom Thurm=Bau zu Babel. 1 Mose, 11te Capitel.

Enda hokunk likhechtite quenaga talli enda luwundasik Babel. 1 Mos. 11. &c.

When on-high when-they-build-it-thusly a-tower in where it-is-called Babel. Genesis 11, etc.

Nach der Sündfluth war nur eine Sprache in der ganzen Welt.

Nane shaki seki nutschiechink psindpekgup haki ngutti schuk liechsowoaganop talli Pemhagamigek.

That so-long until it-begins it-was-flooded the-Earth one only speech-there-was in the-world.

Nachdem sich nun die Menschen wieder gemehret hatten, so nahmen sie einen großen Bau vor. Nämlich sie baueten eine Stadt, und einen Thurm, dessen Spitze bis an den Himmel reichen sollte;

Nane likhikqui wetschitschanquitschik enda lappi mechelhittitup, nane gischipenauwelendamenewo wentschitsch hokunk likhechtit, wentschitsch wulitochtit quenaga. Nane talli uteneyahenewop woak gatta [?go-] likhenewo wulitonewo Quenaga hokunk segek pemihhillak achgumhok.

Then at-that-time human-beings when again they-were-many, that they-decide-it so-that-will on-high they-(will)-make-a-building-thusly, so-that-will they-make-it-well a-tower. Then there they-made-a-city and want-to they-(want-to)-make-a-building-thusly they-make-it-well a-tower on-high the-length which-passes-by a-cloud.

Das thaten sie nun aus Hochmuth, daß sie sich bey der Nach=Welt einen großen Namen machen wollten.

Nane jun wtellenummenewo eli mchelensichtitup, eli litehachtit, nek wetenk ahanhukqui gischigitschik abtschitsch noli nemeschalgooktsch, [32] woak wemi auwen n'machelemukguna.

Then this they-make-it because they-were-proud, for they-think, those after over-and-over-again those-who-are-born always-will me-well they-will-remember-me, **[32]** and every person he-(will)-honor-us.

Da fuhr Gott der Herr hernieder, und besahe die Stadt und den Thurm. Es gefiel aber dem lieben Gott der Bau gar nicht.

Nane Patamawos petschi peninep untschi hokunk mauwi penamen wtuteneyjuwa hokunk elikhechtit, quenaquo enda welitochtit, woak wtelli matta wulinamowunep.

Then God hither He-descended from on-high goes-and He-(goes-and)-looks-at-it their-city on-high how-they-build-it, that-which-is-a-tower where they-make-it-well, and He-thus not He-does-not-like-it.

Weil nun die Menschen davon nicht ablassen wollten, so verwirrete Gott ihre Sprache, daß keiner des andern Sprache vernahm.

Eli matta gachta logahellachtik jun kpitschewi elitehachtit, nane Patamawos untschi ganschi pethackhon wdahsesgawawall espikhetschil woak tschetschpenawall woak wtellihawall, wentschitsch achtschippi liechsichtit woak matta tschitsch nostawachtichtik.

Because not want-to they-do-not-(want-to)-give-up this foolishly what-they-think, then God from terribly there-is-thunder {He-scatters-them} those-who-build-up-the-structure and they-separate and He-does-it-to-them, so-that-will strangely they-speak and not once-more they-do-not-understand-one-another.

Damit konnten sie den Bau nicht fortsetzen, sondern einer zog mit den Seinigen da hinaus, und der andere dort hinaus;

Nane wuntschi tacu kaski gischiaspikhewiwak Quenaga woak alod wemi missii talli elemamek haki haseuchwewak, memajauchsit elangomatschi missii li witschi gathakepannil.

That from-they not able-to they-are-not-(able-to)-finish-building-it-up the-tower and yet all various-places there all-over the-Earth they-are-scattered, each-one his-relations various-places to with they-departed.

Zum Andenken, ward diese neuerbaute Stadt, Babel genennet, weil dieses Wort auf Deutsch eine Verwirrung bedeutet.

Wentschitsch abtschi meshadasik ju gantschi elegup talli enda gotta welitochtit Quenaga, nane wuntschi uteney luwundasik Babel, nan luwejuwu; wiamochhasu, eli talli nutschiechink wiamochgihhillak liechsowoagan.

Therefore-will always it-(will)-be-remembered this terribly as-it-was there where they-want-to they-(want-to)-make-it-well a-tower, that from the-city it-is-called Babel, that it-says; "it-is-mixed," for there it-begins that-which-is-mixed speech.

Nützliche Lehren.
WELAPEMQUO ACHGEGINGEWOAGAN.
PRACTICAL APPLICATION.

1. Gott der Herr giebt Achtung darauf, was die Menschen auf dem Erdboden machen. Das Kann man mit dem Thurm zu Babel beweisen; denn Gott fuhr damals hernieder und besahe den Bau.

1. Patamawos wtelli woatonall woak wuli genachgitonall wemi koecu li elitochtit ju endalauchsitschik jun talli Pemhagamigek.

FORTY-SIX SELECT SCRIPTURE NARRATIVES FROM THE OLD TESTAMENT

Na ju leep Patamawos enda petschi penitup untschi hokunk mauwi penamen nek enda welitochtit Quenaga.

1. God He-thus knows-them and well He-takes-care-of-them every thing toward what-they-establish here those-who-live-here here in the-world-round-about. That here it-was-so God when hither He-came-down from on-high goes-and He-(goes-and)-looks-at-it those where they-make-it-well a-tower.

2. Unter andern können sich die Menschen auch mit prächtigem Bauen an Gott versündigen. Denn der Thurm zu Babel wollte dem lieben Gott nicht gefallen.

2. Nane woak machtauchsinewo ju endalauchsitschik enda kpitschewi woak mchelensuwi wikhechtit, eli pendamank Patamawos elgiqui matta wulinamok Quenaga eli welitochtit.

2. Then also they-sin here those-who-live-here when foolishly and proudly they-make-a-building, for He-looks-at-it God like-as not He-does-not-like-it the-tower how they-make-it-well.

3. Gott der Herr kann die Anschläge der Menschen bald zu nichte machen. Denn zu Babel durste Gott nur die Sprachen verwirren, so mußten sie gleich aufhören zu bauen.

[33] 3. Necama Patamawos Nihillalquonk tepi wunita schai lokenumenall wemi mechelensuwi penauwelendamoaganall ju endalauchsitschi elitehatschi. Nane neichquottop Patamawos enda apui li lihate elikhetschil, wentschitsch achtschippi liechsichtit, nane schai quilalissinewo [L., **quila lissinewo**]

[33] 3. He God our-Lord enough he-skillfully immediately destroys-them all proud considerations here they-who-live-here those-which-they-think. That it-was-seen God when easily to when-He-does-it-to-them those-who-make-buildings-thusly, so-that-will strangely they-speak, then immediately they-are-unable-to-do-anything.

TOWER OF BABEL.

Gottselige Gedanken.
WELAPENDASIK PENAUWELENDAMOAGAN.
PIOUS REFLECTION.

Die Menschen bauen sich oft Häuser und Palläste, Die gleich als wie ein Thurm zu Babel prächtig stehn.

Ju endalauchsitschik m'chelensuwi wawikhenewo woak wulitonewo wikquahemall elinakhokup Quenaga talli Babelink.

Here they-who-live-here proudly they-make-houses-continually and they-make-them-well the-houses as-it-appeared the-tower there in-Babel.

Und sind doch auf der Welt nur Pilgrim und nur Gäste, Die durch das Jammerthal in Himmel sollen gehn.

Bischik wtelsinewo schuk misochwetschik woak tschepsitschik sekachpichtit jun talli Pemhagamigek. Temaki [?Kt-] schuk eschochwenewo jun talli enda pemeuchtink, teek petschi shakochwechtit awossagamewunk.

To-be-sure they-do-so but (are) those-who-wander and those-who-are-strangers they-are-there-a-certain-length-of-time here in the-world. {Pitifully} only they-walk-through here in where there-is-weeping, {there} until they-walk-at-length to-Heaven.

Wer fragt nach Haus und Hof auf dieser schnöden Erde! Wenn ich nur dermaleinst ein Himmels=Bürger werde.

Ni matta koecu nelendamowon wikia woak ntuteney, tepi a schuk leleminke nowitachpintsch talli awossagame.

I not a-thing I-am-not-glad-about-it where-I-dwell and my-city, enough would only if-He-(would)-allow-me I-will-be-there-with-(him) in Heaven.

Die 8te Historie.

[34] 8 ELEGUP.—2083.

---

8 AS-IT-WAS—1921 B.C.

Von Abraham und Sarah.

Naga Abrahama nahellii wikimatschi Saraha enda lauchsichtitup. 1 Mos. 18. Ch.

That-late deceased-Abraham together-with his-spouse the-late-Sarah when they-lived. Genesis 18th Ch.

Als einsten Gott mit Abraham redete, so gab er ihm diese Verheissung: In dir sollen alle Geschlechter auf Erden gesegnet werden.

Ngutten ma leep Patamawos enda nensitawotup Abrahamall wtelli kitaptonalanep wtellapanil: Kakenk untschi wulapensohalgussowaktsch wemi endchagetschik epitschik schigantsch elgigunk Pemhagamigek.

Once in-the-past it-was-so God when He-appeared-to-him Abraham He-thus promised-him He-said-to-him: From-yourself from they-will-be-blessed all those-who-are-as-many-nations-as those-(anim.)-which-are entirely as-wide-as the-world-round-about.

Das hieß so viel, es sollte der Heiland aller Menschen aus Abrahams Nachkommen gebohren werden.

Na jun majawi luejuwu: Untschi hokenk Abrahamink ahanhukqui gischigitschik auwen gischigutsch elitsch kikemhalat wemi ju endalauchsitschi.

Then this rightly it-is-said: "Of of-himself of-Abraham over-and-over-again those-who-are-born a-person he-will-be-born as-will he-make-them-live all here those-who-live-here.

Nun hatte Abraham eine Gemahlin, die hieß Sarah; allein sie hatte keine Kinder, sondern war unfruchtbar. Es war auch keine Hoffnung dazu, weil sie beyde sehr alte Leute waren.

Nane talli leep Abrahama wtelli wikimanep wunachauchschumall elewunsilid Sarah, alod matta wiwunitschaniwon, woak techi matta tschitsch kaski litehewon wtellitsch ihaschi wunitschanin, eli metschi [35] sami kikeyichtit eliwi.

That there it-was-so the-late-Abraham that-he married-her his-old-woman she-who-is-called Sarah, yet not she-does-not-have-children, and utterly not still-more able-to is-not-(able-to)-think that-she-will ever bear-children, because already **[35]** excessively they-are-old both-(of-them).

Demungeachtet glaubte Abraham doch, daß Gott seine Verheissung erfüllen würde:

Schuk ihiabtschi Abrahama matta pallsittawawiwall Patamawossall, wentschitsch tepi pachgantschichtolid wemi koecu endchi kitaptonalguk.

But still the-late-Abraham not he-does-not-disbelieve-Him God, so-that-will enough He-will-fulfill-it every thing as-much-as He-promised-him.

Und dieser Glaube ward ihm von Gott zur Gerechtigkeit gerechnet. Wie nun Abraham einst seine Augen aufhub, so sahe er drey Männer zu ihm kommen, die er nicht kante.

Na jun wulistamoewoaganink untschi uschachachgauchsohalgussinep Patamawos elinquechink talli. Na ma ngutten leep, Abrahama elisquondek lemattachpo lehellemattachpite, tamse

ABRAHAM AND SARAH.

elhoquete wunewawall nacha Lennowall pejatschik, tacu wunennawawiwall auwenil.

That-one this by-(this)-belief by he-was-made-righteous God in-His-presence in. Then in-the-past one-time it-was-so, the-late-Abraham {as-there-is-a-doorway} he-sits as-he-takes-a-seat, sometime when-he-looks he-sees-them three men those-who-come, not he-does-not-recognize-them the-persons.

Es war aber der Sohn Gottes mit zwey Engeln, die alle Menschen Gestalt an sich genommen hatten.

Ulaha juk wemi omenewop untschi Awossagamewunk; mauchsit Gettanittowit Quisall, witscheuchgopanni nischowak Enschellak, linaxopanik elinaxit ju endalauchsit.

Moreover these all they-came-from from from-Heaven; one (is) the-Great-Spirit His-son, those-who-went-with-him they-are-two angels, they-looked-like how-one-looks here one-who-lives-here.

Abraham bat diese drey Männer, daß sie bey ihm einsprechen möchten, und ließ ihnen Wasser geben, damit sie ihre Füsse waschen konnten.

Abrahama wangomawall jul Lennowall woak winuwamapanil wentschitsch mattamigechtit enda wikit woak matta lowiwunewo, woak schawi allogemuin wentschitsch milintschik m'bi, wentschitsch kschiechpattonk wsitowawall.

The-late-Abraham he-greets-them these men and he-beseeched-them so-that-will they-enter where he-dwells and not they-do-not-pass-by, and immediately he-sent so-that-will they-be-given-it water, so-that-will someone-wash-them their-feet.

Darnach führte er dieselben unter einen Baum, und ließ ihnen Kalbfleisch, Kuchen, Milch und Butter vorsetzen.

Nane peschuwawall esquondewink enda nipawit Mhittuk, wuli tahquachtop ne talli, woak schawi chamawall koecu gischtek

tange weuchschumuititii wujus, woak achpoanall, nahelii nonagon woak butel.

Then he-brings-them to-the-door where it-(anim.)-stands a-tree, good there-was-(good)-shade that in, and immediately he-feeds-them a-thing that-which-is-cooked a-little-bit of-calf meat, and bread, together-with milk and butter.

Sarah, seine Frau war zwar nicht mit zu Tische, sie konnte aber in der Küche alles hören, was über der Mahlzeit geredet ward.

Nane Sarah, Abraham wunachauchschumall bischi matta wipomawiwall talli enda lipuink, schuk ihiabtschi enda wiechenink pechotschi untschi tepi hitta pendamen wemi koecu elachgenutink talli enda wipundink.

Then Sarah, Abraham his-old-woman to-be-sure not she-does-not-eat-with-them there where {people-are-eating-thusly}, but still where she-cooked-it close by enough skillfully she-hears-it every thing as-it-is-related there where there-is-feasting.

Unter andern sprach Gott der Herr zu Abraham: Ich will wieder zu dir kommen, so ich lebe, so soll Sarah dein Weib einen jungen Sohn haben.

Nane wtenda Patamawos Nihillalquonk wtellapannil Abrahamall: Lappitsch ta likhikqui ktachelen tpisquihhillake, nanetsch wunitschanu knachauchschum Sarah.

That then-He God our-Lord He-said-to-him Abraham: Again-will definitely at-that-time I-(will)-visit-you when-the-time-is-at-hand, then-will she-bear-a-child your-old-woman Sarah.

Das hörte Sarah hinter der Thür, und lachte darüber. Der liebe Gott aber gab ihr deßwegen einen Verweiß, und sagte dazu: Sollte dem Herrn etwas unmöglich seyn?

Nane necama pendamen neli nipait wtenk undachqui kpahonink woak gelgiechgunall nel aptonaganall. Alod Nihillalquonk

ABRAHAM AND SARAH.

ktschaptonalapannil [36] **eli palistamelid wtaptonaganall woak wtellapanil: Kdite a wtallaiton koecu Patamawos?**

That she she-hears-it while she-stands behind on-this-side of-the-door and she-laughed-at-them those words. Yet our-Lord He-upbraided-her **[36]** because she-disbelieves His-words and He-said-to-her: Do-you-think would He-cease-to-establish-it a-thing God?

Die gute Frau wollte sich zwar entschuldigen, und sagte sie hätte nicht gelacht: Aber Gott strafte sie darum und sagte: Es ist nicht also, du hast gelacht. Unterdessen tras die Verheissung richtig ein,

Schuk na ktemaxit wischasit ochque gatta pallachpin woak luep: Tacu ngagelixiwon. Nane lappi kschaptonalawall wtellapanil: Tacu kschachachgaptonewon, bischik gagelixinep. Nane tpisgauwihhilake ihiabtschi tpisqui leep Patamawos endchi nigani wundamauwotup.

But that poor-one who-is-afraid the-woman wants-to be-innocent and she-said: Not I-do-not-laugh. Then again He-upbraids-her He-said-to-her: Not you-do-not-speak-the-truth, to-be-sure you-were-laughing. Then when-the-time-is-at-hand still exactly it-was-so God as-much-as beforehand that-which-He-declared-to-her.

und derjenige Sohn, den Sarah zur Welt brachte ward Isaac genennet. Das geschah, wie Abraham hundert, und Sarah neunzig Jahr alt war.

Woak Sarah Quisall gischigilitup wtelluwihhillan, Isaac. Na jun likhikqui leep Abrahama enda nguttapachki tchi gachtinamite woak Saraha peschgunktchinachge tchi gachtinamop.

And Sarah her-son he-who-was-born she-named-him, Isaac. Then this at-that-time it-was-so the-late-Abraham when one-hundred so-many when-he-is-(so-many)-years-old and the-late-Sarah when-she-was-ninety so-many she-was-(so-many)-years-old.

Nützliche Lehren.
WELAPEMQUO ACHGEGINGEWOAGAN.
PRACTICAL APPLICATION.

1. Aus dieser Historie lernet man daß die Geister in sichtbarer Gestalt erscheinen können, wenn sie wollen.

1. Jul aptonaganall untschi penundelukgeneen tepi a leu, nek epitschik talli awossagame, matta weuhokeyitschik wtschitschanquinewo, schuk ihiabtschi tepi neichgussinewo woak nensitawawall ju endalauchsitschil, litehachtite woak alogalgussichtite.

1. These words from we-are-shown enough could it-be-so, those those-who-are-there in Heaven, not those-who-are-embodied they-are-(not)-human-beings, but still enough they-are-seen and they-appear-to-them here those-who-live-here, when-they-think and when-they-are-sent.

Denn sie haben mit Abraham geredet, gegessen und getrunken.

Jun tepi neichquot nek lennowak enda dowalachtit [?ndonalachtit] Abrahamall enda wipomachtit.

This enough it-is-seen those men when {?they-seek-him} Abraham where they-eat-with-(him).

2. Man lernet ferner daraus, daß man auf Gastereyen nicht so viel Gerichte aufsetzen soll. Denn Abraham hat dem lieben Gott nicht mehr als Kalbfleisch, Kuchen, Milch und Butter vorgesetzet.

2. Ikalissi kpenundelukgeneen auwen gatta [?gotta] changen tacu gachtalquottowi sami cheleneyachki koecu gatta [?gotta] changen. Abrahama tepelendam, wtelli chaman Patamawossall, endchi koecu wulatagup, wujoos, achpoan, nonagon woak butel.

2. Further we-are-shown who he-wants-to feed-people not it-is-not-desirable too-many many-kinds (of) things he-wants-to feed-people.

The late-Abraham is-satisfied, that-he feeds-Him God, as-many-as the-things he-stored, meat, bread, milk and butter.

3. Man lernet endlich dabey, daß Gott möglich machen kann, was vor aller Menschen Augen unmöglich ist. Denn Sarah bekam einen jungen Sohn, ob sie gleich schon neunzig Jahr alt war.

3. Ikalissi lappi untschi koecu woatelukgeneen eleek; ju endalauchsit bischik quilalissin koecu, schuk Patamawos matta allaitowon koecu. Na jun [37] weitschiechtaguna, Sarah elihindup wtelli nuntschen, quisall gischigilowall, bischi metschi peschgunk tchinachge tchi gachtinamop.

3. Further again concerning a-thing we-are-made-known-about as-it-is; here one-who-lives-here to-be-sure he-lacks-to-do a-thing, but God not He-does-not-cease-to-establish-it a-thing. That-One this **[37]** He-demonstrates-it-to-us, Sarah how-she-was-done-to that-she is-with-child, her-son he-is-born, to-be-sure already nine times-ten she-was-years-old.

Gottselige Gedanken.
WELAPENDASIK PENAUWELENDAMOAGAN.
PIOUS REFLECTION.

Wie Gott von Sarah sprach, sie sollt ein Kind gebähren, So lachte sie dabey, und dacht im Herzen nein: Allein sie maßte darauf die harten Worte hören: Wie? sollte wohl bey Gott etwas unmöglich seyn?

Patamawos enda wundaptonete untschi Sarahall wtellitsch wunitschanilin nane necama gagelixilinep, woak wdehenk talli litehep, ta eet ne lewi. Alod untschi eli pallistank kschaptonalgussin woak lau: Tepi eet leu, Patamawos wtelli allaiton koecu?

God when when-He-speaks-concerning concerning Sarah that-she-in-the-future she-(will)-have-a-child then she she-laughed, and in-her-heart in she-thought, not perhaps that it-is-not-so. Yet from how she-disbelieves she-is-upbraided and she-is-told: Enough perhaps is-it-so, God that-He ceases-to-establish a-thing?

Die Frage will ich mir meiner Nachricht merken, Und meinen Glauben stets mit Gottes Allmacht stärken.

Na ju eli nachgutink aptonagan abtschi nuwingi meschatamentsch, woak Patamawos wtallouchsowoaganink untschi ntschitaniechtagen ktemaki schewek nolsittamoewoagan.

That here how she-answers-it the-word always I-gladly will-remember-it, and God by-His-might by I-am-strengthened poor weak my-(poor)-(weak)-belief.

Die 9te Historie.

[38] 9 ELEGUP.—2107.

---

9 AS-IT-WAS.—1897 B.C.

Von Sodom und Gomorra. 1 Mos, 19te Capitel.

Sodomink woak Gomoraink talli Elegup. 1 Mos. 19

In-Sodom and in-Gomorrah in as-it-was. Genesis 19

In der Stadt Sodom war nicht mehr als ein einziger frommer Mann, mit Namen Lot. Derselbe hatte sich um die Abendzeit unter das Thor gesetzet, und sahe unter andern zwey Engel zum Thor herein kommen.

Nane talli utenink elewundasik Sodom, achpop schuk mauchsit lenno welilissit, elewunsit Loth. Won wulacuniwi wtelli lemattachpin mechinqui esquandewink ika talli utenink. Nane wtenda newawall nischowall Enschelall pentschigewak talli esquandewink.

Then in in-the-city that-which-is-called Sodom, he-was-there only he-is-(only)-one man who-behaves-well, he-who-is-called Lot. This-one of-an-evening he-thus sits the-great gate-at there in in-the-city. Then he-then sees-them they-are-two angels they-come-inside in in-the-gate.

Dieselben nöthigte Lot, daß sie doch das Nacht=Quartier bey ihm nehmen möchten.

Nane schai wunumikitawawall neli wawangomat woak ahi winuwamawall wentschitsch meigechtit wikit.

Then immediately {he-bows-to-them} while he-is-greeting-them and very-much he-beseeches-them so-that-will they-camp where-he-dwells.

Ehe sich die Engel zur Ruhe begeben konnten, so kamen die gottlosen Einwohner in das Haus, und wollten die beyden Engel heraus haben, damit sie Sünde und Schande mit ihnen treiben könnten.

Nesquo gatta gauwichtik juk awossagame wentschijeyitschik Enschellak wemi petscholtinewo schigantsch endchichtit elgikuteneyik epitschik niskalamhattowak kotschemunk talli Lot wikit, gattatamauwanewo Lotall wentschitsch [39] ktochwalat nel tschepsitschil wetchukgil, gatta palihanewo.

Not-yet want-to they-do-not-(want-to)-sleep these Heaven these-who-are-from the-angels, all all-of-them-come-hither wholly as-many-as-they-are as-wide-as-the-city-is those-who-are-there all-of-them-make-an-ugly-noise outside there Lot where-he-dwells, they-desire-it-of-him Lot so-that-will **[39]** he-walk-them-out those strangers those-who-visit-him, want-to they-(want-to)-hurt-them.

Lot gieng zwar zu den Leuten hinaus, und sagte zu ihnen: Lieben Brüder, thut nicht so übel. Ja er that ihnen gar den Vorschlag, sie sollten nur die fremden Männer zufrieden lassen, er wollte ihnen seine beyden Töchtern heraus geben. Sie waren aber damit nicht zufrieden, sondern sagten: du bist der einige Fremdling hier, und willt regieren;

Bischi Lot eli wuliwoatak geta lihachtit, kotschemunk eep, mauwi quitelawall, woak gatta tschitquihillalawall: schuk tacu gelistawawiwawall alod allowi manunxinewo woak wtellawapanil: Ki mejauchsit palli wentschijeyit ju utenink, ihiabtschi ktelli gatta gegeyjumhen jun talli.

To-be-sure Lot as he-well-knows-it want-to they-(want-to)-do-something-to-them, outside he-went, goes-and he-forbids-them, and wants-to he-(wants-to)-silence-them: but not they-do-not-listen-to-him yet more they-are-angry and they-said-to-him: You (are) one-person elsewhere one-who-is-from here in-the-city, still you-thus want-to govern here in.

SODOM AND GOMORRAH.

Indem sie aber die Hände an den frommen Lot legen wollten, so griffen die Engel zur Thüre hinaus, und zogen den Mann in sein Haus.

Nane metschi gatta quihillutawanewo welilissit Lotall neli kotschemink achpit, nane wiechgawotschi wtallemi ktschihillanewo nek Enschellak, ika wdannanewo Lotall, wiquahemink wtellochwalawawall woak gobhamenewo esquandey

Then already want-to they-(want-to)-attack-him the-well-behaved-one Lot while outside he-is-there, then unexpectedly they-begin-to they-(begin-to)-come-out those angels, there {they-grab-him} Lot, in-the-house they-bring-him and they-close-it the-door

Die bösen Leute wollten zwar die Thüre aufbrechen; sie wurden aber mit Blindheit geschlagen, daß sie dieselbe nicht finden konnten.

woak wtellihanewo wentschi wiechgawotschi achgepinquechtit woak schaschgunemawak, eli matta koecu nemhittik, matta kaski lappi machgamowunewo esquandey.

and they-do-it-to-them so-that unexpectedly they-are-blind and {they-are-squeezing}, for not a-thing they-do-not-see-it, not able-to again they-are-not-(able-to)-find-it the-door.

Wie sie von der Thüre weg waren, so redeten die Engel mit Lot, und sagten ihm, daß sie von Gott gefandt wären, diese Stadt zu zerstören.

Nane metschi allumsgepannik eli wiquihillachtit enda schaschgunemachtitup, nan Enschellak wtellanewo Lotall: Patamawos npetalogalguna wentschitsch wemihenk jun uteney, woak nek woagai epitschik, eli gantschi mattauchsichtit;

Then already they-went-away because they-are-weary where {they-were-squeezing}, that-one the-angels they-say-to-him Lot: God He-sends-us-hither so-that-will we-eradicate this city, and those around those-who-are-there, for terribly they-sin;

Sie gaben ihm auch den Rath, daß er sich mit allen den Seinigen ohne Verzug aus der Stadt machen sollte.

woak ikalissi wtellawapanil luewak: Schuk ki woak wemi wikijan wentschijeyitschik, genachgiechgussihhimo, katschi wauchtamsihek, schai schimuik, ngattumook uteney.

and further they-said-to-him they-say: But you and all your-house those-who-are-of, you-are-taken-care-of, don't do-not-tarry, immediately flee, leave-it the-city.

Lot redete hierauf mit denen, die seine Töchter nehmen sollten; aber es war ihnen lächerlich.

Nane Lot wentschimawall nel nischowall geta wunatonamaquitschi, woak wemi atschimolchapanil, woak gihimapanil wentschitsch schai ngattumichtit uteney; schuk techi matta gelsittawawiwa ulahah gelchgiechgook.

Then Lot he-calls-them those they-are-two want-to those-who-(want-to)-be-his-sons-in-law, and all he-counsels-them, and he-admonished-them so-that-will immediately they-leave-it the-city; but utterly not they-do-not-listen-to-him moreover {he-makes-them-laugh}.

So bald als die Morgenröthe anbrach, so sagten die Engel: Lot sollte fortmachen;

Nane petapanke Enschellak wtellawawall Lotall: Schauwelenda, wentschitsch matta achogaguwon kschaptonalgussowoagan.

Then when-it-is-daybreak the-angels they-say-to-him Lot: Hurry, so-that-will not {it-will-not-come-upon-you} the-chastisement.

und wie er noch lange zögern wollte, führten sie ihn und seine Frau nebst seinen zwey Töchtern mit Gewalt zur Stadt hinaus.

SODOM AND GOMORRAH.

Schuk [40] Lot eli wauchtami lissit, nane Enschellak ika wtannanewo, necama woak wikimatschil woak elii wdanall woak guttochwalawawall untschi utenink.

But **[40]** Lot because tarrying he-does-so, then the-angels there {they-grab-him}, he and his-wife and both his-daughters and they-bring-them-out of of-the-city.

Vor dem Thor befahlen die Engel, sie sollten eilen, und sich nicht umsehen, bis sie auf den Berg kommen wären.

Metschi ktschichtite untschi utenink, nane Nihillalquonk wtellawall Lotall: schauwelenda, ktenni kpommauchsowoagan, wachtschunk pemameek lischimuil, katschi wdukhoquehan, katschi nagihhillahan shaki teek ika petschi pajan talli wachtschunk.

Already when-they-go-out of of-the-city, then our-Lord He-says-to-him Lot: hurry, hold-onto-it your-life, to-the-hills straight flee-toward, don't do-not-turn-your-head, don't do-not-stop until {there} there unto you-come in in-the-hills.

Aber Lot wollte nicht auf dem Berge bleiben, sondern nahm seine Zuflucht in das Städtlein Zoar. Dasselbige sollte auch mit untergehen, aber um Lots willen wurde es mit der Strafe verschonet.

Schuk Lot quitamen nundawi paan wachtschunk, eli metschi nenk petschihhilleu machtapan, nan winuwamawall nihillalgukgil, wentschitsch lelemind lischimuil ne utenetitink, Zoar elewundasik pechotschi eteek. Nane wuntschi Patamawos tacu witschi pallitowon nen utenetit, Lotink wuntschi eli ika lischimuit.

But Lot he-dreads-it needing to-come to-the-hills, for already he-sees-it it-draws-near a-bad-morning, that-one he-beseeches-them his-lords, so-that-will he-be-allowed to-flee-to that village-to, Zoar that-which-is-called near where-it-is. That for God not with-(them)-He does-not-ruin-it that village, for-Lot for because there he-flees-to.

Der Engel aber sagte nochmals: Eile und rette dich daselbst, denn ich kann nichts thun, bis daß du da hinein kommest. Eben nun wie die Sonne aufgegangen war, so erreichte Lot das Städtlein Zoar,

Schuk Nihillalquonk lappi wtellawall: Schauwelenda, gatta pommauchsil, ta a n'kaski koecu mikindamowi, gintsch ika nalawi pajanne ki. Nanne likhicqui tschinquehhelleu gischuch, Lot Zoarink utenetitink pejate.

But our-Lord again He-says-to-him: Hurry, want-to live, not could I-(be)-able-to a-thing work-it, until there safely when-you-come you. Then at-that-time he-shows-his-face the-Sun, Lot to-Zoar to-the-village when-he-comes.

und gleich darauf fiel Feuer und Schwefel auf Sodom und Gomorra, und verheerte die ganze Gegend.

Nane nihillalquonk schai wtelliton sokelanhawawall nachpi tindey woak wisawek achsin, awossagame wentschihhillak wtenda tchitonall uteneyall Sodom woak Gomorrah, woak nel woagai pemhattekil uteneyall.

Then our-Lord immediately He-makes-it-so He-rains-on-them with fire and yellow stone, heaven it-flows-from when-He destroys-them the-cities Sodom and Gomorrah, and those around those-which-are-thereabout the-cities.

Sein Weib aber sahe hinter sich, ob es ihr gleich der Engel verboten hatte, und ward zur Salt=Säule.

Schuk Lot wikimatschil eli guluphoquete, bischi quitelindup lau: Katschi guluphoquehan, nane wiechgawotschi nipain taat msink wtellinaxin, tschitanihhilleu hokey, nan nipachteu taat sikewiachsin.

But Lot his-wife as as-she-turns-her-head, to-be-sure she-was-warned she-was-told: Don't do-not-turn-your-head, then unexpectedly she-stands as-if a-graven-image she-appears, it-became-stiff her-body, that-one it-stands as-if a-stone-of-salt.

Nützliche Lehren.
[41] **WELAPEMQUO ACHGEGINGEWOAGAN.**
PRACTICAL APPLICATION.

1. Man lernet hieraus, daß die heiligen Engel der frommen Leute Häuser behüten.

1. Nhittami penundelukgeneen jun elsittamank, geschiechsitschik Enschellak elgiqui natschitochtit, tachpatamachtit nel welsittamelitschil enda wikichtit.

1. First we-are-shown this as-we-listen, those-who-are-holy angels like-as they-take-care-of-things, they-maintain-them those believers where they-dwell.

Denn hier wurden die bösen Leute mit Blindheit geschlagen, daß sie die Haus=Thüre nicht finden konnten.

Ikalissi woak knemeneen, eliechgussichtitup nek metapeitschik lennowak, achgepinqueuhalgussowak, wuntschitsch matta hittawi lappi mochgamowiwak kpahon enda esquondewink.

Further also we-see-it, what-they-were-done-to those impious men, they-are-blinded, therefore-will not skillfully again they-(will)-not-find-it the-door where there-is-a-gateway.

2. Man lernet daraus, daß Gott nicht die Bösen und Frommen mit einander dahin reiffet. Denn wie Gott Sodom verderben wollte, so ließ er den frommen Lot zuvor heraus führen.

2. Woak lappi ikalissi untschi neichquot Patamawos wtelli matta wingi kschaptonalawiwall woak tchihawiwall nel welilissitschil enda palihat pelsittankgil. Patamawos enda gotta palihat

epitschil Sodomink, nane nhittami allogemuin wentschitsch ktochwalind welilissit Lot.

2. And again further by it-is-seen God that-He not like-to He-does-not-(like-to)-chastise-them and He-does-not-destroy-them those those-who-behave-well when He-hurts-them the-disbelievers. God when He-wants-to He-(wants-to)-hurt-them those-who-are-there in-Sodom, then at-first He-sends-people so-that-will he-be-brought-out the-well-behaved-one Lot.

3. Was Gott befohlen oder verboten hat, daß muß man genau beobachten. Denn Lots Weib sollte sich nicht umsehen, und wie sie solches dennoch that, so ward sie zur Salz=Säule.

3. Patamawos wemi koecu li tachpamatup schitta quithigetup talli wtaptonaganink, nane woak gachtalquot auwen wulistank woak nosogank. Lot wikimatschil quitelindup, lan: katschi ktukhoquehan, schuk ihiabtschi wtellenummenep, nane wuntschi schai mamukquihhilleu.

3. God every thing toward He-maintained-him or He-advised-him there by-His-words, that also it-is-desirable a-person he-believes and he-follows-Him. Lot his-wife she-was-warned, she-is-told: don't do-not-turn-your-head, but still she-did-it, that from immediately she-is-destroyed.

Gottselige Gedanken.
WELAPENDASIK PENAUWELENDAMOAGAN.
PIOUS REFLECTION.

Daß Gott die frommen nicht vertilgt mit den Bösen, Da kann der fromme Lott uns zum Exempel stehn:

Patamawos matta ngutteli lihawiwall nel welilissitschil elihat metschilissitschil, jun weitschiechtageneen elihatup welsittangil Lotall.

God not singly He-does-not-do-it-to-them those well-behaved-ones as-He-does-it-to-them the-evil-doers, this we-are-demonstrated (by) how-He-did-it-to-him the-believer Lot.

Ach ja! Gott weiß sie schon vorhero zu erlösen, Eh er sein Gericht und Strafe läßt ergehn.

Patamawos nhittami alogemuin wentschitsch palli lochwalind welsittangil woak wschimohalawall untschi mamukuwoaganink, nane gintsch kschaptonalapanil metauchsitschil pelsittankgil.

God at-first he-sends-people so-that-will elsewhere they-(will)-be-brought the-believers and He-makes-them-flee from from-destruction, then until He-chastises-them the-sinners those-who-disbelieve.

Auch ich will schlecht und recht in meinem Hause wohnen, Wenn Gott die Bösen straft, so wird er mich verschonen.

Nepe woak ngatta nolauchsi talli wikija, wentschitsch matta witschi linamowon, pelsittank elinanktsch enda kschaptonalgussit.

I-likewise also I-want-to I-(want-to)-live-well in my-house, so-that-will not with-(him) I-(will)-not-be-treated-so, he-who-disbelieves how-He-will-treat-him when he-is-chastised.

Die 10te Historie.

[42] 10 ELEGUP.—2133.

---

10 AS-IT-WAS.—1871 B.C.

Von Isaacs Opferung. 1 Mose, 22ste Capitel.

Isaaca enda gachta wihundinke. 1 Mos. 22.

The-late-Isaac when wanted-to when-he-is-(wanted-to)-be-sacrificed. Genesis 22.

Abraham hatte mit der Sarah den einzigen Sohn Isaac gezeuget, und Gott hatte ihm die Verheissung gethan, daß in seinem Saamen alle Völker auf Erden sollten gesegnet werden.

Naga Abrahama schuk mauchsilowall quisall elewunsilid Isaac, gischigilowall untschi wunachauchschumink elewunsilid Sarah. Bischik Patamawos metschi wtellapanil, kakenk untschi auwentsch gischigu, nan wtellapendamenewotsch wemi elchagewitschik epitschik elgigunk pemhagamigek.

That-late deceased-Abraham only he-is-one his-son he-who-is-called Isaac, he-is-born of of-his-old-lady she-who-is-called Sarah. To-be-sure God already He-said-to-him, from-yourself from a-person-will he-(will)-be-born, that-one they-will-make-use-of-it all tribesmen where-they-are as-wide-as the-world-round-about.

Es bekam aber der liebe Mann den unverhofften Befehl von Gott daß er diesen Sohn der Verheissung schlachten und opfern sollte. Und solches that Gott darum, daß er Abraham versuchen wollte, ob er ihm auch würde gehorsam seyn.

Schuk nane talli leep, enda matta litehak, Patamawossall wtellgol: Naten Quis, nigani wundamagejan ehoalatt Quis, nhill woak wihungel. Patamawos jun wuntschi wtellihawall Abrahamall wentschitsch tepi woachquo elsilid wdehall, gachenetsch a wemi koecu li wingi awulsittawawall Patamawossall.

But then there it-was-so, when not he-does-not-think, God He-says-to-him: Take-him your-son, beforehand it-is-declared-to-you him-whom-you-love your-son, kill-him and offer-him-up. God this for He-does-it-to-him Abraham so-that-will enough it-(will)-be-revealed how-he-acts his-heart, whether-in-the-future would every thing toward willingly he-(will)-obey-Him God.

Abraham that, was ihm Gott befohlen hatte, und reisete mit seinem Sohne nach dem Berge Morija. Der Vater nahm das Feuer und das Messer in seine Hand. Der Sohne aber mußte das Hol; zum Opfer auf dem Rücken tragen.

Nane Abrahama schai wtellenumen eland lissil, woak allumsgewak necama woak Quisall Isaac teek ika [43] **petschi wachtschunk elewundasik Moria. Nane wetochemuxit wtelli gelennemen tindey woak bachkschigan untschi wunachkink. Schuk Quisall Isaac nejundamenall nel tachanall geta ewegenk enda wihundink.**

Then the-late-Abraham immediately he-does-it as-he-is-told: Do-so, and they-go-away he and his-son Isaac {there} there **[43]** unto unto-the-mountain that-which-is-called Moriah. Then the-father he-thus holds-it fire and a-knife by by-his-hands. But his-son Isaac he-carries-them-on-his-back those pieces-of-wood wants-to one-who-(wants-to)-use-them where there-is-a-sacrifice.

Unterwegens fragte der Sohn den Vater, wo denn das Schaaf zum Opfer wäre? Der Vater aber gab zur Antwort: Gott der Herr hätte sich schon ein Schaaf ausersehen.

Nawotschi li ejachtite, quisall wtellgol: Nocha! Ta ha na untschi gohellaneen mekis nhillind enda wihundink. Nane Abrahama

ABRAHAM OFFERETH ISAAC.

nechgutink wtellawall: Patamawos metschi pipinawawall memekschall.

{Along-the-way} toward when-they-go, his-son he-says-to-him: My-father! Where it-is-asked (is) that-one for {we-take-him-(for)} the-sheep to-be-killed where there-is-the-sacrifice. Then the-late-Abraham he-answers he-says-to-him: God already He-chooses-him the-sheep.

Wie sie an den Ort kamen, so bauete Abraham einen Altar, und leate das Holz darauf.

Medchi ika pejachtite, geta pachtit, nane Abraham maniton enda lipuink enda lagenk, woak tachanall ika wtatonall.

As-soon-as there when-they-come, want-to they-who-(want-to)-come, then Abraham he-makes-it where there-is-eating when there-is-a-ceremony, and the-pieces-of-wood there he-places-them.

Hernach band er seinen Sohn, und legte denselben auf das Holz.

Nane gintsch wundamauwan Quisall, Gettanittowit eli wulelendank. Nane Isaac pendawote ochwall, wingi leleman wentschitsch gachpilguk. Nane aschitte gachpilapanil Quisall woak wochgitschi wtahhellawall, tachanall enda gischiwulitagup.

Then a-little-while he-declares-it-to-him his-son, the-Great-Spirit how He-is-glad-about-it. Then Isaac when-he-hears-him his-father, willingly he-allows-him so-that-will he-bind-him. Then next he-bound-him his-son and on-top he-places-him, the-pieces-of-wood where he-finished-making-it-well.

Als er nun das Messer schon in der Hand hatte, und den Knaben schlachten wollte, so rief der Engel des Herrn vom Himmel: Abraham! Abraham!

Nane metschi weteninke pachkschigan, wtaspenumen wentschitsch nhillat Pilawesissall, nane Patamawos wtenschellumall pendaxu,

amangiechsin untschi awossagamewunk wtellawall, lueu: Abraham! Abraham!

Then already when-he-takes-it the-knife, he-lifts-it-up so-that-will he-kill-him the-lad, then God His-angel he-is-heard, he-speaks-loudly from from-Heaven he-says-to-him, he-says: Abraham! Abraham!

Er sagte darauf: Hie bin ich! Der Engel sprach weiter in ihm: Leae deine Hand nicht an den Knaben; den nun weiß ich, daß du Gott fürchtest. Wie nun Abraham hinter sich sahe, so ward er einen Widder gewahr, der mit seinen Hörnern in einer Hecke hieng. Diesen Widder nahm Abraham, und opferte denselben anstatt seines Sohnes.

Nane nechgutink lue: Katschi pallihahan Quis; juke tepi wochquot ktelli awulsittawan woak quittajalan Patamawos. Nane Abrahama guluphoquete, wunewawall mchinqualuppawewall, uschumunk talli etschgagenechin; nan nel wulaphallan palipaewall, enda gachta wihungetup quisall.

Then he-answers he-says: Don't do-not-hurt-him your-son; now enough it-is-revealed that-you obey-Him and you-fear-him God. Then the-late-Abraham when-he-turns-his-head, he-sees-him a-great-ram *[lit., a-great-buck]*, by-his-horns there {he-is-stuck}; that-one that-one he-replaces-him-(with) the-ram *[lit., the-buck]*, where wanted-to he-(wanted-to)-sacrifice his-son.

Diesen Gehorsam gefiel Gott aus dermassen wohl,

Na jun awulsittamoewoagan Abrahama eli penundhigete, enda techi mesitsche wdehenk untschi wingi lissit, eland lissil, Patamawos wtelli wulachgenutemen, woak wulinamenep,

That-one this obedience the-late-Abraham as as-he-shows, when utterly quite from-his-heart from willingly he-does-so, as-he-is-told: Do-so, God He-thus talks-well-about-it, and He-observed-it,

ABRAHAM OFFERETH ISAAC.

und Abraham erhielt nochmals den Segen, daß in seinem Saamen alle Völker auf Erden sollten gesegnet warden. Was erhielt Abraham für eine Verheissung?

wentschi lappi antschi mechinqui wulapensohalat [44] woak kitaptonalat Abrahamall, woak lapaptonalan elindup: Owochganimink untschitsch wulapensohenaktsch wemi ekhogewitschik wochgithagamique epitschik.

so-that again anew greatly He-blesses-him **[44]** and He-promises-him Abraham, and He-speaks-to-him-again as-he-was-told: From-his-seed from-will He-bless-them all the-tribesmen upon-the-Earth those-who-are-there.

Nürtzliche Lehren.
WELAPEMQUO ACHGEGINGEWOAGAN.
PRACTICAL APPLICATION.

1. *Gott der Herr prüfte den Abraham, ob er auch würde gehorsam seyn. Daraus siehet man, daß Gott seine Gläubigen bißweilen in Versuchung führet.*

1. Patamawos Nihillalquonk gutschillachtiganehenep Abrahamall, gachenatsch a tepi awulsittagol. Nane untschi neichquot Patamawos wtelli hank lihan welsittagil, wentschitsch achquetschiechgussichtit welhikink li.

1. God our-Lord {He-made-a-trial} (of) Abraham, whether-in-the-future would sufficiently he-obey-Him. That from it-is-seen God that-He as-said does-it-to-him the-believer, so-that-will they-be-tempted toward-that-which-is-good toward.

2. *Gott der Herr sandte einen Engel, der Abraham von dem Blutvergießen abhalten mußte. Daraus siehet man, daß Gott die Seinigen auch wieder aus der Versuchung erlöset.*

2. Patamawos wtelli allogemuinep wtenschellumall, wentschitsch genachgihind Abrahama woak matta sogate'hemok mhuk. Nane untschi knemeneen Patamawos elgiqui lappi ktinnat wtamemensumall enda achquetschiechgussichtit.

2. God He-thus sent His-angel, so-that-will he-be-taken-care-of the-late-Abraham and not {he-does-not-shed-it} blood. That from we-see-it God like-as again He-pulls-them-away His-children when they-are-tempted.

3. Gott der Herr gab Abraham aufs neue den Segen. Daraus siehet man, daß den Gläubigen alle Versuchungen zum besten dienen müssen.

3. Patamawos nihillalquonk wuskitawanall Abrahamall nel wulapensowoaganall. Nane guntschi penundelukgeneen elgiqui abtschi lapendank welsittank nhagalate Patamawossall, enda achquetschiechgussit.

3. God our-Lord {He-renews-them-with-him} Abraham those blessings. That from-we we-are-shown like-as always he-finds-it-useful the-believer if-he-trusts-(in)-Him God, when he-is-tempted.

Gottselige Gedanken.
WELAPENDASIK PENAUWELENDAMOAGAN.
PIOUS REFLECTION.

Gott sprach: In Isaac will ich die Völker segnen, und sprach doch auch zugleich: Geh, schlachte deinen Sohn!

Patamawos laptonep: Isaacink elitsch gischigit, nolapensohenak wemi endchitschik elhagewitschik; woak guluppatschi aschitte luep: Mauwi nhil quis knitschan!

God He-spoke-thusly: From-Isaac as-in-the-future he-(will)-be-born, I-bless-them all those-who-are-as-many-as the-tribesmen; and {also} then He-said: Go-and kill-him your-son your-child!

ABRAHAM OFFERETH ISAAC.

Nichts härters konnte wohl dem Abraham begegnen: und dennoch hielt er aus, und trug den Sieg davon!

Tacu hittai allowi koecu sesachquoak meschigaguwunep Abrahama: Ihiabtschi matta tschanelendamowon, matta logahellewi, alod wtelli patachwilsin.

Not could more a-thing {that-which-is-troubling} it-(could)-not-(have)-drawn-near the-late-Abraham: Still not he-is-not-in-doubt-about-it, not he-is-not-discouraged, yet he-thus wins.

Ach wenn Gott mich und dich so in Versuchung führte, Wer weiß, ob er bey uns dergleichen Glauben spührte.

Kiluna auwen achquetschiechgussite Abrahama elgiqui achquetschiechgussitup, tamse matta tepi penundhikewon elinaquo tschitanek awulsittamoewoagan.

We who when-he-is-tempted the-late-Abraham like-as he-was-tempted, sometimes not enough he-does-not-show-it that-which-looks-like strong obedience.

Die 11te Historie.

[45] 11 ELEGUP.—2148.

---

11 AS-IT-WAS.—1856 B.C.

Von Isaacs Vermählung. 1 Mose, 24ste Capitel.

Isaaca enda wikingetup. 1 Mos. 24, &c.

The-late-Isaac when he-married. Genesis 24, etc.

Wie Abraham nunmehro alt war, so wünschte er, daß sein Sohn Isaac heyrathen möchte.

Abrahama metschi kikeyjop, nane wdehenk lachauwelendamen woak liteheu: Jukella Nquis Isaac wtelli wikingen.

The-late-Abraham already he-was-old, then in-his-heart he-is-concerned and he-thinks: Oh-that my-son Isaac that-he marries.

Abraham aber wollte nicht, daß sein Sohn eine Heydnische Tochter aus dem Lande Canaan heyrathen sollte, sondern er wollte eine Schwieger Tochter von seiner Freundschaft haben.

Schuk matta techi wtelli gattatamowunep, schilendamelin quisall, nel epitschil nalowauchsitschi; schuk liteheu: ngatta n'chumi auwen wdanissall elangomachgik welsittangik epitschik.

But not utterly he-thus did-not-desire-it, to-take-a-wife his-son, those those-who-are-there heathens; but he-thinks: I-want my-daughter-in-law a-person his-daughter those-who-are-my-relations the-believers those-who-are-there.

Er schickte deßwegen seinen Haus=Vogt oder den ältesten Knecht seines Hauses, mit Namen Elieser, nach seiner Heymath. Es wohnten aber die

Unverwandten Abrahams in der Stadt Nahor, und vor dem Thore war ein Brunnen, daraus das Vieh getränket wurde.

Nane wtallogalan wentschi ika aat haki wengup Abrahama, na allowi gegeyit wdallogaganall, elewunsit Elieser. Nik Abrahama elangomatschik achpopanik talli utenink elewundasik Nahor. Nane giechgi utenink hattep ehelilamank nane ehenda michmenachhind awessissak.

Then he-sends-somebody so-that there he-goes the-land from-whence-he-came the-late-Abraham, that-one more he-is-old his-servant, he-who-is-called Eliezer. Those the-late-Abraham those-who-are-his-relations they-were-there in in-the-city that-which-is-called Nahor. That near to-the-city it-was-there a-well that where-habitually they-are-habitually-given-a-drink the-beasts.

Zu diesem Brunnen kamen des Abends die Töchter aus der Stadt, Wasser zu schöpfen.

Nek ochquewak utenink wentschijeyitschik wtellileninewo eheschi giechki wulaquik ika pewak ehelilamank eteek, mauwi anshamenewo m'bi.

Those women of-the-city those-who-are-of they-customarily every nearly evening there they-come the-well where-it-is, go-and they-(go-and)-draw-it water.

Da bat Elieser den lieben Gott, daß er ihm doch Isaacs zukünstige Liebste bey diesem Brunnen zeigen wollte.

Nane metschi ika pate elogalgussit [46] Elieser, wdenda papatamauwan Patamawossall wtelli penundelukgun pipinund ochque wentschitsch wikimat Isaacall.

Then already there when-he-comes he-who-is-sent [46] Eliezer, he-there prays-to-Him God that-He He-shows-him she-who-is-chosen the-woman so-that-will she-marry-him Isaac.

MARRIAGE OF ISAAC.

Indem kam eine sehr schöne Jungfer, mit Namen Rebecca aus der Stadt. Ihr Vater war Bethuel, ein Anverwandter von Abraham.

Nane quajaqui papatamate ika paan ehelilamank Rebecca elewunsit, pilsit wuskochque, utenink wentschijeyit. Ochwall luwunsu Bethuel, Abrahama elangomatschi.

That still when-he-is-praying there comes (to) the-spring Rebecca she-who-is-called, she-who-is-pure a-young-woman, from-the-city she-who-is-from. Her-father he-is-called Bethuel, the-late-Abraham his-relation.

Wie dieselbe ihren Krug voll Wasser geschöpfet hatte, so sagte Elieser zu ihr: Laß mich ein wenig Wasser aus deinem Kruge trinken. Das that Rebecca, und gab seinen Cameelen auch zu trinken.

Won metschi anshanke m'bi Elieser wtellapanil, kechitti menahil m'bi eteek ktasisguwakhakunk. Nane wingi wtellihan woak happi menahawall wdallemunsall.

This-one already when-she-draws-it water Eliezer he-said-to-her, a-little give-me-to-drink the-water which-is-there in-your-earthen-bottle. That willingly she-does-it-for-him and in-the-bargain she-gives-them-a-drink his-domestic-animals.

Weil nun dieses das Kennzeichen war, welches der Knecht von Gott ausgebeten, hatte, so schloß er daraus, daß Gott Gnade zu seiner Reise gegeben hätte. Elieser beschenkte hierauf die Dirne mit einer gütdenen Spange, und mit zwey gütdenen Arm Ringen.

Jun kikenolowoagan Elogalgussit Abrahama wdallogagan eli ajandangup milgussin untschi Patamawossink, nane untschi wtelli woawelendamen Patamawos wtelli wulelendamowi wulapensohatamen wtellochwewoagan. Nane Elieser schai welhigi nguldii manschapiall milapanni na wuskochquewall.

This sign he-who-is-sent the-late-Abraham his-servant as he-wished-it he-is-given-it by by-God, that by he-thus witnesses-it God that-He gladly blesses-it his-trip. Then Eliezer immediately those-which-are-good golden beads he-gave-them-to-her that young-woman.

Er fragte auch zugleich, ob er nicht bey ihrem Vater Herberge haben könnte. Rebecca tief gleich nach Hause, und wieß ihren Eltern das Präsent, das sie von dem fremden Manne bekommen hatte.

Woak ntutemawall, wtellawall: Tepi hatsch tauwalachgat goch wikit, mawigejenk a ika talli? Rebecca schai ika schihhillan wikit, woak penundelawall gegeyjujumall endchi milguk na tschepsit lennowall.

And he-inquires-of-her, he-says-to-her: Sufficiently it-will-be-asked is-it-open your-father his-house, (could)-we-camp could there in? Rebecca immediately there runs where-she-dwells, and she-shows-them her-parents as-much-as he-gives-her that-one who-is-a-stranger the-man.

Unterdessen dankte der Knecht dem Herrn seinem Gott, daß er Gnade zu seiner Reise gegeben hätte.

Neli allumsgat Rebecca na Lenno wtelli gagenamawall Patamawossall nihillalgukil untschi eli genachgiechguk nawotschi li, woak na ju petschi witahemguk, wentschi tepi leek, wentochwet nhagalgussitup.

While she-goes-away Rebecca that man he-thus continually-thanks-Him God his-Lord for how He-takes-care-of-him {along-the-way} towards, and then here unto He-helps-him, so-that enough it-is-so, he-who-walks-for he-was-trusted.

Es währte nicht lange, so kam ihr Bruder Laban aus der Stadt, und empfieng diesen Elieser mit diesen Worten:. Komm herein, du Gesegneter des Herrn, warum stehest du draussen?

MARRIAGE OF ISAAC.

Nane schai untschi utenink peu Rebecca chansall Laban elewunsilid, woak nachpi jul aptonaganall wangomapanil Elieserall woak wtellawall: Pintschigel ki welapensohalgussian untschi nihillalquongunk, quatsch kotschemunk nipawijan?

Then immediately from from-the-city he-comes Rebecca her-older-brother Laban he-who-is-called, and with these words he-greeted-him Eliezer and he-says-to-him: Come-inside you you-who-are-blessed of of-our-Lord, why outside do-you-stand?

So bald der Knecht in das Haus kommen war, so brachte er seine Werbung an.

Nane medchi ika pate wiquahemink nane schai wtellatschimuin woak wemi wundamen lue: Jun nundochwen, jun untschi ndallogalgun nihillalid [47] **Abraham.**

Then as-soon-as there when-he-comes in-the-house then immediately he-relates-it and all he-declares-it he-says: this I-travel-for, this for he-sends-me my-lord **[47]** Abraham.

Die Antwort bestand darinnen: Das kommt vom Herrn, darum können mir nichts dawider reden, weder Böses noch Gutes.

Nane nachgutemenewo gegeyitschik woak luewak: Jun pejeju nihillalquongunk untschi, ta a niluna nitai koecu laptonehumena kakenk, welhik schitta medhik.

Then they-answer-it the-elders and they-say: This it-comes from-our-Lord from, not could we we-skillfully a-thing (could)-we-speak-thusly of-yourself, that-which-is-good or that-which-is-evil.

Darauf sagte der Vater zu seiner Tochter: Willt du mit diesem Manne ziehen? Sie gab zur Antwort: Ja ich will mit ihm ziehen. Damit gieng die Reise vor sich

Nane wentschi Rebecca ochwall wtellgol: Guwingi eet witschewon wo Lenno? Necama nechgutink luep: Nuwitschewantsch a. Nane

schai wetschpinewo pili gischquike wentschitsch allumsgachtit.

Then therefore Rebecca her-father he-says-to-her: Willingly-you perhaps accompany-him this man? She she-answers she-said: I-(would)-go-with-him-in-the-future would. Then immediately they-get-dressed another when-it-is-(another)-day so-that-will they-go-away.

[Luckenbach only]

Woak Rebecca chansall wemi wimachtall milawawall chesse-mussowawall allogagan ochquewall, wentschitsch genachgiechguk Rebecca,

And Rebecca her-older-brothers all her-brothers they-give-her-to-her their-younger-sibling a-servant woman, so-that-will she-take-care-of-her Rebecca,

und ihr Geschwister gab ihr folgenden Segen mit auf den Weg: Du bist unsere Schwester machse in viel tausend mal tausend

woak allowi wtellaptonalawawall jul wulapensowaptonamik luewak: Ki nchessemussena kakey, allumikil li kitapachki tchen kitapachki shaki..

and more they-speak-to-her-thusly these words-of-blessing they-say: You our-younger-sibling yourself, grow to a-thousand so-many-times a-thousand so-long.

Nützliche Lehren.
WELAPEMQUO ACHGEGINGEWOAGAN.
PRACTICAL APPLICATION.

1. Eltern sollen ihre Kinder zur Arbeit halten. Denn hier mußte Rebecca das Vieh beschicken, und war doch eines vornehmen Mannes Tochter in der Stadt.

MARRIAGE OF ISAAC.

1. Husca gachtalquot wenitschanitschik wtelli a achgegimanewo wunitschanowawall wentschi wingi mikemossichtit. Jun ktelli nemeneen Rebecca eleninkgup, wtelli wingi genachgihawall awessissall, bischi pewallessit lenno wdannissall utenink wentschijeyit.

1. Exceedingly it-is-desirable those-who-have-children that-they should they-(should)-teach-them their-children so-that willingy they-work. This we-thus we-see-it Rebecca that-which-she-did, that-she willingly takes-care-of-them the-beasts, to-be-sure one-who-is-rich a-man his-daughter in-the-city he-who-is-from.

2. Kinder sollen ohne Vorwissen ihrer Eltern nicht heyrathen. Denn hier sorgte Abraham für seinen Sohn, und Bethuel für seine Tochter.

2. Tacu wulittowi quisak schitta wdanisak mattelemanewo gegeyjujumowawall woak nihillapewi wikingechtit. Ktelli nemeneen jun eli wuliechink elilenink welsittank. Abrahama wtelli penauwelemawall quissall woak Bethuel wtelli penauweleman wdansall.

2. Not it-is-not-good sons or daughters they-despise-them their-parents and freely they-marry. We-thus we-see-it this how it-is-good that-which-one-customarily-does the-believer. The-late-Abraham he-thus considers-about-him his-son and Bethuel he-thus considers-about-her his-daughter.

3. Die Eltern aber sollen ihre Kinder zu keiner Heyrath zwingen. Denn hier wurde die Rebecca erst gefragt, ob sie auch mit ihm ziehen wollte.

3. Alod matta wulittowi wenitschanitschik gatta achtschinkhallanewo wunitschanall wentschi wikingelid, matta lhilchpique. Gintsch kpendameneen elihindup Rebecca, nhittami eli ntutemund, wingi eet witschewan nel lennowall?

3. Yet not it-is-not-good those-who-have-children want-to they-(want-to)-force-her one's-child so-that she-marries, not if-she-is-not-

willing. Just-now we-hear-it how-she-was-treated Rebecca, first how she-is-asked, willingly-she perhaps does-she-accompany-him that man?

Gottselige Gedanken.
[48] **WELAPENDASIK PENAUWELENDAMOAGAN.**
PIOUS REFLECTION.

Wie Elieser soll ein wichtig Werk vollbringen, so läßt er das Gebät sein allererstes seyn, und wie er sieht das Gott ihm läßt sein Werk gelingen. So giebt er auch dafür die Ehre Gott allein;

Elieser enda nhagalgussit wentschitsch mikindank koecu welhik; nane nhittami nesquo mikindamok papatamawawall Patamawossall. Woak enda metschi nenkgup Patamawossall elgiqui witahemguk woak wulapensohalguk, nane untschi wingi genamawall woak nechoha necama m'chelemawall.

Eliezer when he-is-trusted so-that-will he-work-it a-thing that-which-is-good; that first not-yet he-does-not-work-it he-prays-to-him God. And when already he-saw-it God like-as He-helps-him and He-blesses-him, that for willingly he-thanks-Him and alone he praises-Him-(alone).

so will ich ebenfalls in allen meinen Sachen den Anfang mit Gebät, den Schluß mit Lobe machen.

Jun nepe nuwingi lissi ta koecu geta mikindama, abtschitsch nhittami npapatama, woak wtenk untschitsch ngagenamantsch N'Patamawos.

This I-likewise I-willingly do not a-thing want-to I-(want-to)-work, always-will first I-pray, and after wards-will I-will-repeatedly-thank-Him my-God.

Die 12te Historie.

[49] 12 ELEGUP.—2245.

---

12 AS-IT-WAS.—1467 B.C.

Wie Isaac seine Kinder gesegnet hat. 1 Mose, 27ste Capitel.

Isaaca enda mamtschitsch wulapensohalat wunitschanall. 1 Mos. 27, &c.

The-late-Isaac when lastly he-blesses-them his-children. Genesis 27, etc.

Isaac hatte mit Rebecca zwey Söhne gezeuget, die waren Zwillinge. Der Erstgebohrne hieß Esau, und war rauh; der jüngste aber hatte eine glatte Haut, und hieß Jacob.

Isaac nischigopannil quisineyall untschi Rebeccaink gachpesak. Netamiechinelid elewunsilid Esau, gachktschessu, techi mesitschewi hokey, schuk chessemusall aschitte schachsu, woak luwunsop Jacob.

Isaac he-raised-those-two sons by by-Rebecca, twins. He-who-was-first who-is-called Esau, he-is-rough, utterly whole his-(whole)-body, but his-younger-sibling instead he-is-smooth, and he-was-called Jacob.

Esau war ein Jäger und Ackermann; Jacob aber war ein frommer Mann, und blieb in seiner Hütten.

Esau ehalait woak ekihet; schuk Jacob welilissit schachachgapeit lenno woak abtschi winkachpo wikquahemink woak clami lehellecheu.

Esau (is) a-hunter and a-planter; but Jacob (is) well-behaved one-who-is-upright a-man and always he-likes-to-be-there in-the-house and quietly he-lives.

Bey dem Vater war Esau der liebe Sohn; und hingegen bey der Mutter stund Jacob in großen Gnaden.

Ochuwawall Isaac, allowi wdahoalawall netami gischigitschi elewunsitschi Esau, aschitte wtellsin Rebecca wtelli aholalan tenktititschi Jacoball.

Their-father Isaac, more he-loves-him first he-who-is-(first)-born he-who-is-called Esau, instead she-does-so Rebecca, she-thus loves-him the-little-one Jacob.

Wie nun Isaac alt war, so waren seine Augen dunkel geworden, daß er nicht mehr sehen konnte. Er nahm sich deßwegen vor, seine Kinder zu segnen:

Nane metschi mihillusite Isaac matta tschitsch wulapandamowun, techi [50] achgepinqueu. Nane gischiliteheu, nolapensohalawak nitschanak nesquo allalechewa.

Then already when-he-is-a-very-old-man Isaac not once-more he-does-not-see-well, utterly **[50]** he-is-blind. Then he-decides, I-bless-them my-children not-yet I-do-not-(yet)-expire.

und zwar so hatte er den besten Segen nicht dem frommen Jacob, sondern dem gottlosen Esau zugedacht.

Woak alakqui gotta [L., gatta] tschanilissin, eli matta litehak, nolapensohalantsch welilissit Jacob, schuk gotta [L., gatta] milan wulapensowoagan metapewitschi Esauall.

And 'tis-a-pity he-wants-to do-wrong, because not he-does-not-think, I-will-bless-him the-well-behaved-one Jacob, but he-wants-to give-it-to-him a-blessing he-who-is-wicked Esau.

[vi] ISAAC BLESSETH JACOB.

In diesem Vorsatz sprach er zu Esau: Gehe aufs Feld, sahe mir ein Wildpret, und mache mir ein Essen, wie ichs gerne habe, und bringe mirs herein, daß ich esse daß dich meine Seele segne, ehe denn ich sterbe.

Nel elitehenemoalat wtellawall: Juh gattati, glen kdadapi woak kpindalan, allail, ndonamail wujus; petawonne, wulitail mitschewoagan, ni eli wingandama, natsch kpetain ju epia wentschitsch mitschija, woak wulapensohalgejan ntschitschankunk untschi, nelema angelowa.

That-one {as-he-wishes-to-tell-him} he-says-to-him: Well! Come! Grab your-bow and your-quiver, hunt, seek-it-for-me meat; when-you-bring-it, make-it-well-for-me the-food, I how I-like-the-taste-of-it, then-will you-bring-it-to-me here where-I-am so-that-will I-eat-it, and you-be-blessed from-my-soul from, not-yet I-do-not-(yet)-die.

Dieses hörete Rebecca, und dachte gleich darauf, wie sie den Segen ihrem jüngsten Sohne zuwenden wollte.

Jun wemi elaptonenk pendamen Rebecca, woak schai pennauwelendamen, wentschitsch a milind wulapensowoagan tenktititschi quisall Jacob.

This all which-is-spoken she-hears-it Rebecca, and immediately she-considers-about-it, so-that-in-the-future would he-be-given-it the-blessing the-little-one her-son Jacob.

Sie sagte demnach zu Jacob, er sollte zwey Böcklein von der Heerde holen, daraus wollte sie ein Essen machen,

Nane wentschi wtellawall Jacoball: Icka schihillal epichtit kmekisemak, woak nal nischowak wewulsitschik paluppawetittak wentschitsch wulitawak Goch michmitschit koecu wingank;

That therefore she-says-to-him Jacob: There hurry where-they-are your-sheep, and fetch-them they-are-two those-who-are-very-good little-rams [*lit.*, little-bucks] so-that-will I-fix-it-for-him your-father that-which-he-eats a-thing which-tastes-good;

das sollte Jacob dem Vater bringen, und sich für seinen Bruder Esau ausgeben.

natsch ktellochwachton Goch epit, wentschitsch mitschit, woak ktellantsch: Ni quis Esau nhakey, wentschitsch milquon wulapensowoagan.

then-will you-take-it-along your-father where-he-is, so-that-will he-eat-it, and you-will-say-to-him: I (am) your-son Esau myself, so-that-will he-give-it-to-you a-blessing.

Jacob sagte zwar zu seiner Mutter: Siehe, mein Bruder ist rauh, und ich bin glatt, mein Vater möchte mir, als einem Betrüger, den Fluch für den Segen geben.

Schuk Jacob schwilaweu wentschi apatschi lat Gahoesall: Nachasi, noch tamse meschenite nachkink, wdamandamen ni eli wschachsia, woak nchans eli gachktschessit, nuntschitsch milgun gendelemuxowoagan, npallihellan wulapensowoagan, woahite ntelli achgiwalan.

But Jacob he-is-discouraged so-that coming-back he-says-to-her his-mother, Take-care, my-father sometimes when-he-receives-it from-my-hand, he-feels-it I how I-am-smooth, and my-older-brother how he-is-rough, me-thereby-will he-give-it-to-(me) a-condemnation, I-miss-the-time the-blessing, when-he-knows-me that-I deceive-him.

Die Mutter aber sprach: Der Fluch sey auf mir, mein Sohn, gehorche nur meiner Stimme.

Gahoesall apatschi wtellgol, luep: Wemi gendelemuxowoagan woak mandundowoagan machtechentsch nhakenk, ki nquis schuk wulistawil.

[vi] ISAAC BLESSETH JACOB.

His-mother coming-back she-says-to-him, she-said: Every condemnation and blame it-will-land on-myself, you my-son only believe-me.

Wie das Essen fertig war, so zog sie dem Jacob die Kleider seines Bruders Esau an, und darnach band sie ihm die Felle von dem Böcklein um die Hände und um den Hals.

Nane gischi wulitaque mitschewoagan, nane Rebecca natenummenall Esau ehachquitschi welhiki, woak pintschillachsolan Jacoball, schuk nel chettitall untschi [51] palupppawetittink gachptawan wunachkink shaki sagiechink, woak enda schachsit ochqueganganink.

Then done when-she-is-(done)-fixing-it the-food, then Rebecca she-takes-them Esau his-clothes those-which-are-good, and she-puts-them-on-him Jacob, but those little-hides of [51] of-the-little-rams [*lit., of-the-little-bucks*] she-ties-them-on-him on-his-hands so-long-as they-stick-out, and where he-is-smooth on-his-neck.

Wie er nun hinein kam, so sagte der alte Vater: Wer bist du mein Sohn? Jacob gab zur Antwort: Ich bin Esau dein erstgebohrner Sohn, stehe auf und iß von meinem Wildpret.

Nane pintschigete mihillusis ochwall wtelgol: Auwen ha, ki nquis? Nane Jacob wtellawall: Ni Esau nhakey, netami gischigit quis. Amuil, lemattachpil, mizil untschi ndalauwiwoagan.

Then when-he-comes-inside the-aged-man his-father he-says-to-him: Who it-is-asked, (are) you my-son? Then Jacob he-says-to-him: I (am) Esau myself, first he-who-is-(first)-born your-son. Arise, sit-down, eat of my-hunt.

Isaac fragte weiter: Wie hast du so bald funden, mein Sohn? Jacob sprach: Der Herr dein Gott bescherte mirs.

Nane Isaac ikalissi wtellawall: Ta ha leu nquis, wentschi metschimi mochgaman tekeni wujus? Jacob nachgutinke lue: Nihillalquonk KPatamawos nemilgun.

Then Isaac further he-says-to-him: How it-is-asked is-it-so my-son, so-that soon you-find-it of-the-woods meat? Jacob when-he-answers he-says: our-Lord your-God He-gives-it-to-me.

Isaac merkte wohl, daß es nicht recht zugieng; deßwegen mußte ihm Jacob erstlich die Hände geben. Da nun dieselben rauh waren, wie Esaus Hände,

Nane wtschanelendamen mihillusis, wentschi lat: Undachal nquis wentschi mischenelan. Nane Jacob giechgi Ochunk nipain wentschi tepi meschenguk,

That he-doubts-it the-aged-man, so-that he-says-to-him: Come-this-way my-son so-that I-receive-you. Then Jacob near to-his-father stands so-that sufficiently he-receives-him,

so sagte der alte Vater: Die Stimme ist Jacobs Stimme, aber die Hände sind Esaus, er fragte darauf nochmals: Bist du mein Sohn Esau?

nan wtellowen: ntschanelendam untschi liechsowoagan Jacob eliechsit, schuk wunachkall allesche Esau wunachkall. Lappi ntutemawawall, wtellawall: Ki nquis Esau kakey?

that-one he-says: I-am-in-doubt by the-language Jacob how-he-speaks, but his-hands (are) like Esau his-hands. Again he-asks-him, he-says-to-him: (Are) you my-son Esau yourself?

Jacob antwortete: Ja ich bins. Hierauf aß Isaac von dem Essen, und trank von dem Weine, den ihm Jacob vortezte. Als er gegessen hatte, so sagte er zu Jacob: Komm her, mein Sohn, und küsse mich.

Jacob apatschi late: Gohan nane ndellsin: Nane petawan, mizin woak menen endchi pataguk Jacoball. Nane metschi gischi mizite wtellawall Jacoball: Undachall nquis, woak moskdonamil.

Jacob comes-back when-he-says-to-him: Yes that I-am-so: Then he-brings-it-to-him, to-eat and to-drink as-much-as he-brings-it-to-him Jacob. Then already done when-he-is-(done)-eating he-says-to-him Jacob: Come-this-way my-son, and kiss-me.

[vi] ISAAC BLESSETH JACOB.

Wie Jacob das that, so roch der Vater den Geruch seiner Kleider, und glaubte nunmehro gewiß daß es Esau wäre. Darauf gab er ihm einen schönen Segen und gebrauchte sich unter andern diese Worte:

Nane Jacob neli moskdonawate, majawelendam wetochwink eli melank ehachquitschi welhiki Esau eli ahimaquo wtelli Esauilin: Nane wtenda milawall quisall schigi wulapensowoagan woak wtellawall nel aptonaganall:

Then Jacob while while-he-kisses-him, he-is-certain-of-it the-father as he-smells-them his-clothes those-which-are-good Esau because {there-is-a-strong-odor} that-he is-Esau: That he-then gives-it-to-him his-son a-fine blessing and he-says-to-him those words:

Sey ein Herr über deine Brüder und deiner Mutter Kinder müssen dir zu Fusse fallen! Verflucht sey, wer dir fluchet; gesegnet sey wer dich segnet.

Nihillal kimachtak, woak gahoes wunitschanall schengie-chinhittitetsch petschi ksitink. Gendelemuxutsch auwen gendelemukquon, wulapensohalgussutsch auwen wulapen-sohalquon. Nan wdendchi wulapensohenall quisall.

Be-master-of-them your-brothers, and your-mother her-children they-will-lie-down hither at-your-feet. He-will-be-condemned a-person who-condemns-you, he-will-be-blessed a-person who-blesses-you. That-one as-much-as-he blesses-him his-son.

Wie Jacob kaum hinsaus gegangen war, so kam Esau von der Jagd, und brachte dem Vater auch Essen.

Nane medchi untschi ktschite, Jacob enda wulapensohenk, nane paan Esau wdappalain, schai ika wtellochwachton wingank mitschewoagan, [52] **wetochwink epit.**

Then as-soon-as from when-he-goes-out, Jacob when being-blessed, then comes Esau he-comes-from-hunting, immediately there he-brings-it that-which-is-savory food, **[52]** the-father where-he-is.

Isaac fragte alsobald, wer bist du? Esau gab zur Antwort: Ich bin Esau, dein erstgebohrner Sohn: Darüber erschrack der Vater hestig, und sagte:

Nane Isaac schai ntutemawawall: Auwen Kakey? Nechgutinke lue: Esau nhakey netami gischigit quis. Nane husca ganschelendam wetochwink, woak nechgutinke lue:

Then Isaac immediately he-asks-him: Who (is) yourself? When-he-answers-it he-says: Esau (is) myself first he-who-is-(first)-born your-son. Then exceedingly he-is-astonished the-father, and when-he-answers he-says:

Dein Bruder ist kommen mit List, und hat den Segen hinweg, und wird auch wohl gesegnet bleiben.

Chesemus gintsch peep woak ktschikenukgun wulapensowoagan woaktsch abtschi wtellatschessowen, metschi nolapensohala, woaktsch wulapensohalgussutsch.

The-younger-sibling a-little-while-ago he-came and he-takes-it-away-from-you the-blessing and-will always he-(will)-possess-it, already I-bless-him, and-in-the-future he-will-be-blessed.

Esau betrübte sich anfangs herzlich darüber, sieng an zu weinen, und sagte unter andern: Hast du denn nur einen Segen; mein Vater, segne mich doch auch!

Nane Esau nhittami eli pendank elek husca schiwelendamenep, wtallemi sasalamo woak luep: Nocha! schuk ngutti wulapensowoagan gulaton? Nepe wulapensohalil nocha! nepe.

Then Esau at-first as he-hears-it how-it-is exceedingly he-is-grieved-about-it, he-begins-to he-(begins-to)-howl-continually and he-said: My-father! only one blessing do-you-have? Me-too bless-me my-father! Me-too.

Hierauf bekam er zwar auch einen Segen; aber was Jacob einmal voraus hatte, das konnte der Vater nunmehr nicht widerrufen.

[vi] ISAAC BLESSETH JACOB.

Bischi woak milan wulapensowoagan, schuk endchi koecu welhik Jacob metschi mescheninkgup wundamundup, ta a tschitsch hittai wulokenumowi wetochwink.

To-be-sure also he-gives-it-to-him a-blessing, but as-much-as a-thing which-is-good Jacob already he-received-it he-was-shown-it, not could once-more skillfully he-(could)-not-pull-it-apart the-father.

Nun geschahe hierinnen zwar dem Esau kein arosses Unrecht: Denn er hatte das Recht der ersten Geburt seinem Bruder Jacob um ein schnödes Linsen=Gerücht verkaufet:

Bischi matta majawi achgiwaluxiwon Esau elihindup, eli mhallamaguk chesemussall wunetami gischiguwoagan, untschi machtitti koecu wingank mitschewoagan.

To-be-sure not rightly he-is-not-cheated Esau how-he-was-treated, for he-bought-it-from-him his-younger-sibling his-first birthright, by a-very-little thing that-which-is-savory food.

Gott hatte es auch der Mutter zuvor gesagt, daß ihr größerer Sohn dem kleinern dienen würde:

Patamawos woak nigani metschi wtellapanil wenitschanitschi gachoesall, junitsch leu: Gegeyit quis wtellitsch allogetawantsch tenktititschi.

God also beforehand already He-said-to-her the-parent his-mother, this-will it-be-so: He-who-is-the-elder your-son he-thus-will work-for-him the-little-one.

Aber er wurde doch seinem Bruder gram deßwegen, und sprach in seinem Herzen: Es wird die Zeit bald kommen, daß mein Vater Leid tragen muß, denn ich will meinen Bruder Jacob erwürgen.

Schuk nan untschi ganquilawall schingalawall chesemussall, woak wdehenk liteheu: Auwijewitsch wschiwelendamentsch noch; elitsch ngattonallak [?gattonallak] nchesemus.

But that-one from he-envies-him he-hates-him his-younger-sibling, and in-his-heart he-thinks: Yet-will he-will-be-sorry-about-it my-father; for-in-the-future I-want-to-kill-him my-younger-sibling.

Nützliche Lehren.
[53] **WELAPEMQUO ACHGEGINGEWOAGAN.**
PRACTICAL APPLICATION.

1. Der Segen der Eltern hat eine große Kraft? Isaac sagte: Jacob ist einmal gesegnet, und wird auch wohl gesegnet bleiben.

1. Husca welapemquo koecuniki nel wulapensowoaganall wenitschanitschik enda wulapensohalachtit wunitschanowawall. Isaac luep: Jacob nolapensohalap, woaktsch abtschi wulapensohalgussutsch.

1. Exceedingly beneficial {those-which-are-real} those blessings parents when they-bless-them their-children. Isaac he-said: Jacob I-blessed-him, and-in-the-future always he-will-be-blessed.

2. Die Frömmigkeit bleibt nicht unbelohnt. Jacob war ein frommer Mann, dafür bekam er den Segen, auch wider des Vaters Willen.

2. Nek welilissitschik tacu wtankhittowunewo wulapensowoaganowa. Jacob eli welilissit lenno, nane untschi mischenumenep wulapensowoagan, bischi ochwall matta wtelitehenemoalguwunep.

2. Those those-who-behave-well not they-do-not-lose-it their-blessing. Jacob because he-is-well-behaved a-man, that from he-received-it a-blessing, to-be-sure his-father not {he-did-not-wish-it-to-be-him}.

3. Was Gott beschlossen hat, das muß ergeben. Gott sagte: Der Grössere sollte dem Kleinern dienen, und so mußte es auch geschehen.

3. Wemi koecu endchi Patamawos gischipenauwelendank, nanitsch leu, quila allai lewi. Patamawos eli luetup: Gegeyit wtellitsch allogetauwan tenktititschi nall ne tpisqui leu.

3. Every thing as-much-as God he-decides-it, so-will it-be-so, nothing in-vain it-is-not-so. God because he-said: The-older-one he-thus-will work-for-him the-little-one then that exactly it-is-so.

Gottselige Gedanken.
WELAPENDASIK PENAUWELENDAMOAGAN.
PIOUS REFLECTION.

Was einem Gott beschert, daß bleibet unvermehret, Diß alte Sprichwort trifft bey Jacob richtig ein: Es ist der Segen ihm einmal von Gott bescheret,

Ta endchi koecu meguk Patamawos, ta auwen hittai tschigenhigewon. Jun ejilaptonenk aptonagan, tpisqui leu talli Jacobink elinankgup. Nel wulapensowoaganall milindtschi untschi Patamawossink, eliechingup nane abtschi liechenop.

Where as-much-as a-thing He-gives-it-away God, not (by) a-person skillfully it-is-not-taken-away. This {which-is-repeatedly-spoken-thusly} the-word, exactly it-is-so there of-Jacob how-he-was-treated. Those blessings which-he-is-given from from-God, as-it-came-down that always it-came-down.

Deßwegen soll er auch, und muß gesegnet seyn. Was mir Gott zugedacht; das wird mir auch wohl bleiben, und niemand auf der Welt wird solches hintertreiben.

Ta endchi koecu milit Patamawos, abtschitsch nolaton, woak tacu eet auwen achpiwon talli Pemhagamigek, tepi a ndajumaguwon.

Where as-much-as a-thing He-gives-it-to-me God, always-will I-have-it, and not perhaps a-person he-is-not-there in the-world-round-about, sufficiently could he-(could)-not-(sufficiently)-purchase-it-from-me.

Die 13te Historie.

[54] 13 ELEGUP.—2245.

---

13 AS-IT-WAS.—1467 B.C.

Von der Himmels=Leiter im Traum. 1 Mose, 27 und 28ste Capitel.

Jacob enda lonquongup, woak elinangup awossagame sachgehican. 1 Mos. 28. &c.

Jacob when he-dreamed, and how-he-observed-it Heaven (its)-ladder. Genesis 28, etc.

Jacob war in seines Vaters Hause seines Lebens nicht sicher: Denn sein Bruder Esau hatte sich vorgesezt, daß er ihn erwürgen wollte.

Nane likhikqui Jacob matta tschitsch wulamalsiwon wentschi nalai achpit talli ochunk wikit, chansall eli metschi gischipenauwelendamelid [L., gischi penauwelendamelid] wtelli gachtonalugun.

Then at-that-time Jacob not once-more he-does-not-feel-well so-that safely he-is-there in in-his-father his-house, his-older-brother because already he-is-decided, that-him he-wants-to-kill-him.

Wie seine Mutter Rebecca Nachricht davon bekam, so gab sie Jacob den Rath, daß er zu ihrem Bruder Laban ziehen, und eine von seinen Töchtern heyrathen sollte.

Nane Rebecca jun metschi tepi woataque, gihimapanil Jacoball wtellawall schimuil, ika all wahellemi, epit n'chans Laban, woak ika talli mauchsilowall wdansall ktellitsch wikiman.

Then Rebecca this already enough when-she-knows-it, she-exhorted-him Jacob she-says-to-him run-away, there go far-away, where-he-is my-older-brother Laban, and there in she-is-one-of-them his-daughter that-you-will marry-her.

Der Vater war es auch zufrieden, und gab ihm nochmals einen schönen Segen mit auf den Weg.

Jun aptonagan woak wtelli wulinamen Isaac wentschi woak gihimat woak gischenaxohalot quisall Jacoball, woak schiki wulapensowoagan milan wentschitsch nachpowelid nawotschi ejalid wdankquall [55] Labanall epilid.

This word also he-thus he-observes-it Isaac so-that also he-exhorts-him and he-makes-him-ready his-son Jacob, and fine a-(fine)-blessing he-gives-it-to-him so-that-will he-take-it-along-also {along-the-way} where-he-goes his-brother-in-law **[55]** Laban where-he-is.

Unterwegens gieng die Sonne eher unter; als er die Herberge erreichen konnte: Er mußte deßwegen im freyen Felde bleiben, und mit einem Stein anstatt des Haupt=Küssens verlieb nehmen.

Nane nawotschi li ika ejate netami gischquik allumsgate, nane wsigau pisgeu, nundawi nesquo pejak utenink eteek. Nane quila wiquahemink mawiken wentschitsch bischuwi talli gauwit, woak enda gauwit achsin meloqueho.

Then {along-the-way} to there as-he-goes first the-(first)-day when-he-goes-away, then it-is-sunset it-is-dark, wanting not-yet he-does-not-come to-the-city where-it-is. Then lacking in-a-house to-encamp therefore-will the-wilderness in he-(will)-sleep, and where he-sleeps a-stone he-has-for-a-pillow.

In derselben Nacht sahe Jacob im Traum ein Leiter die stand auf der Erde, und rührte mit der Spitze bis an den Himmel. Auf dieser Leiter stiegen die heiligen Engel auf und nieder,

JACOB'S VISION.

Neli gauwilid, talli lunquamuaganink Jacob wtelli wunemenep sachgehicanall, nane epit wuntschi allumamen ika petschi achgumhokunk. Getanittowit wtenschellumall wunewawall wtelli aschundehotilin, liechitschik woak aspachgositschik.

While he-sleeps, in in-a-dream Jacob he-thus he-saw-it a-ladder, that where-he-is from {to-begin-to-run-in-a-line} there unto unto-the-clouds. The-Great-Spirit His-angels he-sees-them that-they {all-of-them-change-places}, those-who-climb-down and those-who-climb-up.

und Gott der Herr stand oben darauf, und sprach: Das Land, da du auf liegest, will ich dir und deinem Saamen geben,

Ika wochgitschi sachgehicanink eli wiquamet, wunipawin Nihillalquonk, wtellawall Jacoball, Na haki juke eli schengiechinan kmilentsch, woak nek wemi kakenk untschi ahanhokqui gischigitschik, nektsch wtelsinewo taat punk jun talli haki, matta a kaski achgimgussiwiiwak.

There on-top of-the-ladder as {there-is-a-house}, He-stands our-Lord, He-says-to-him Jacob: That land now as you-lie-on I-will-give-it-to-you, and those all from-yourself from over-and-over-again those-who-are-born, those-will they-be-so as-if dust here in-the-Earth, not could able-to they-(could)-not-be-(able-to)-be-counted.

und durch dich und deinen Saamen sollen alle Geschlechter auf Erden gesegnet werden.

Kakenk untschi ahanhokqui gischigitschik tpisquihillaque auwentsch gischigo, wemitsch wulapensohenak wemi ekhogewitschik epitschik talli wochgithagamique.

From-yourself from over-and-over-again those-who-are-born when-the-time-is-at-hand a-person-will he-be-born, all-will he-bless-them the-nations those-who-are-there there upon-the-Earth.

Wie Jacob aufwachte, so sieng er sich an zu fürchten, und sagte: Wie heilig ist diese Stätte! hier ist nichts anders denn Gottes Hause, hier ist die Pforte des Himmels.

Nane togihhilleu Jacob wtallemi wischamallsin woak luep: Wo kschiechek pilhik jun epia! Kitschiwi leu jun talli wikiu Gettanittowit, tauwiechen awossagame jun petschi.

Then he-wakes-up Jacob he-begins-to feel-frightened and he-said: O that-which-is-holy that-which-is-pure (is) this where-I-am! Truly it-is-so here in He-dwells the-Great-Spirit, it-opens Heaven here unto.

Des Morgens nahm Jacob den Stein darauf er mit seinem Haupte geruhet hatte, und richtete denselben zu einem Denkmal auf. Die Stätte aber nennte er Bethel, und that zugleich ein Gelübde,

Nane petapanke wtamuin woak wtapachtschiechton jun achsin melhoquehitup, wentschitsch abtschi meschadasik. Nane wtellowendamen enda gewitup: Bethel, nane luwundasu Patamaeigawan.

Then when-it-is-daybreak he-rises-up and he-sets-it-up this stone which-he-had-for-a-pillow, so-that-will always it-(will)-be-remembered. That he-called-it where he-slept: Bethel, that it-is-called house-of-prayer.

wenn ihn Gott mit Frieden wieder heim zu seinem Vater brächte,

Woak wtenda wundangoman Patamawossall nigani wtellawall: Ki nihillalian witawemijanne genachgihijanne ta ejaja, woak lappi wdukii loochwalijanne, nochunk wulamalsowii,

And then-he promised-Him God beforehand he-says-to-Him: You my-Lord if-You-accompany-me if-You-take-care-of-me definitely where-I-go, and again {back} if-You-bring-me-({back}), to-my-father healthy,

so wollte er auf deiselbe Stelle ein Gotteshaus bauen, und dazu den zehnten Theil von allem seinem Vermögen anwenden?

natsch ne ndelsin, Patamaeigawan ndendatsch wuliton, nuntschitsch meken endchi latschessoweja wemi metellen endcheleneyachga ngutti ika nuntschitsch nemeken.

then-will that I-(will)-do-so, a-house-of-prayer I-then-will make-it-well, thereby-will-I give-it-away as-much-as I-possess every ten as-many-kinds-as-there-are one there from-will-I I-(will)-give-it-away.

Nützliche Lehren.
[56] **WELAPEMQUO ACHGEGINGEWOAGAN.**
PRACTICAL APPLICATION.

1. Hieraus hat man zu lernen, was man den Kindern mit auf die Reise geben soll. Nämlich einen guten Segen, wie hier Isaac seinem Sohne Jacob gegeben hat.

1. Jun talli wundamagejank ta koecu majawi welhik milank ktamemensemenanak nek ta undachqui wahellemi ejatschik, nane gachtalquot wulapensohalgussowak nachpi Patamawos wulapensowoagan, Isaac elihat quisall Jacoball.

1. This in we-are-shown definitely a-thing rightly that-which-is-good we-give-it-to-them our-children those indeed that-way far-off those-who-go, that it-is-desirable they-are-blessed with God (His)-blessing, Isaac as-he-does-it-to-him his-son Jacob.

2. Mann kann ferner daraus lernen, daß man seinen Feinden aus dem Weg gehen soll. Das that Jacob, welcher lieber seines Vaters Haus verließ, als daß er mit seinem Bruder im Streit leben sollte.

2. Woak ikalissi lappi knemeneen wuliechen a auwen hitta lissin, wtelli wingi schiman getonalukgil. Nane woak wtellsin Jacoba allowi wingi ngattumen Ochunk wikit, eli schingelendank machtangoman Chansall.

2. And further again we-see-it it-is-good should a-person skillfully he-do-so, that-he willingly flees-him he-who-wants-to-kill-him. That also he-does-so the-late-Jacob more willingly-he leaves from-his-father his-house, as he-detests-it to-be-mean-to-him his-older-brother.

3. Man hat endlich daraus zu lernen, daß sich Gott den Seinigen oftmals in der Einsamkeit offenbaret.

3. Woak ikalissi ju untschi elekil kpenundelukgeneen Patamawos wdihilissin wtelli wingi nensitawan nihillalatschi enda nechohalenid.

3. And futher here from how-they-are we-are-shown God He-does-so-repeatedly He-thus willingly appears-to-him himself when he-is-alone.

Denn hie sahe Jacob etwas im freyen Felde da er ganz allein war, welches er schwerlich in dem größten Gast=Hose würde gesehen haben.

Bischi Jacob ktemaki gauwinep talli bischuwi enda nechohalenid, husca koecu welhik wtellinamen, ta eet elinaquo penundeluxiwunep, sokhupesink talli gauwitpanne.

To-be-sure Jacob poorly he-slept in-the-wilderness where he-is-alone, exceedingly a-thing that-which-is-good he-observed-it, not perhaps that-which-appears he-was-not-shown-it, in-an-inn there if-he-slept.

Gottselige Gedanken.
WELAPENDASIK PENAUWELENDAMOAGAN.
PIOUS REFLECTION.

Was dorten Jacob sah, erscheint uns zwar nicht weiter, doch zeigt mir Gottes Wort dergleichen in der That; ich sehe vor mir stehn auch eine solche Leiter. Die bis gen Himmel reicht,

Quonna ta juke ni matta ndellinamowon Jacob elinangup, nane ihiabtschi Patamawos elinaquo kitschiwi npenundelukgun talli

JACOB'S VISION.

wtaptonaganink. Nepe woak nemen elinquechina talli ndehenk nipachteu sachgehican, allummamek teek petschi awossagame.

Even-if definitely now I not I-do-not-observe-it Jacob what-he-observed, then yet God that-which-appears truly He-shows-it-to-me in in-His-word. I-likewise also see-it in-my-presence in in-my-heart it-stands a-ladder, {beginning-to-go-in-a-line} {there} unto Heaven.

und nur drey Stuffen hat; die sind des Vaters Huld: Herr Jesu! deine Schmerzen und Herr Gott Heiliger Geist! den Glaubin meinem Herzen.

Nane ika schuk hattewall nachenol pomitstschechinkil elhigenkil, nel elewundasiki: Wetochwink goktomagelowoagan, Nihillalid NJesus omamchachwelendamoagan woak welsit mtschitschank eli tachpatank wulistamoewoagan talli ndehenk.

Then there only they-are-there they-are-three {those-which-lay-sidewards} {steps}, those those-which-are-called: The-Father His-mercy, my-Lord Jesus his-suffering and the-Holy Spirit because he-maintains-it truth in in-my-heart.

Die 14te Historie.

[57] 14 ELEGUP.—2245.

---

14 AS-IT-WAS.—1467 B.C.

Von Jacobs gedoppelter Heyrath. 1 Mose, 29ste Capitel.

Jacob enda wikingete. 1 Mos. 29, &c.

Jacob when he-marries. Genesis 29, etc.

Jacob reißte zu Laban, der war seiner Mutter Bruder, und wohnte zu Haran. Derselbe Laban hatte zwey Töchter: Die älteste hieß Lea, und hatte ein blöd Gesicht: die jüngste aber hieß Rahel, und war hübsch und schön.

Nane Jacob wtelli allumsgan gotta [L., gatta] paan schisall Laban epilid. Won wtelli wikilin utenink Haran elewundasik, woak nischilowall wdanissall, gegeyitschi eluwihillind Lea, woak matta wulissuwi [L., wulapandamowi], woak tenktititschi luwunsop Rachel, schiki woak wulinaxu ochque.

Then Jacob he-thus goes-away he-wants-to come (to) his-uncle Laban where-he-is. This-one he-thus dwells in-the-city Haran that-which-is-called, and they-are-two his-daughters, the-older-one who-is-named Leah, and not she-is-not-good-looking *[L., she-does-not-see-well]*, and a-little-one she-was-called Rachel, pretty and she-looks-good the-woman.

Als nun Jacob nicht mehr weit von Haran war, so traf er unterwegens einen Brunnen an, bey welchem die Hirten aus derselben ganzen Gegend ihre Schaafe zu tränken gewohnet waren.

Nane Jacob giechki pejate utenink elewundasik Haran, nane wtenda paan eteek ngutti ehelilamank, nutemekschetschi enda menahachtit omekisemowawall.

Then Jacob near when-he-comes to-the-city that-which-is-called Haran, then he-there comes where-it-is one well, shepherds where they-give-them-a-drink their-sheep.

Jacob fragte die Hirten, ob sie nicht zu Haran einen Mann mit Namen Laban kenneten? Sie gaben zur Antwort: Wir kennen ihn gar wohl.

Jacob ntutemauwawall nutemekschetschi wtellapanil: Gowoahawa eet lenno Laban elewunsit, utenink Haranink epit. Nachgutemichtit luewak, nuli woahawuna.

Jacob he-asks-them the-shepherds he-said-to-them: Do-you-know-him perhaps a-man Laban he-who-is-called, in-the-city in-Haran where-he-is? They-answer they-say, well-we we-know-him.

Wie er nun weiter fragte, ob es ihm noch wohl gienge? so kam Labans Tochter, mit Namen Rahel mit den Schaafen ihres Vaters zum Brunnen.

Nane Jacob wtallemi luen: Ta hatsch wtellsin? Luewak: quila likhikqui [

] **wulilehellecheu sche penau won pejat wdansall elewunsitschil Rachel nahellii omekisumowawall.**

Then Jacob he-begins-to say: How it-will-be-asked is-he-doing? They-say: {greatly} at-this-time **[58]** he-lives-well see-there! look-at-her this-one she-who-comes his-daughter she-who-is-called Rachel together-with their-sheep.

Mit derselben machte sich Jacob gleich bekannt, er wältzte den Stein von dem Brunnen, er tränkte die Schaafe und gab ihr endlich einen Kuß.

Nelaptonechtite nan paan Rachel ehelilamank eteek. Jacob jun pendanke wtelli wulelendamen, palli lennemen achsin kpahican

JACOB'S MARRIAGE.

untschi ehelilamank, menahawall mekisemall, woak wtenk untschi mosktonamawall.

While-they-speak that-one comes Rachel (to) the-well where-it-is. Jacob this when-he-hears-it he-thus is-glad-about-it, elsewhere he-puts-it the-stone the-lid of the-well, he-gives-them-a-drink her-sheep, and after wards he-kisses-her.

Rahel ließ unverzüglich in die Stadt, und sagte ihrem Vater an, daß seiner Schwester Sohn Jacob vor der Stadt bey dem Brunnen ware.

Nane Rachel schai allumamehhelleu ochunk li, mauwi wundamauwan, wtellapanil: Klunwachsis N'Jacob peu, ika wtappin giechki utenink ehelilamank eteek.

Then Rachel immediately {she-swiftly-goes-away} to-her-father to, goes-and she-declares-it-to-him, she-said-to-him: Your-nephew Jacob he-comes, there he-is-there near to-the-city the-well where-it-is.

Laban gieng ihm gleich entgegen, und nachdem sie einander vor Freuden gehertzet und geküsset hatten, so nahm er Jacoben mit sich in sein Haus.

Nane Laban pendanke eluenk nachpi mchinqui wulelendamoagan ika schihilleu ehelilamank eteek, woak ika pejate okikoch-quenawawall Jacoball, mosktonamawall woak mattemigalawall wikit.

Then Laban when-he-hears-it what-is-said with great joy there he-runs the-well where-it-is, and there when-he-comes he-hugs-him-around-the-neck Jacob, he-kisses-him and he-takes-him-in his-house.

In demselben gefiel Jacoben nichts so sehr als die schöne Rahel. Wie nun ihr Vater Laban den Vorschlag that, ob ihm Jacob um emen gewissen Lohn dienen wollte?

Schuk ne talli NJacob allowi winginawawall Rachelall wemi epitschik. Nane matta guni achpik Jacob, Labanall wtelgol luep: Tatsch hatsch ktelenholen [?ktenholen] mikindamauwijanne?

But that in Jacob more he-likes-the-look-of-her Rachel (than) all those-who-are-there. That not long he-is-not-there Jacob, Laban he-says-to-him he-said: How-will it-will-be-asked (will)-I-pay-you if-you-work-for-me?

So gab Jacob alsobald zur Antwort: Ich will dir sieben Jahre um deine jüngste Tochter Rahel dienen.

Nane Jacob nechgutink luep: Nitsch newingi kmikindamolen nischasch tchi gachtinewi shaki, milijanne wo Rachel na tenktitit ktanis.

Then Jacob he-answers he-said: I-will willingly-I I-(will)-work-for-you seven so-many of-years so-long-as, if-you-give-her-to-me this Rachel that little-one your-daughter.

Laban bedachte sich nicht lange, sondern sagte gleich: Es ist besser, ich gebe sie dir, denn einem andern.

Nane Laban matta gunipenauwelendamowon, alod liteheu, allowi wulit nemilan ndanis elangomak auwen, machta nuwingi nemilawi auwen tschepsit nalowauchsit.

That Laban not he-does-not-long-consider-it, yet he-thinks, more it-is-good I-give-her-to-him my-daughter my-relation a-person, not willingly-I I-do-not-give-her-to-him a-person a-stranger one-who-is-a-heathen.

Also diente Jacob um Laban [H., Rahel] sieben Jahre, und es deuchte ihn, als wären es einzelne Tage, so lieb hatte er sie.

Nane Jacob wachtschangun Labanall, shaki nischasch tchi gachtinewi, woak tacu techi gunelendamowunall nel nischasch gachtinall, schuk wtellelendamenall taat, nane tchi gischguwall, eli ahoalat woak mchelemat Rachelall.

JACOB'S MARRIAGE.

Then Jacob he-serves-him Laban, so-long-as seven so-many of-years, and not utterly he-does-not-think-it-is-a-long-time those seven those-are-(seven)-years, but he-thinks-about-it as-if, that so-many days, for he-loves-her and he-honors-her Rachel.

Als aber die Hochzeit gehatten ward, so betrog ihn der Schwieger=Vater, und legte die älteste Tochter Lea in das Brautbette.

Nane metschi lowihillake enda wachtschangussit, nane gachtalan ochquewall nechgomintschi, schuk nane tpisquihillaque enda wikindohalgussichtite, achgiwalan Jacob, schilhillusall gogiwalukgol, [59] eli kimi petund Leahall,

That already when-it-passes-by when he-is-enslaved, then he-wants-her the-woman {her-answer}, but then when-the-time-is-at-hand when they-are-married, he-is-cheated Jacob, his-aged-uncle he-deceives-him, **[59]** as secretly she-is-brought Leah,

Der gute Jacob ward es nicht eher inne, als auf den Morgen: Da sagte er zwar zu Laban: Habe ich dir nicht um deine jüngste Tochter Rahel gedienet, warum hast du mich den betrogen?

bischi Jacob tacu owoatowun, nane untschi leu, wtelli ihiabtschi wikiman na ochquewall Gettanittowit eli pipinamoelchat.

to-be-sure Jacob not he-does-not-know-it, that from it-is-so, that-he yet marries-her that woman the-Great-Spirit because He-chooses-her-for-him. *[Not a complete match with the German text.]*

Er mußte aber mit der Entschuldigung verlieb nehmen; es wäre nicht Sitte im Land, daß man die Jüngste vor der Aeltesten ausgebe.

Nane Jacob gatta migomate Labanall eli achgiwalukguk, nane Laban nutschque wtellowen: Gohan, schuk nane leu jun talli epijenk, ta a kaski auwen schilemai tenktititschi wdanall, gintsch nhittami misall wikingelide.

Then Jacob wants-to when-he-(wants-to)-remind-him Laban how he-deceives-him, then Laban for-nothing he-says: Yes, but that it-is-so here in where-we-are, not could able-to a-person (could)-not-be-(able-to)-marry-into-a-family a-little-one his-daughter, until at-first her-older-sister when-she-marries.

Er that ihm aber alsobald den Vorschlag, daß er die schöne Rahel dazu haben sollte, wofern er ihm noch andere sieben Jahre dienen wollte?

Schuk ne wtellsin na schaxit lenno, quajaqui penamen, Jacob eli allowi ahoalat Rachellal, nane untschi laan: Sche jun ktellihellen, won Lea wulahellachte woak tschitsch nischasch tchi gachtinewi shaki mikindamaijanne, woaktsch Rachel kmilelen.

But that he-does-so that one-who-is-greedy the-man, yet he-looks-at-it, Jacob how more he-loves-her Rachel, that therefore he-says-to-him: See-here! this I-do-it-for-you, this Leah if-you-keep-her and once-more seven so-many of-years so-long if-you-work-for-me, also-will Rachel I-(will)-give-her-to-you.

Das ließ sich Jacob gefallen, und nahm also zwey Schwestern zu Weibern. Unter denen hatte Jacob zwar die schöne Rahel viel lieber, als die häßliche Lea:

Nane Jacob wunachgoman woak wikimapanik nek elii witgochgunditschik, schuk allowi wdahoalawall welinaxit Rachellall, woak nundai wtellelemawall matta welinaxik Leahall.

Then Jacob he-answers-him-(in-the-affirmative) and he-married-them those both those-who-are-sisters-to-each-other, but more he-loves-her she-who-looks-good Rachel, and less he-allows-her *[i.e., he thinks less of her]* not she-who-does-not-look-good Leah.

Als aber Gott der Herr sahe, daß Lea unwerth war, so machte er sie fruchtbar, und hingegen Rahel unfruchtbar.

JACOB'S MARRIAGE.

Schuk Patamawos achgettemageluwi penawawall metelemuxitschi Leahall, woak wtelihawall wulapensohalawall hokeyall wentschi schai wunitschanit, schuk Rachelall matta schai wulapensohalawiwall wentschi cheli gachtin matta wunitschanik.

But God mercifully He-looks-at-her she-who-is-despised Leah, and He-does-it-for-her He-blesses-her herself so-that immediately she-has-a-child, but Rachel not immediately He-does-not-bless-her so-that many it-is-(many)-a-year not she-does-not-have-a-child.

Weil nun die beyden Schwestern einander deßwegen neideten, so mußte der gute Jacob gar viel Verdruß dabey ausstehen.

Juk witgochgunditschik eli ju wuntschi jane ganquiltichtit, nane wuntschi cheli sacquauchsowoagan woak machtangundawoagan machtechen hokenk Jacob.

These these-who-are-sisters-to-each-other because this from at-all-times they-envy-each-other, that from much troublesome-living and {bad-relations} it-falls-hard on-himself Jacob.

Nützliche Lehren.
WELAPEMQUO ACHGEGINGEWOAGAN.
PRACTICAL APPLICATION.

1. Wer mit Schönheit des Leibes begabet ist, der soll deßwegen nicht hochmüthig seyn; weil es ihm vielleicht an etwas anders fehlen wird.

1. Auwen wulinaxit hokey, katschitsch untschi mchelensihitsch, na elsit ihiabtschi schachachki pipili koecu li wtelli nundehhellan.

1. A-person who-looks-good his-body, don't-in-the-future from do-not-honor-him, that one-who-is-so yet surely various things toward he-thus is-in-need.

Das siehet man deutlich an der einen Schwester, nämlich and der Rahel, die war schön von Leibe, aber unvergnügt am Gemüthe.

Jun kschiechi neichquot talli elsitup mauchsit ochque Rachel [60] elewunsit, wtelli wulinaxinep hokey schuk ihiabtschi matta wulelendamoagan wunachpauchsiwon.

This clearly it-is-seen in what-she-did one-of-them the-woman Rachel **[60]** she-who-is-called, that-she looked-good her-body but yet not gladness she-does-not-enjoy-it.

2. Leute die nicht schön sind, die soll man unverachtet lassen, weil sie Gott dafür vielleicht mit etwas anders begabet hat.

2. Tacu wulittowi mattelemau medsisit auwen, eli ihiabtschi lissit, pili koecu welhik wtellatschessowen, milgussit untschi Patamawosink.

2. Not it-is-not-good she-despises-her she-who-is-ugly the-person, for yet she-does-so, another thing that-which-is-good she-possesses, she-is-given-it by by-God.

Daß siehet man klärlich an der andern Schwester, nämlich an der Lea, die war blöd von Gesichte, aber fruchtbar im Ehestande.

Na ju neichquot wulamoewoagan elsitup takan witgochgunditschik ochquewak, eluwihhillind Lea, won bischi machtissisu wuschgink, alod Patamawos wulapensohalawall hokeyall, wentschitsch mecheli wunitschanit.

Then here it-is-seen the-truth she-who-did-so the-other (of) those-who-are-sisters-to-each-other the-women, she-who-is-named Leah, this-one to-be-sure she-is-ugly in-her-face, yet God He-blesses-her herself, so-that-will many she-(will)-have-(many)-children.

3. Kinder sind eine Gabe Gottes, und Leibes=Frucht ist ein Geschenke des Höchsten.

JACOB'S MARRIAGE.

3. Patamawos kmilguna ktamemensemenanak, woak auwen wunitschanite tepi liteheu: Na welilissit eluwilissit Patamawos nemilgun.

3. God He-gives-them-to-us our-children, and who if-she-has-children enough she-thinks: That-One He-Who-does-good the-Most-Holy-One God He-gives-them-to-me.

Das siehet man klärlich an beyden Schwestern: Denn Gott hatte Lea fruchtbar, und Rahel hingegen auf eine Zeit unfruchtbar gemacht.

Jun kschiechi penundelukgeneen elsitschik juk nischowak, witgochgunditschik, Patamawos elihat Leahall wentschitsch cheluntschet, woak Rachelal wtellihawall wentschitsch quin matta wunitschanik.

This clearly we-are-shown those-who-are-so these they-are-two, those-who-are-sisters-to-each-other, God how-He-does-it-for-her Leah so-that-will {she-be-pregnant-many-times}, and Rachel He-does-it-to-her so-that-will a-long-time not she-(will)-not-have-children.

Gottselige Gedanke.
WELAPENDASIK PENAUWELENDAMOAGAN.
PIOUS REFLECTION.

Es hatte Jacob sich was schönes auserlesen, und was er sich gewünscht, das ließ auch Gott geschehn; doch daß sein Ehestand auch ein Wehstand sey gewesen, das kann man Sonnenklar aus vielen Dingen sehn.

Wewulinaxilid ochquewall Jacob wtelli pipinawan, woak pipinawotschi Patamawos wtellelemawall wentschitsch wulahhellat, schuk nihillii eli ajandankgup wikingen ochquewall, wtelli untschi cheli sasacquauchsin, jun tepi neichquot, untschi wtellauchsowoaganowawink.

She-who-is-really-good-looking the-woman Jacob he-thus chooses-her, and her-whom-he-chooses God He-allows-him so-that-will he-keep-her, but by-himself because he-wished to-marry the-woman, he-thus from much has-a-troublesome-life, this sufficiently it-is-seen, of of-their-lives.

Mich deucht die Schrift hat uns hiermit erinnern wollen daß wir auf Tugend mehr, als Schönheit sehen sollen.

Ni ndite eet untschi ju elekil penundelukgeneen, allowi wulit a allowelendamank wulauchsowoagan woak nundai mchelendameneen wulinaxowoagan.

I I-think perhaps from this as-they-are we-are-shown, more it-is-good should we-esteem-highly a-good-life and less we-(should)-honor-it good-looks.

Die 15te Historie.

[61] 15 ELEGUP.—2265.

---

15 AS-IT-WAS.—1447 B.C.

Wie Jacob mit Gott gerungen hat. 1 Mose, 32ste und 33ste Capiitel.

Jacob enda papatamaete woak achquepenalguk Patamawosall. 1 Mos. 32, &c.

Jacob when when-is-praying and {he-wrestles-with-Him} God. Genesis 32, etc.

Jacob zog wieder nach Hause zu seinem Vater, und hatte seine Weiber und seine Kinder, und alles was ihm Gott gegeben hatte, bey sich. Es hatte aber Jacob zwölf Söhne.

Nane metschi liteheu Jacob, nguttgi, lappitsch nda nochunk wikit epijakup. Nane wtelli guttgin woak witscheuchgopanik wunachauchschumall, unitschanall woak awessissak, wemi koecu endchi milguk Patamawossall. Schuk Jacob metellen woak attach nischa quisineyall.

Then already he-thinks Jacob, {I-am-moving} again-will I-go to-my-father his-house where-I-was. Then he-thus {moves} and they-went-with-him his-wives, his-children and-the-beasts, every thing as-much-as He-gives-it-to-him God. But Jacob ten and moreover two (are) his-sons.

Sechse waren von der Lea, und hiessen Ruben und Simeon, Levi und Juda, Isaschar und Sebulon.

Guttasch endchitschik gischiginewo untschi Leahink woak luwunsowak: Ruben woak Simeon, Levi woak Juda, Isaschar woak Sebulon.

Six those-who-are-as-many-as they-are-born of of-Leah and they-are-called: Reuben and Simeon, Levi and Judah, Issachar and Zebulon.

Die jüngsten zwey waren von der Rahel, und hiessen Joseph und Benjamin. Die übrigen vier waren von ihren beyden Mägden, und hiessen Dan und Naphtali, Gad und Assar.

Nek allowi tenktititschik gischiginewo [L., **gischiginenewo**] **untschi Rachelink woak luwunsowak Joseph woak Benjamin. Nek takanik luwunsowak: Dan woak Naphthali, Gad woak Asser.**

Those more those-who-are-little they-are-born of of-Rachel and they-are-called Joseph and Benjamin. Those others they-are-called: Dan and Naphtali, Gad and Asher.

Als er unterwegens war, so begegneten ihm erstlich die Engel Gottes, und da er sie sahe, sprach er: Es sind Gottes Heere.

Neli wtukgii li lochwet Jacob, kitelook Enschelak newop nek achpishigakgil [62] **wentschitsch metakquikgaguk. Jul newote ganschalamuin woak luep: Penno juk pejatschik Gettanittowit wtellenapejumall.**

While {he-returns} toward-(there) he-who-walks-thusly Jacob, there-is-a-host (of) angels it-(anim.)-is-seen those they-go-to-meet-him **[62]** so-that-will they-cover-him. These when-he-sees-them he-cries-out and he-said: Behold these these-who-come (are) the-Great-Spirit His-people.

Hierauf bekam er zur Nachricht, daß ihm sein Bruder Esau mit vier hundert Mann entgegen käme.

Nane talli likhikqui schai pendamen Jacob, wtelli pechotschi maigen Esau, wtellitsch unagisgagun chansall nachpi newapachki tchowak lennowak.

Then there at-that-time immediately he-hears-it Jacob, that-he nearby encamps Esau, that-he-will he-(will)-meet-him his-older-brother with four-hundred they-are-so-many men.

JACOB WRESTLETH WITH GOD.

Darüber erschrack Jacob heftig, und nahm seine Zuflucht zum Gebät, Unter andern sprach er zu Gott: Herr, ich bin zu geringe aller Barmherzigkeit und Treue, die du an deinem Knechte gethan hast.

Jun pendankil, ahi wischamgun Jacob, wentschi schai patamat, woak wtellawall Patamawossall: Woh nihillalian NPatamawos, nusami ngettemaxi, taku ni tepi likhixiwon, wemi nel goktomagelowoaganall woak wulamwewoaganall elatschahatt ktemaki ktallogagan nhakey.

Here he-hears-them, very-much they-frighten-him Jacob, so-that immediately he-prays, and he-says-to-Him God: O my-Lord my-God, excessively-I I-am-poor, not I enough am-not-worthy, all those mercies and truths him-whom-you-nourish poor your-(poor)-servant myself.

Darnach schickte Jacob seinem Bruder ein Geschenk, welches aus Ziegen, Schafen, Cameelen und Eseln bestand,

Nane Jacob wtellsin quischiechton welhiki miltowoaganall, wentschitsch milat Chansall, nan wtenda gatta milan mekisall, woak wehiwachschitschik awesissall woak weuchschumuisall woak oxschenall woak wequanitawakatschi.

Then Jacob he-does-so he-finishes-making-them good gifts, so-that-will he-give-them-to-him his-older-brother, that-one he-then wants-to give-them-to-him sheep, and those-(anim.)-which-repeatedly-carry-bundles the-beasts [i.e., camels] and cows and oxen and asses.

die ließ er in unterschiedenen Haufen vor sich hintreiben.

Jull miltowoaganall niganoochachtasuall, nhittami gintschinan allumoochwalan, nan nhittami ngutti meniechink, nan wahellemitschi wtenk pipili wauchtegawachtowak.

These gifts {they-are-taken-ahead}, first he-dispatches-people to-remove-them, that first one flock, that not-far after variously they-follow-one-another-continually.

Seine übrige Heerde vertheilte er auch in etliche Haufen; denn er dachte, wenn Esau den einen Haufen unterdessen entrinnen.

Woak ikalissi wtellsin Jacob wentschitsch wuli penauwelemat hokeyall, wtelli pachsinan wemi endchi nihillalatschi woak nihillatangi, nischeleneyachgenawall. Jun wuntschi lennemen, wentschitsch Esau ngutteli palihat, takquakiltsch piwunawall eli metschi wschimohet.

And further he-does-so Jacob so-that-will well he-consider-about-him himself, he-thus {halves-them} all as-much-as those-whom-he-owns and those-things-which-he-owns, {they-are-divided-into-two-parts}. This he-thereby does-it, so-that-will Esau singly he-(will)-hurt-him, others-will they-be-left-over as already he-runs-away.

Die Nacht darauf, wie Jacob ganz alleine war siehe da rang ein Mann mit ihm, und zwar mit solcher Heftigkeit, daß sich Jacob eine Hüfte darüber verrenkte, daß er hernach Lebenslang hincken mußte. Dieser Kampf währte, bis die Morgenröthe anbrach, da wollte der Mann seines Weges gehen: aber Jacob hielt ihn fest, und sagte zu ihm: Ich lasse dich nicht, du segnest mich denn. Darauf gab der Mann zur Antwort: Du hast mit Gott und Menschen gekämpfet, und hast obgelegen. Dieser Mann gab sich zwar nicht zu erkennen: aber Jacob merkte wohl, daß es der Sohn Gottes wäre. Deßwegen rief er aus: Ich habe Gott von Angesicht gesehen, und meine Seele ist genesen! Damals sagte Gott auch zu Jacob: Du sollt nicht Jacob heissen, sondern Israel soll dein Name seyn.

[Luckenbach's text, here, doesn't really follow the German and adds much more detail to this story than is found in Hübner's version, so it must be given separately.]

Nane nesquo petapano'k, enda nechohalenite Jacob, wiechgawotschi tschepsitschil lennowall quihillutagul.

Then not-yet it-is-not-daybreak when when-he-is-alone Jacob, unexpectedly a-stranger a-man he-attacks-him.

JACOB WRESTLETH WITH GOD.

↓↓↓

Nane husca wischixinep Jacob eli litehat: Nall eet wo schingalit N'Chans Esau, schitta mauchsit auwen wtellenapejumall, woak amintschi gotta [L., gatta] pachganechwin untschi hokenk, elitehat schi [L., eliitehatschi], ngatonaluk.

Then exceedingly he-is-afraid Jacob for he-thinks: At-last perhaps this-one (is) he-who-hates-me my-older-brother Esau, or he-is-one person (of) his-people, and absolutely he-wants-to {break-him-away} from from-himself, as-he-thinks see-here, he-wants-to-kill-me.

↓↓↓

Nanquepenaltowak teek ika petschi tschinquehhellak gischuch, woak metschi [63] giechgi patahawall, nane na lenno tschitane alennan ulocanink, nan Jacob gulquihillan tschipoame talli, wentschi abtschi segauchsit gugulukquihillat.

{They-wrestle-with-each-other} {there} there until it-(inan.)-shows-its-face the-Sun, and already **[63]** nearly he-subdues-him, then that man strongly touches-him on-his-hip, that-one Jacob he-is-lame {the-hollow-of-the-thigh} in, so-that always so-long-as-he-lives he-is-continually-lame.

↓↓↓

Nane amandanke wtelli tschilihillan talli poamink, nane wulohgahhellan, nane wunutschi mehemendowaman quihillutak'gil, wtellawall: Ponimil guwinuwamel.

Then when-he-feels-it that-he has-a-sprain in in-his-thigh, then he-is-discouraged, then he-begins-to entreat-Him Him-by-Whom-he-is-attacked, he-says-to-Him: Let-me-be I-beseech-you.

↓↓↓

Nane metschi kschiechi petapanke, wulelendam Jacob nauwat patachgukgil, nall nel [L., ne] ehoalatschi Patamawossall, nane

aschitte tschitane gelenawall wentschi aski lukguk: Kponi, metschi petapan. Schuk Jacob apatschi wtellawall: Ta kponenellowi, gintsch wulapensohalijanne.

Then already clearly when-it-is-(clearly)-daybreak, he-is-glad-about-it Jacob he-recognizes-Him Him-whom-he-subdues, that that-one (is) Him-Whom-he-loves God, then afterwards strongly he-holds-Him so-that must He-say-to-him: you-let-Me-be, already it-is-daybreak. But Jacob coming-back he-says-to-Him: Not I-do-not-let-You-be, unless if-You-bless-me.

↓↓↓

Nane Patamawos wtellan: Koecu ktellewunsi? Lue: Jacob ntellewunsi. Nane Patamawos nechgutinke wtellawall: Tacu tschitsch allowi li ktellewunsiwi, Jacob, schuktsch Israel ktellewunsi, eli metschi achquepenalatt Gettanittowit, woak ju endalauchsit, woak ki kpatahowen.

Then God He-says-to-him: What are-you-called? He-says: Jacob I-am-called. Then God when-He-answers He-says-to-him: Not once-more more here you-are-not-called, Jacob, but-will Israel you-(will)-be-called, because already {you-wrestle-Him} the-Great-Spirit, and here one-who-lives-here, and you you-overcome.

↓↓↓

Schuk Jacob husca wdajandamen wentschi pendank Nihillalgukil nihillatschi wdonink untschi, ta ewenikit, nane untschi wunatutemauwan Patamawossall lue: Gulah kwundamauwin elewunsian ki?

But Jacob exceedingly he-wishes-it so-that he-hears-it Him-Whom-he-masters Himself from-His-mouth from, definitely who-He-is, that from he-asks-Him-for-it God he-says: {Oh-that} You-declare-it-to-me what-You-are-called You?

JACOB WRESTLETH WITH GOD.

↓↓↓

Schuk Patamawos nechgutinke wtellawall: Quatsch ntutemauwijan? Metschi gowoahi, elewunsia. Nane Patamawos schai nan wtenda wulapensohalan.

But God when-He-answers He-says-to-him: Why do-you-ask-Me-for-it? Already you-know-Me, what-I-am-called. Then God immediately That-One He-then blesses-him.

↓↓↓

Nane Jacob tacu kaski tepi petschitehawon elgiqui wulelendank, eli nentsitaguk pilsitschi, wentschi amangaptonet woak lue: Ni newan Gettanittowit untschi neschginkgunk, woak quajaqui npomauchsi, woak nolapendamen, ntschitschank eli kikeuchgussit.

Then Jacob not able-to enough he-is-not-(able-to)-to-think-(enough)-so-far like-as he-is-glad-about-it, because He-appears-to-him He-Who-is-pure, therefore he-speaks-loudly and he-says: I I-see-Him the-Great-Spirit by by-my-eyes, and yet I-live, and I-am-glad-about-it, my-soul as it-(anim.)-is-healed.

Wie er hierauf seine Augen aufhob, so sahe er seinen Bruder Esau daher kommen. Gegen demselben bucket sich Jacob siebenmal gegen die Erde, und seine Weiber und Kinder neigten sich auch gegen ihm. Esau aber lief ihm entgegen und herzte ihn, und fiel ihm um den Hals, und küßte ihn, und sie weinten beyde miteinander.

Nane Jacob asphoque wtelli newan chansall palin. Nane unimigitawawall Chansall nischasch tchenol petschi hakink, woak wunachauchschumall [64] **ngutteli lenemawawall unimigitawawapannil. Esau aschitte ika schihilleu ohikochquenawall chessemusall woak elii lepakgok seki wawangundichtit.**

Then Jacob he-lifts-up-his-head he-thus sees-him his-older-brother is-coming. Then he-bows-down-to-him his-older-brother seven they-are-so-many-times hither on-the-ground, and his-wife **[64]** the-same she-does-it-so-to-him she-bowed-down-to-him. Esau then there he-hurries he-hugs-him-around-his-neck his-younger-sibling and both they-weep so-long they-greet-each-other-warmly.

Die Geschenke wollte zwar Esau anfangs nicht annehmen, doch ließ er sich endlich dazu bereden.

Nel welhiki miltowoaganall, nhittami schingi wunatenumen Esau, schuk wtenk untschi ihiabtschi wtelli ajumenep wentschi wulilawehat chesemussall.

Those good gifts, at-first unwilling he-is-(unwilling)-to-take-them Esau, but after wards yet he-thus got-them so-that he-appeases-him his-younger-sibling.

Hierauf zog Esau wieder des Weges, da er herkommen war, und Jacob zog auch seine Strasse.

Nane tepi wawangundichtite, Esau lappi matschiu, wtellochwen anenk wentochwetup, woak Jacob wtallemussin elhagechink gotta [L., gatta] paan ochunk epilid.

Then enough when-they-greet-each-other-(enough), Esau again he-goes-home, he-travels on-the-road from-which-he-walked, and Jacob he-goes-away {as-the-road-goes} he-wants-to come to-his-father where-he-is.

Nützliche Lehren.
WELAPEMQUO ACHEGEGINGEWOAGAN.
PRACTICAL APPLICATION.

1. Wenn man in Roth ist, so soll man seine Zuflucht zum Gebet nehmen. Das that Jacob, wie er sich vor seinem Bruder fürchten mußte.

JACOB WRESTLETH WITH GOD.

1. Wischasite auwen enda nachanaquo achpite nane papatamawatetsch. Nane wtellenumenep Jacob enda quitajalat chansall.

1. When-he-is-afraid a-person when {there-is-danger} if-he-is-there then let-him-pray-repeatedly. That he-did-it Jacob when he-fears-him his-older-brother.

2. Einen Feind kann man nicht besser versöhnen, als wenn man ihm Böses mit Gutem vergült. So machte es Jacob, der schickte seinen Bruder Geschenke, wie er auf ihn los gieng.

2. Allowi apuat patahau schingalowetschi, auwen welhik penundelate schingalgukil, quonna aschundei medhik liechguke. Nane wtellsinep Jacob allogemuinep miltowoaganall, wentschitsch milind chansall enda nagisgawate.

2. More it-is-easy he-subdues-him he-who-hates-him, who good if-he-shows-him him-whom-he-hates, even-if exchanging evil when-it-is-done-to-him. That he-did-so Jacob he-sent gifts, so-that-will he-be-given-them his-older-brother when when-he-meets-him.

Nichts ist in der Welt so stark, als der Glaube. Denn durch den Glauben hat Jacob mit Gott gekämpfet, und den Sieg davon getragen.

3. Tacu hattewi koecu allowi allouchsojuwik, wulistamoewoagan schuk. Wulistamoewoaganink Jacob quepenalap Patamawossall woak patahowenep.

3. Not it-is-not-there a-thing more it-is-not-(more)-mighty, faith only. In-faith Jacob he-wrestled-with-Him God and he-overcame.

Gottselige Gedanken.
WELAPENDASIK PENAUWELENDAMOAGAN.
PIOUS REFLECTION.

Es mußte Jacob dort mit einem Manne ringen, wer war denn dieser

Mann? Wahrhaftig Gott der Sohn. Und siehe da, Got ließ von Jacob sich bezwingen; der trug den Segen auch auf diesen Kampf davon.

Quilalissop Jacoba enda achquepenalguk Lennowall. Auwen eet na Lenno? Nechgutink: Kitschii Gettanittowit Quissall. Jun wuntschi nemen Patamawos wlilchpinep wentschi patachguk Jacoball. Alod gintsch patahinde, Jacob aschitte wtelli wsihowen enda nundajelensowi mehemendowet, woak nane gintsch wulapensohalgussop.

He-was-at-a-loss-what-to-do the-late-Jacob when he-wrestles-with-him the-man. Who perhaps (is) that man? Answer: Truly the-Great-Spirit His-son. This from-he sees-it God he-was-diligent therefore he-subdues-Him Jacob. Yet just-now when-He-is-subdued, Jacob then he-thus wins when humbly he-begs-pardon, and that until he-was-blessed.

Mein Gott! ich will dich auch mit starken Glauben fassen, und will dich eher nicht, bis du mich segnest, lassen.

Woh N'Patamawos nepe woak ntschitanaktschita kakenk nolsittamoewoagan untschi. Tacu kponenellowi gintsch wulapensohalijanne.

O my-God I-too also I-hold-on-tight-to-Him to-Yourself my-faith by. Not I-do-not-let-you-be until when-You-bless-me.

Die 16te Historie.

[65] 16 ELEGUP.—2276.

---

16 AS-IT-WAS.—1436 B.C.

Wie Joseph von seinen Brüdern verkauft ward. 1 Mose, 37ste Capitel.

Joseph Wimachtall enda mhallamundup Chessemusowawall Josephall. 1 Mos. 35, &c.

Joseph his-brothers when he-was-bought their-younger-sibling Joseph. Genesis 35, etc.

Jacob hatte zusammen zwölf Söhne. Der Liebste darunter war Joseph, weil er denselben im Alter mit der schönen Rahel gezeuget hatte,

Jacob tellen attach nischa tchilopanni quisineyall. Nan mauchsilitschi allowi ahoalatschi luwunsop Joseph, won ehoalatschi Rachelall wentschigilid, metschi mihillusite,

Jacob ten plus two they-were-so-many his-sons. That one-of-them more he-loves-him he-was-called Joseph, this-one him-whom-he-loves Rachel (is) he-who-is-born-of, already when-he-is-aged,

deßwegen er ihm auch einen schönen bunten Rock hatte machen lassen. Es waren ihm aber seine Brüder feind, und konnten ihm kein freundlich Wort zusprechen.

woak won allowi welhiki ehachquinkgi milawall, takquakgil elihat. Schuk wimachtineyall gehella schingalguk [L., -gu] tacu kaski tschitsch wulangunduwi aptonalguwiwall.

and this-one more good clothing he-gives-it-to-him, (than) the-others what-he-does-for-them. But his-brothers indeed they-hate-him not able-to once-more peacefully they-are-not-(able-to)-speak-to-him.

Die Hauptursache war wohl diese, weil Joseph seine Brüder bey dem Vater verrieth, wenn sie dann und wann was Böses gestiftet hatten.

Nane untschi eet majawi schingalgun wimachtall, eli ta koecu newot woak linawot pallalogasichtit necama matta witschgenemowon, ulahah abtschi gutschihillalawall wimachtall wemi koecu wtellan ochwall.

That for perhaps rightly they-hate-him his-brothers, because definitely what those-whom-he-sees and those-whom-he-observes they-transgress he not {he-does-not-go-along-with-it}, moreover always he-betrays-them his-brothers every thing he-tells-him his-father.

Ueber dieses hatte Joseph auch zwey Träume gehabt, welche seinen Brüdern nicht anstunden.

Nane Joseph nischen wtellunquamen, nane nallai wdatschimolchapannil wimachtall woak eli matta nostamhittik [66] eluwejuwik, nane allowi schingalawawall.

That Joseph twice he-dreams, then unconcernedly he-related-them-for-them his-brothers and because not they-do-not-understand [66] what-is-being-said, then more they-hate-him.

Den ersten Traum erzählte Joseph seinen Brüdern mit diesen Worten: Mich deuchte, wir banden Garben auf dem Felde und meine Garbe richtete sich auf, und stand, und eure Garben neigten sich gegen meiner Garben.

Nane nhittami elaschimuite [?lasch-] wtellapannil: Ehoalachgik gelistauwik elaschimuija! Ndellaschimui, ktahansiptigehhena hagihacanink, woak ni elamptawak nihillatschi amuin nipachteu; woak kiluwa elamptigejeek wiwunigapachtewall woak wtamachgitamenewo ni elamptawa.

JOSEPH'S BRETHREN SELL HIM.

Then first when-he-dreams he-told-them: You-whom-I-love listen-to-me what-I-dream! I-dream, we-are-repeatedly-binding-sheaves in-the-field, and I that-which-I-bind itself rises-up it-is-standing; and you that-which-you-bind they-stand-in-a-circle and they-bow-down-to-it I that-which-I-bind.

Da sprachen seine Brüder zu ihm: Sollst du unser König werden, und über uns herrschen? und wurden ihm noch feinder.

Jun pendamichtite wimachtall schai manunkaptonalawawall, wtellawapanil: Nosakimajumineentsch kakey, wentschitsch knihillalihhena? Woak untschi allowi schingalawawall.

This when-they-hear-it his-brothers immediately they-angrily-speak-to-him, they-said-to-him: Will-we-have-a-king yourself, so-that-will you-own-us? And therefore more they-hate-him.

Zum andern mal träumete Joseph, als wenn die Sonne, der Mond und elf Sterne sich vor ihm neigten.

Ikalli wendachquiechink laschimoagan wundamauwate wimachtall, wtellawall: Ntellaschimui, schela gischooch, woak nipai gischooch, woak attach ngutti alanquewak nemigitagook.

Further {the-second} dream when-he-declares-it-to-them his-brothers, he-says-to-them: I-dream, see-there! the-Sun, and of-the-night the-luminary *[i.e., the moon]*, and ten-plus one stars they-bow-down-to-me.

Darüber strafte ihn zwar der Vater mit diesen Worten: Was ist das für ein Traum, der dir geträumet hat?

Nane enda wundank jun mamtschitsch laschimoagan, nane ochwall schai quitelukgun, wtelgul: Ta linaquo elaschimuijan?

That when he-declares-it this last dream, then his-father immediately he-warns-him, he-says-to-him: How does-it-appear that-which-you-dream?

Soll ich und deine Mutter und deine Brüder kommen, und dich anbeten? Er behielt aber doch den Traum, in seinem Herzen.

Koecu hatsch ktiteha, gehella eet ni woak gahoes, npaneentsch ki elinquechinan talli, woak wemi kimachtak, wentschitsch wemi nemigitolenk petschi hakink? Schuk Jacob ihiabtschi gulenumenall nel lunquamoaganall talli wdehenk.

What it-will-be-asked do-you-think, indeed perhaps I and your-mother, we-will-come (to) you in-your-presence in, and all your-brothers, so-that-will all we-(will)-bow-down-to-you hither to-the-ground? But Jacob still he-holds-them those dreams in in-his-heart.

Nach diesem weideten Josephs Brüder das Vieh ihres Vaters zu Sichem.

Nanne wuntschi metschimi wdallemusganewo Joseph wimachtall, Ochuwawall wdallemunsall, nguttigischquackat Sichemink li enda wulaskat.

That from soon they-go-away Joseph his-brothers, their-father his-animals, {it-is-one-day's-journey} to-Shechem to where there-is-good-pasture.

[Luckenbach only]

Nane untschi kechokunakhake, nane ochuwawall wunutschi lachauweleman, eli litehat: Tamse eet juke leu, nek pemuteneya-hetschik gatta allutamoelchauwawall hokeyjuwawall, nitschanak eli ahi pallichquichtitup, nitschanak eli juke nechohalenichtit ne talli.

That from when-it-is-a-few-nights, then their-father he-begins-to be-concerned-for-them, as he-thinks: Sometimes perhaps now it-is-so, those those-who-made-the-towns-round-about want-to they-(want-to)-exact-revenge-on-them-for-them themselves, my-children because deeply they-hurt-them, my-children because now they-are-alone there in.

JOSEPH'S BRETHREN SELL HIM.

Da sagte Jacob zu seinem Sohne Joseph: Gehe hin, und siehe zu, ob es wohl stehet um deine Brüder, und um das Vieh, und sage mirs wieder.

Nane Jacob wtellawall quisall Josephall: Ika all woak pennau kimachtak ta elsichtit, woak lappi atschimolchime pajanne.

Then Jacob he-says-to-him his-son Joseph: There go and look-on-them your-brothers definitely how-they-are-doing, and again relate-it-to-me-in-the-future when-you-come.

[Luckenbach only]

Nane Joseph schai wetschpo, [67] allumsgeu, woak ika pejate Sichemink tacu mochgawawiwall wimachtall ika talli; metschi ksunga enda luwundasik Dothanink ewak. Ngutti Lennowall ika pomusgajeu neli awonit enda mamgukek, wtellgol: Auwen netonawatt?

Then Joseph immediately he-dresses, **[67]** he-goes-away, and there when-he-comes to-Shechem not he-does-not-find-them his-brothers there in; already {they-moved} where it-is-called at-Dothan they-go. One man there he-walks-about while he-is-lost where there-is-a-treeless-plain, he-says-to-him: Who do-you-seek?

[Luckenbach only]

Wtellawall nimachtak natonawawak. Nane apatschi lan: Tpisqui all Dothanink natsch ne kmochgawan kimachtak. Nane Joseph wdallemusgan, nane tpisqui wdan elind aal.

He-says-to-him my-brothers I-seek-them. Then coming-back he-says-to-him: Exactly go to-Dothan then-will that you-(will)-find-them your-brothers. Then Joseph he-goes-away, then exactly he-goes as-he-is-told go.

Wie sie nun Joseph von ferne kommen sahen, so sagten sie gleich; Da kommt der Träumer her, kommt laßt uns ihn erwürgen.

Nane wahellemi li newochtite pejatschil, nane schai littowak: Sche woh! pejat ehelaschimuit; juh gattatook, nhillatamook.

Then far-off toward when-they-see-him he-who-comes, then immediately they-say-to-one-another: See! Oh! he-who-comes (is) he-who-continually-dreams; well! come!, let-us-kill-him.

Hierauf war der älteste Bruder Ruben nicht zufrieden, sondern sagte: Vergießet nicht Blut, sondern werfet ihn in die Grube, dir in der Wüsten ist. Das that aber Ruben in guter Mennung, daß er ihn darnach aus der Gruben heimlich herausziehen, und wieder zu seinem Vater bringen wollte.

Nane Ruben, nall nen gekeyit matta wulelendamowon woak wtellawall: Katschi sogatehankhek mhuk; ulaha lanechwik wuli enda walik haki. Nanne luen eli gachta kimi ktinnat, wentschitsch lappi peschuwat ochunk.

Then Reuben, that one he-who-is-the-elder not he-is-not-glad-about-it and he-says-to-them: Don't do-not-spill-it blood; better cast-him there where it-is-pitted the-ground. That he-says because wants-to secretly he-(wants-to)-take-him-out, so-that-will again he-bring-him to-his-father.

Die Brüder waren es zufrieden, und zogen Joseph den bunten Rock aus, und wurfen ihn in eine Grube, darinnen kein Wasser was.

Nane schai nachgutemenewo woak guttenummauwanewo uschakhoquiwanall welhikil mamalekhasikil, nane wtellochwalanewo enda woalik haki, wtelli pindanechwinewo, peki matta m'bi ika hattewip.

Then immediately they-answer-it and they-pull-it-off-of-him his-coats those-which-are-good those-which-are-striped, then they-take-him-along where it-is-a-pitted the-ground, they-thus they-cast-him-inside, by-chance not water there it-was-not-there.

JOSEPH'S BRETHREN SELL HIM.

Hierauf setzten sie sich nieder zu essen, gleich als wenn sie alles gar wohl asgerichtet hätten.

Nane lemattachpoak mizachtowak woak wulelendamoak eli metschi pallihachtit ochwall eluwelematschi, necamawa schingalachtitschi.

Then they-sit-down all-of-them-eat and they-are-glad because already they-hurt-him his-father him-whom-he-values, they they-hate-him.

Ungesehr reiseten einige Kaufleute mit Cameelen vorbey. Da sprach Juda zu seinen Brüdern; Kommt laßt uns unsern Bruder verkaufen.

Neli ju lissichtit newepannik wahhellemi li peltitschik Ismaelii memhallemunditschik, gachta lowoltowak. Nane Judas wtellapanil wimachtall mhallamagetam kimachtena.

While this they-do-so they-saw-them far-off toward many-of-those-who-come Ishmaelite merchants, want-to all-of-them-(want-to)-pass-by. Then Judah he-said-to-them his-brothers let-us-sell-him our-brother.

Die Brüder gehorchten seiner Stimme, zogen Joseph aus der Grube, und verkauften ihn für zwanzig Silberlige.

Nane pendamichtite Judas elaptonet, nane olsittamenewo woak guttenanewo wimachtowawall untschi hakialachgunk, woak mhallamawanewo chessemusowawall li Ismaelitink, wtellawachtohenewo nischinachge sillebelall.

That when-they-hear-it Judah how-he-spoke, then they-believe-it and they-take-him-out their-brother from from-the-hole-in-the-ground, and they-sell-him their-younger-sibling to to-the-Ishmaelites, they-set-a-price twenty pieces-of-silver.

Der älteste Bruder Ruben mußte hievon nichts, sondern gieng heimlich zur Grube, und wollte Joseph heraus ziehen:

Nane Ruben tacu weuchsii eleek, eli allumsgatup, nane lappi pejate enda woalik haki, nane wunemen wtelli matta [68] **ika achpiwon pilawetschitsch.**

Then Reuben not he-does-not-know how-it-is, because he-went-away, then again when-he-comes where it-is-the-pitted the-ground, then he-sees-it that-he not **[68]** there he-is-not-there the-boy.

Wie er nun den Knaben nicht fand, so zerriß er seine Kleider, und sagte: Der Knabe ist nicht da, wo soll ich hin?

Nane quilalikhikqui wdenda sallachgihhillan, ganschelendamen; wtatoochgillachton equit, eli schiwelendank wsami, ika schihhilleu wimachtall epilid woak luep: Tatsch hatsch juke ndellsin: Tatsch hatsch juke nda?

Then {at-a-loss-at-that-time} he-then is-terrified, he-is-amazed; he-tears-it his-clothing, for he-is-sad excessively, there he-runs (to) his-brothers where-they-are and he-said: How-will it-will-be-asked now (will)-I-act: Where-will it-will-be-asked now (will)-I-go?

Da nahmen sie Josephs Rock, und schlachteten einen Ziegenbock, und tauchten den Rock in das Blut.

Nane wunihillanewo weitoneyitschik palippawetittall, woak mhukhoatonewo mamalekhasikil schakhokquiwanall Joseph,

Then they-kill-them goats the-little-bucks, and {they-put-blood-on-them} the-striped-ones the-robes (of) Joseph,

Darnach schickten sie dieses blutige Kleid zu dem alten Vater, und liessen ihm sagen: Dieses haben wir funden, siehe obs deines Sohnes Rock sey?

woak pili auwenil wdallogalawawall wentschitsch allumoch-wachtasik schakhokquiwanall ochuwawink li wentschitsch lachtit: Jun nemochgameneen, ki penna, quonna eet ta quis uschakhokquiwan schitta matta?

and other persons they-send-them so-that-will it-be-carried-away the-robes to-their-father to so-that-will they-tell-him: This we-find-it, you look-at-it, even-if perhaps definitely (is) your-son his-coat or not?

Der gute Vater kannte den Rock alsobald, und riefte laut: Es ist meines Sohnes Rock, ein böses Thier hat ihn gefressen, ein reissendes Thier hat Joseph zerrissen.

Schuk gettemaxit wetochwink medchi nenke, wunennamen wentschi ganschalamuit woak luep: Quatsche nane leu, nall jun nquis oschakhokquiwan; menunxit awessis mohawall. Woh! gettemaki N'Josephum, tatochgenukgol sechsisenowetschil awessisall.

But he-is-miserable the-father as-soon-as as-he-sees-it, he-recognizes-it so-that he-cries-out and he-said: Oh! then it-is-so, that this (is) my-son his-coat; an-angry-one a-beast it-(anim.)-eats-him. Oh! poor my-(poor)-Joseph, it-(anim.)-tears-him-to-apart a-clawing-one a-beast.

Es traten zwar alle seine Söhne und Töchtern auf, und wollten ihn trösten; aber er wollte sich nicht trösten lassen, sondern sprach: Ich werde mit Leid hinunter fahren in die Grube zu meinem Sohne.

Nane wemi quisall pewak gotta liwilawemawawall [?wulilawemawawall], woak wemi wikit epitschik pachsucquiwak gotta wulilawemawawall eli wsamelendank quisinga, ta a kaski wunatenummowon elind, schuk lue: Newimbenema nquis, ika petschi ni enda woalhalgeja nachpi schiwelendamoagan.

Then all his-sons they-come they-want-to {they-(want-to)-comfort-him}, and all his-house where-they-are they-stand-up they-want-to they-(want-to)-comfort-him because {he-feels-it-excessively} his-late-son, not could able-to he-(could)-not-be-(able-to)-take-it what-he-is-told, but he-says: I-would-twist-and-turn-for-him my-son, there until I when I-am-buried with sorrow.

Die Kaufleute brachten unterdesen Joseph nach Egypten, und verkauften ihn dem Potiphar, welcher ein Hofmeister des Königs in Egypten war.

Nane nek Ismaelii memhallamunditschik, wtellochwalanewo Josephall Egyptenink li woak m'hallamawanewo Sakima Pharao mchelemuxit wtallogagan elewunsilid Potiphar.

Then those Ishmaelite merchants, they-take-him-along Joseph to-Egypt to and they-sell-him-to-him King Pharao one-who-is-honored his-servant he-who-is-called Potiphar.

Nützliche Lehren.
WELAPEMQUO ACHGEGINGEWOAGAN.
PRACTICAL APPLICATION.

1. Was Joseph geträumet hat, das ist ihm auch nachher begegnet. Man siehet daraus, daß nicht alle Träume schlechterdings zu verwersen sind.

1. Wemi koecu Joseph elaschimuitup nane woak wtellinamenep. Jun untschi woatelukgeneen leu, tamse auwen koecu laschimuit Gettanittowitink wentschijeyik wulamoewoagan. [69]

1. Every thing Joseph that-which-he-dreamed that also he-observed-it. This from we-are-made-acquainted-with-it it-is-so, sometimes a-person what he-dreams from-the-Great-Spirit that-which-is-from (is) truth. **[69]**

2. Josephs Brüder thaten erst böse Dinge, darnach verkauften sie den Bruder, und endlich betrogen sie den Vater.

2. Joseph wimachtall nhittami mamachtauchsinewo, aschitte mhallamawanewo wimachtowawall, nane wtenk untschi achgiwalanewo ochuwawall.

2. Joseph his-brothers first they-sin-repeatedly, then they-sell-him their-brother, then after wards they-deceive-him their-father.

Man siehet daraus, wie immer eine Sünde aus der andern kommt, wenn ihr im Anfang nicht widerstanden wird.

Jun guntschi nemeneen eleek machtauchsowoagan ahallowi gischiechen woak gagelutasuall, auwen matta schai wischasique woak bonenemoque koecu pallalogasite, schitta machtauchsit.

This from-we we-see-it how-it-is sin more-and-more it-is-done and {?they-are-done-repeatedly}, a-person not immediately if-he-does-not-fear and if-he-does-not-avoid-it a-thing if-he-transgresses, or he-sins.

3. Jacob war ein frommer Mann, und seine Söhne waren doch moistens böse Buben.

3. Bischi Jacob schachgauchsit lenno, ihiabtschi unitschanall gachti wemi machtapewinewo machtauchsinewo.

3. To-be-sure Jacob he-is-upright the-man, yet his-children nearly all they-are-impious they-commit-sins.

Man siehet daraus, daß auch fromme Eltern böse Kinder haben können, und deswegen hat man sich in seinen Urtheilen nicht zu übereilen.

Jun guntschi nemeneen eleek, quonna welilissit welsittank wenitschanit, ihiabtschi tamse machtapeit pelsittank wnitschanall. Nane wuntschi matta abtschi wuliechenowi wenitschanit witschi mandomgussite, wnitschanall ta koecu elauchsilid.

This from-we we-see-it how-it-is, even-if one-who-is-well-behaved the-believer one-who-has-children, still sometimes he-is-impious a-disbeliever his-child. That from not always it-is-not-good one-who-has-children with if-he-is-blamed-(with) his-children indeed a-thing as-they-live.

Gottselige Gedanken.
WELAPENDASIK PENAUWELENDAMOAGAN.
PIOUS REFLECTION.

Geht doch, wie Joseph dort die bösen Buben hassen! Hört doch, wie kläglich er in seiner Grube schreyt!

Pennamook! elgiqui schingalgussit Joseph untschi metapewitschik wimachtall. Glistamook elgiqui ktemaki sasalamuit enda pindanehhemalind hakialachgunk talli.

Behold! like-as he-is-hated Joseph by those-who-are-impious his-brothers. Listen! like-as poorly he-cries-out when he-is-cast-inside in-a-hole-in-the-ground in.

Denkt doch, wie er zulezt sich muß verkaufen lassen! Was war denn Schuld daran? Nichts als die Frömmigkeit.

Pennamook wtenk untschi eliechgussit m'hallasu hokey woak wachtschangussu. Koecu eet majawi untschi wtellinamenep: Nanne untschi wtelliechgussinep eli gachta schachachgapewi lehelechet, Patamawos eli wulelendank.

Behold! After wards how-he-was-treated it-is-sold his-body and he-is-enslaved. A-thing perhaps rightly therefore he-observed-it: That from he-was-treated how wants-to righteously he-(wants-to)-live, God how He-is-glad-about-it.

Du liebe Frömmigkeit! Nichts soll mich von der scheiden; und sollt ich auch so viel, als Joseph drüber leiden.

Nane nepe newingi lissi, matta nponelendamowon welhik, quonna tpisqui liechgeja Joseph elihindup.

That I-likewise I-willingly do-so, not I-do-not-give-it-up that-which-is-good, even-if exactly I-am-treated Joseph as-he-was-treated.

Die 17te Historie.

[70] 17 ELEGUP.—2286.

---

17 AS-IT-WAS.—1426 B.C.

Wie Joseph wegen seiner Keuschheit ins Gesängniß kam. 1 Mose, 39ste Capitel.

Joseph enda wachtschangussitup woak enda kpahasitup talli Egyptenink. 1 Mos. 39, &c.

Joseph when he-was-enslaved and when he-was-imprisoned in-Egypt. Genesis 39, etc. *[Delaware caption totally different than the German one.]*

Joseph war ein Knecht in Egypten, und sein Herr hieß Potiphar. Derselbe sezte Joseph über sein ganzes Haus, und nahm sich seines Dinges an, als daß er aß und trank. Von der Zeit an segnete Gott das Haus Potiphars um Josephs Willen, und war eitel Segen des Hrn. in allem was er hatte, zu Hause und zu Felde.

[Once again, Luckenbach's text, here, doesn't follow the German and adds much more detail than is found in Hübner's version, so it is given separately.]

Nane Joseph allummochwalau Egyptenink, woak nek Ismaelitschik memhallemunditschik peschuwatschik, nane talli lappi mhallamauwanewo Potipharink elewunsit, Sakima Pharao m'chelemuxitschi wdellenojuma. Nelachpit talli wiquahemink, mhitschohai neichgussop, Pemauchsohalquonqui wtelli witawemgun.

Then Joseph he-is-taken-along to-Egypt, and those Ishmaelites the-merchants those-who-bring-him, then there again they-sell-him-to-him to-Potiphar he-who-is-called, King Pharao he-who-is-honored his-man. While-he-is-there in in-the-house, bodily he-was-seen, our-Savior that-he he-is-with-him.

Nihillalgukil eli pili linawot gutschquiwoaganink talli, nane wunemen Joseph endchi natenink mikemossowoagan, abtschi wuliechen, woak gischitasu nachpi schachachgapewoagan woak Gettanittowitii wewoatamoagan.

His-master as he-observes-him in-his-movements in, then he-sees-it Joseph as-much-as he-accepts-it work, always it-is-well-done, and it-is-finished with righteousness and of-the-Great-Spirit the-wisdom.

Nane wuntschi ahoalan Josephall, woak nhagalan, wentschi gischimat wtelli niganigapawin allogaganink talli, woak [71] ikalissi milan wentschi genachgitak nihillalgukil wikilid wemi koecu etekil, nachpi wemi endchi latschessowelid, necama li wunachkink.

That from-he loves-him Joseph, and trusts-him, so-that he-nominates-him that-he stands-foremost of-the-servants there, and [71] further he-gives-it-to-him so-that he-takes-care-of-it his-master his-house every thing those-which-are-there, with all as-much-as he-possesses, his to to-his-hands.

Nane wuntschi Patamawos wulapensohatamenall Nihillalgukil wikilid woak ekihelid, untschi Joseph eli wulelemuxit untschi Patamawosink;

That for-He God blesses-them his-master where-he-dwells and where-he-plants, for Joseph as he-was-considered-to-be-someone of of-God;

wemi elgiqui nihillatank Egyptsit Potiphar techi shuck [?schuk] neichquot Patamawos wulapensowoagan, wentschi nehellatank tacu tschitsch lachauwelendamok mikemossowoagan schuk nalauwi wtelli mamizin.

JOSEPH'S CHASTITY AND IMPRISONMENT.

all so-as he-owns-it the-Egyptian Potiphar utterly only it-is-seen God His-blessing, so-that that-which-he-owns not once-more he-is-not-concerned-about-it work but peacefully he-thus eats-leisurely.

Es war aber dieser Joseph schön und hübsch von Angesicht. Deßwegen warf Potiphars Weib ihre Augen auf ihn, und sprach: Schlaf bey mir.

Schuk ma leep, Joseph nesquo gunih achpique Nihillalgukil wikilid, nall ne [?na] ochque Potiphar witawematschil gotta pallihawall wentschitsch mattauchsilid li Patamawossink.

But in-the-past it-was-so, Joseph not-yet long when-he-was-not-there-(long) his-master where-he-dwells, then that woman Potiphar his-spouse she-wants-to hurt-him so-that-will he-sin toward toward-God.

Joseph aber gab zur Antwort: Wie sollte ich ein so grosses Uebel thun, und wider Gott sündigen?

Joseph nechgutink wtellawall: Koecu hatsch a wuntschi nelikhicqui mchinqui pallalogasia woak mescheki mattauchsia elinquechink Gettanittowitink, won genachgihuk woak ntapaluk?

Joseph he-answers he-says-to-her: What it-will-be-asked would for at-this-time greatly (would)-I-transgress and every-bit (would)-I-sin in-His-presence the-Great-Spirit-in, This One-Who-takes-care-of-me and He-maintains-me?

Das wollüstige Weib ließ sich zwar damit nicht abweisen, sondern wiederholte dergleichen Worte täglich: Aber Joseph gehorcte ihr nicht, sondern gieng ihr aus dem Weg, wo er mußte und konnte.

Schuk na metapewit Ochque matta logahhellewi, abtschi lachlappi wdachgenutemauwan getatank medhik. Schuk Joseph matta awulsittawawiwall [L., olsitta-], alod abtschi wingi tpassu untschi ochquewunk, woak matta wingi pechuwigawawiwall.

But that one-who-is-impious the-woman not she-is-not-dicouraged, always again-and-again she-relates-it-to-him that-which-she-desires that-which-is-evil. But Joseph not he-does-not-obey-her, yet always likes-to he-(likes-to)-dodge from from-the-woman, and not he-likes-to he-does-not-(like-to)-be-near-her.

Einmal kam Joseph in das Haus, und mußte nicht daß die Frau ganz allein darinnen war; da erwischte ihn die Frau bey seinem Kleide,

Schuk ngutten ma leep eli pintschiget wiquahemink, tacu woatowon na ochque wtelli nachohalenilin. Nane schai ika wdalihhellalan, tschitane achgenenawall, glennemen equilid,

But once in-the-past it-was-so as he-comes-inside in-the-house, not he-does-not-know-it that woman that-she is-alone. Then immediately there she-goes-toward-him, strongly {she-holds-fast-to-him}, she-holds-onto-it his-garment,

und sprach nochmals; Schlaf bey mir. Aber Joseph ließ das Kleid in ihrer Hand, und flohe, und lief zum Hause hinaus.

wtellapanil Glistawil elelan; schuk necama amintschi pachgibhawall ochquewall wunukachteschimuin equit, wunachgink ochque gunummen, woak kdeschimo.

she-said-to-him listen-to-me what-I-say-to-you; but he absolutely {he-breaks-free-from-her} the-woman he-flees-leaving-it-behind his-garment, in-her-hand the-woman she-holds-it, and he-runs-out.

Wie sie nun sahe daß alle Mühe vergebens war, so rief sie mit einem Zeter=Geschrey alles Gesinde im Hause zusammen, und sagte: Joseph hätte mit Gewalt bey ihr schlafen wollen; sie aber hätte angefangen zu schreyen, damit wäre er davon gelaufen, und hätte sein Kleid legte sie so gelassen.

Schuk na metapeit ochque, nenke wtelli matta koecu patatowon medhikink li, nane manunxu, quilalikhicqui niskalamo,

JOSEPH'S CHASTITY AND IMPRISONMENT.

wentschitsch ikalli mawehhellachtit, wemi na wiquahemink epitschik [72] **wdallogaganowawall,**

But that one-who-is-impious the-woman, when-she-sees-it that-she not a-thing she-does-not-gain towards-evil towards, then she-is-angry, {at-a-loss-at-that-time} she-makes-an-ugly-noise, so-that-will thither they-assemble, all there in-the-house those-who-are-there [72] their-servants,

Dasselbe Kleid legte sie so lange neben sich, bis ihr Herr nach Hause kam, zu dem sagte sie eben so; der Hebräische Knecht, den er ins Haus gebracht hätte, der wäre zu ihr kommen, und hätte sie wolle zu Schanden machen.

woak equink Joseph wtelli wulaton, wechitschil pejalide, nane achgiwalan wechitschi eli glonet woak wtellawall: Na Israelii allogagan ki eli peschuwatt, notchukgop ngatta miechanihuk, schuk eli ganschalamuija, wunukachteschimuin equit woak allumhattachgihhilleu.

and the garment Joseph that-she saves-it, her-husband when-he-comes, then he-is-deceived her-husband as she-lies and she-tells-him: That-one of-Israel the-servant you because you-bring-him, he-came-to-me wants-to-me he-(wants-to)-shame-me, but because I-cry-out, {he-runs-away-leaving-it-behind} his-garment and he-leaves-running.

Potiphar, dachte, es wäre wahr, was ihm seine Gemahlin sagte, und ließ den unschuldigen Joseph alsobald unverhörter Sache in ein Gefängniß werfen, darinnen die Gefangenen des Königs lagen.

Nane Potiphar jun pendanke manunxu, eli litehat, wemi eet leu, nachauchschum elit, woak schai allogemuin wentschitsch lochwalind pelachpit Joseph enda kpahotink, enda kpahasichtit Sakima wtallogaganall metschilissitschik.

Then Potiphar this when-he-hears-it he-is-angry, as he-thinks, all perhaps it-is-so, my-old-lady what-she-tells-me, and immediately sends-people so-that-will he-be-brought he-who-is-innocent Joseph where people-are-imprisoned, where they-are-imprisoned the-king his-servants those-who-do-evil.

[Luckenbach only]

Nane Potiphar matta tepi litehewi nhittami nattonamentsch talli leu schitta matta, elachgenimind; schuk eli metschi machtagenimgussit Joseph, nane wuntschi schai kpahoan.

Then Potiphar not enough he-does-not-think first I-will-seek-it there it-is-so or not, as-he-is-informed; but because already he-is-spoken-ill-of Joseph, that for-he immediately imprisons-him.

Aber Gott der Herr war mit ihm, und ließ ihn Gnade finden vor dem Amtmann, welcher über das Gefängniß gesetzet war.

Bischik Joseph enda kpahasit wtellsin nekgalind elsit, schuk ehoalatschi Patamawossall quajaqui witawemgol, woak wtelliechgussin wentschitsch mochgank tgauchsowoagan woak nhagatamoewoagan elinquechinelid talli na genachgitak gechkpahotink,

To-be-sure Joseph when he-is-imprisoned he-does-so he-is-left as-he-does, but Him-Whom-he-loves God still he-is-with-him, and he-is-done-to so-that-will he-find-it kindness and trust in-his-presence in that one-who-takes-care-of-it {the-prison}.

Derselbe that alle die andern Gefangenen unter die Hand Josephs, und nahm sich keines Dinges an.

wentschitsch wunachkink hattauwat wemi gebhasitschil epitschik talli kpahotink, woak necama nihillatschi matta tschitsch genachgihawiwall.

so-that-will in-his-hand he-(will)-place-them all the-prisoners where-they-are in {the-prison}, and he himself not once-more he-does-not-take-care-of-them.

Und siehe, der Herr war auch im Gefängnisse mit Joseph, und alles was er that, da gab der Herr Glück darzu.

Woak penna, Patamawos nihillalquonk woak witawemawall Josephall talli kpahotink, woak wulapensohatamenall wemi koecu endchi mikindamelid, wentschitsch wuliechink.

And behold, God our-Lord also He-is-with-him Joseph in {in-the-prison}, and He-blesses-it every thing as-much-as he-works, so-that-will it-be-done-well.

Nützliche Lehren.
WELAPEMQUO ACHGEGINGEWOAGAN.
PRACTICAL REFLECTION.

1. Gott verläßt die Frommen nicht, wenn sie gleich in groß Unglück gerathen. Denn auch im Gefängniß war Gott mit Joseph, und gab Glück zu allem das er that.

1. Patamawos matta ihaschi wunukgalawiwall nel schachachgauchsitschil, quonna meschikgakhittit ganschi sacquauchsowoagan woak mamukuwoagan. Enda kpahasit Joseph [73] talli kpahotink Patamawos ihiabtschi achpitawawall, woak wulapensohatamen wemi koecu endchi mikindamelid.

1. God not ever He-does-not-leave-them-behind those those-who-are-righteous, even-if it-draws-near-to-them terribly a-troublesome-life and destruction. When he-is-imprisoned Joseph **[73]** in {the-prison} God still He-abides-with-him, and He-blesses-it every thing as-much-as he-works.

2. Durch Gottes Gnade kann man sich gar wohl vor groben, wissentlichen und vorsetzlichen Sünden hüten.

2. Patamawos owitahendowoagan auwen ewegete talli wdehenk, tepitsch a genachgiechgussin [?-gussit] untschi wemi medhikink li achquetschiechgussite woak tepi allohigamenall wemi machtauchsowoaganall.

2. God His-help a-person when-he-uses-it in in-his-heart, enough-in-the-future would he-be-taken-care-of from all evil-towards towards if-he-is-tempted and enough he-overcomes-them all sins.

Also ließ sich Joseph weder mit guten noch mit bösen Worten dahin bringen, daß er wider Gott gesündiget hätte.

Nane wtelsinep Joseph matta kaski mguwi wentschitsch natenink medhik woak pallalogasin Gettanittowitink, quonna wulaptonalind schitta kschaptonalind, quonna mattelemind schitta wischamende.

That he-did-so Joseph not able-to he-is-not-(able-to)-surrender so-that-will he-accept-it evil and transgress by-the-Great-Spirit, even-if he-is-spoken-of-favorably or he-is-verbally-chastised, even-if he-is-despised or if-he-is-frightened.

3. Ein jeder Hausvater soll sich auf frommes und gottesfürchtiges Gesinde befleitzigen.

3. Nek Gegeyjumhetschik welahellatschik mikemossitschik, lachauwelendamenewotsch wentschitsch abtschi schuk welahellachtit welilissitschil welauchsitschi mikemossitschil.

3. Those elders those-who-keep-them those-who-work, they-will-be-concerned-about-it so-that-will always only they-keep-them those-who-behave-well those-who-live-well those-who-work.

Denn um eines frommen Knechts willen ward Potiphars ganzes Haus reichlich gesegnet.

Untschi mauchsit welilissit Potiphar wtallogagan Patamawos wtelli wulapensohatamenall wemi koecu eteekil talli wikit nehellatangil.

For he-is-one who-behaves-well Potiphar his-servant God He-blesses-them all things those-which-are-there in his-house his-master.

Gottselige Gedanken.
WELAPENDASIK PENAUWELENDAMOAGAN.
PIOUS REFLECTION.

Laß, keuscher Joseph, zu, daß ich von dir was lerne! Komm, sprach das Weib, du solst in meinen Armen ruhn. Du aber gabest ihr zur Antwort: Das sey ferne.

Gulah ntepe achgegimgen untschi Joseph wtellsowoaganink, nepe a nkaski lissin neca elelingup. Ochque enda latup Josephall: Glistawil elelan, necama nechgutink luep: Quatsch a elikhiqui ganschi palalogasija elinquechink Gettanittowit?

{Oh-that} enough-I am-taught concerning Joseph concerning-his-actions, I-likewise would I-(be)-able-to do-so he as-he-was-permitted. The-woman when she-said-to-him Joseph: Listen-to-me what-I-say-to-you, he he-answers he-said: Why would at-this-time terribly (would)-I-transgress in-His-presence the-Great-Spirit?

Das ich sollt wider Gott ein solches Uebel thun. Das will ich ebenfalls der Welt zur Antwort geben, Wenn sie mich reizen wird zu ihrem Sündenleben.

N'tupisqui nepe juke ntellawaktsch nachgomawaktsch nekik wawinkhallitschik elitschik; machtauchsil.

I-exactly likewise-I now I-will-tell-them I-will-answer-them those those-who-entice-me-by-words those-who-tell-me: Commit-sin.

Die 18te Historie.

[74] 18 ELEGUP.—2289.

---

18 AS-IT-WAS.—1423 B.C.

Wie Joseph wegen seiner Keuschheit ins Gefängniß kam. 1 Mose, 39ste Capitel.

Joseph enda ktennind untschi enda kpahasitup talli enda kpahotink. 1 Mos. 40.

Joseph when he-is-taken-out from where he-was-imprisoned, there where people-are-imprisoned. Genesis 40.

Wie Joseph im Gefängniß war, so fielen zwey Bedienten des Königs in Ungnade.

Joseph neli achpit talli enda kpahotink, nane talli woak leep, nischowall Sakima Pharao wdallogaganall m'chelemuxitschik pallalogasowak talli nihillalquichtitschi elinquechinelid.

Joseph while he-is-there in where people-are-imprisoned, then there also it-was-so, they-are-two King Pharao his-servants those-who-are-honored they-transgress in their-lord in-his-presence.

Der eine war ein Amtmann über die Schenken: und der andere über die Becker bey Hofe. Beyde wurden in das Gefängniß gworfen, und Joseph mußte Aufsicht über sie haben.

Mauchsit wtelli mikindamenep wtelli abtschi menahan Pharaoall, woak takquak majawi necama ehachpoanha'kgil. Nane elii hallawak ehenda kpatotink, Joseph enda kpahasit woak necama genachgihawall.

He-is-one he-thus worked that-he always gives-him-a-drink Pharao, and the-other rightly he he-bakes-bread-for-him. Then both they-are-placed where-continually people-are-imprisoned, Joseph where he-is-imprisoned and he he-takes-care-of-them.

Einsten, wie Joseph des Morgens zu ihnen hinein kam, so fand er sie beyde ganz niedergeschlagen. Joseph redete sie alsobald an, und fragte, warum sie so traurig wären?

Ngutten ma leep ajapawunii wetchate, wunewawall wtelli schiwelendamuwinaxinewo. Nane wunatochtawawall wtellawall: Quatsch eet schiwelendamowinaxijeek juke elachpajeek?

Once in-the-past it-was-so of-an-early-morning when-he-comes-to-them, he-sees-them that-they they-look-sorrowful. Then he-inquires-of-them he-says-to-them: Why perhaps do-you-look-sorrowful now early-in-the-morning?

Sie gaben zur Antwort: Es hätte ihnen beyden in der vergangenen Nacht was sonderliches geträumt, und es wäre niemand vorhander, der ihnen diese Deutung sagen könnte.

Nachgutemenewo luewak: Eliwi [75] ndelunquamhumena wentschi koecu litehajenk, woak nschiwelendamohhena, eli ktemaki lissijenk jun talli enda kpahasijenk, matta eet auwen achpiwi negalenk wentschitsch wundamaquenk eluwejuwik ndellunquamoaganena.

They-answer-it they-say: Both **[75]** we-dream so-that a-thing we-think, and we-are-sorrowful, because poorly we-do-so here in where we-are-imprisoned, not perhaps a-person he-is-not-here one-whom-we-trust so-that-will he-show-us what-it-says our-dream.

Joseph sagte zwar: Träume auslegen wäre Gottes Werk; jedoch sollten sie ihm die Sache nur erzehlen.

JOSEPH DELIVERED FROM IMPRISONMENT.

Nane Joseph nechgutink lue: Nane leu, tacu auwen pili hitta wundamowun eluwejuwik lunquamoaganall Gettanittowit nechoha, schuk ihiabtschi wundamauwik elaschimuijeek.

Then Joseph he-answers he-says: That it-is-so, not someone else skillfully he-does-not-declare-it what-they-(inan.)-say dreams the-Great-Spirit alone, but still declare-it-to-me what-you-dream.

Da sprach der oberste Schenke: Mir hat geträumet als wenn ein Weinstock vor mir wäre, der hatte drey reife Trauben;

Nane gegeyit Pharao memenachgukgil wunutschi atschimuin lue: Ni ndellaschimui elinquechina talli nipo weinimintschi, nane nacheleneyachgi pachgegu, nel nemenall li woataweju, woak nel ika glitakil wisachgim, nemenall li gischtewall.

Then the-chief-one Pharao he-who-gives-him-drinks he-begins-to tell-a-story he-says: I I-dream in-my-presence in it-(anim.)-stands a-grapevine, then three-different-sorts it-branches, those I-see-them here it-blossoms, and those there they-are-fruitful grapes, I-see-them here they-are-mature.

ich aber hätte den Becher Pharao in meiner Hand, und drückte die Trauben in den Becher, und gäbe sie dem König in die Hand. Joseph sagte gleich, die drey Trauben bedeuten drey Tage:

Ne npachgenumenall nsillgennemenall li Pharao mechmenetak, nane nemeken Sakima. Jun ndendchi laschimui. Nane Joseph wtellawall, sche jun eluwejuwik: Nel nachelenawachgi pachgeginkgil luewejujuwall, nacha gischguwall juke untschi.

That I-beat-them I-press-them to Pharao his-cup, then I-give-it (to) the-king. This (is) as-much-as-I dream. Then Joseph he-says-to-him, see! this (is) what-it-says: Those three-different-sorts the-branches they-say, three days now from.

Denn über drey Tage würde Pharao sein Haupt erheben und ihn wieder in sein Amt setzen. Dabey gab er dem Oberschenken eine gute Vermahnung und sagte: Gedenke meiner, wenn dirs wohl geht.

Nischogunakhake Pharao lappitsch kdaspenuk, wentschitsch lappi gischimgejan ktellitsch lappi mikindamauwan elgiqui gischimgejannup ninutschi, enda michmenahachtup. Schuk quinuwamel meschalime endatsch lappi wulilehellechejan.

When-it-is-two-nights Pharao again-will he-raise-you-up, so-that-will again you-(will)-be-nominated that-you-will again serve-him like-as you-were-nominated in-the-beginning, when-you-gave-him-drinks-habitually. But I-beseech-you remember-me-at-that-future-time when-will again you-live-well.

Darauf sagte der oberste Becker: Mir hat auch geträumet, ich trüge drey weiße Körbe auf meinem Haupte,

Nane mchinqui achpoanhes pendanke schai necama wtellatschimuin wdellunquamoagan lue: Ni ndellaschimuin, nachenol tankhaganall, nilink ntenda glennemenall nachi pitaichenol,

Then great the-(great)-baker when-he-hears-it immediately he he-relates his-dream he-says: I I-dream, they-are-three baskets, on-my-head where-I hold-them three they-are-in-layers,

und in dem obersten Korbe allerhand gebackene Speisen dem Pharao, und die Vögel assen aus dem Korbe auf meinem Haupte.

woak na hokunk eliechink, chelenawachgattol wewulikil achpoantittall, Pharao schuk mechmitschitschi, schuk tscholensak petschihillewak, woachgitschi eliechink tankhakanink mitschinewo.

and then on-high that-one-which-lies, they-are-many-different-kinds those-which-are-really-good cakes, Pharao only those-which-he-eats-repeatedly, but birds they-fly-hither, on-the-top that-which-lies in-the-basket they-eat-it.

JOSEPH DELIVERED FROM IMPRISONMENT.

Joseph machte darüber diese Auslegung: Drey Körbe bedeuten drey Tage, denn nach drey Tagen würde der König sein Haupt erheben und ihn an den Galgen henken, da würden die Vögel sein Fleisch von ihm fressen.

Nane Joseph schai wtellan jun wundamawachtowoagan, lue: Nel nachenol tankhaganall luejujuwall nacha [76] **gischguwall kepetsch ktaspenuk ksakimajum nischogunakhage, schuktsch pili leu ki enda aspenuxijann, kschelhellalukge woak tscholensak mehowaktsch [?mitschowaktsch] gujosum.**

Then Joseph immediately he-tells-him this message, he-says: Those they-are-three baskets they-say three **[76]** days you-likewise-will he-raise-you-up your-king when-it-is-two-nights, but-will otherwise it-(will)-be-so you when you-are-raised-up, when-you-are-hanged and birds they-will-eat-it-(anim.) your-flesh.

Ueber drey Tage, als der König eben seinem Jahrstag begieng, wurden beyde Träume erfüllet.

Nane leep, nane wuntschi nischogunakhake, Pharao elilenitup enda tpisquihhillak mechigischquen endchen heschi ngutti gachtinamite, nane wtenda gischiechtawan wdallogaganall m'chinqui wipundewoagan,

That it-was-so, then from when-it-is-two-nights, Pharao as-was-his-custom when the-time-is-at-hand there-is-a-great-day as-often-as every one when-he-is-(one)-year-older, then he-then prepares-it-for-him his-servant great a-(great)-feast,

Denn der Oberschenke kam wieder an sein Amt,

woak kteminaguwi gischimawall mechmenachgukil pachkitatamawall wentschitsch lappi wuski mikindank enda mikindangup.

and happily he-appoints-him his-cup-bearer he-forgives-him so-that-will again anew he-(will)-work where he-worked.

und Oberbecker ward an den Galgen gehangen. Aber der Oberschenke gedachte nicht an Joseph, sondern vergaß seiner.

Schuk aschitte allogemo, li schehellan mchinqui ehachpoanhes Joseph elgiqui nigani wundamauwatup. Schuk Pharao mechmenachgukgil matta meschalawiwall Josephall, elinquechink talli nihillalgukil.

But then he-sends-people, to hang-him great the-(great)-baker Joseph like-as beforehand he-declared-it-to-him. But Pharao his-cup-bearer not he-does-not-remember-him Joseph, in-his-presence in his-lord.

Zwey Jahre darnach hatte König Pharao emen gedoppelten Traum.

Nane metschi nischagachtinke, Pharao laschimop nischenawachki ngutti tpoqueii, ngutteli luejujuwall enda lonquongup.

Then already when-it-is-two-years, Pharao he-dreamed two-of-the-same-kind one of-(one)-evening, singly they-(inan.)-say when he-dreamt.

[Luckenbach only]

Sche jun leu talli Egyptenink ngutti sipu, mechachenneu, elewundasik Nil. Nane Pharao netami laschimuit, laschimuin wtelli nipawin scheyjaunque jun sipunk, eli wemi koecu talli wulikink.

See! this it-is-so in in-Egypt (is) one river, it-is-a-great-stream, that-which-is-called the-Nile. That Pharao first he-dreams, dreams that-he stands on-the-edge-of-the-bank this river-of, as every thing there it-grows-well.

Erstlich sahe er aus dem Wasser steigen sieben schöne fette Kühe,

Neli nan nipawit neweu nischasch tchowak wewulisitschik wisitschik weuchschumuisak petschi gachpatschik, nane wdenda tiasinewo enda wulaskat;

While that-one he-stands he-sees-them seven they-are-so-many those-who-are-really-good-looking those-who-are-fat cows hither those-who-climb-onto-land-from-the-water, then there-they they-graze where there-is-good-grass;

und darnach sieben heßliche und magre Kühe.

nan wtenk untschi neweu pili petschi gachpatschik, ihiabtschi nischasch tchoak wechschumuisak memachtissisitschik alogitschik, giechgi nipawinewo netami gachpatpannik epichtit japewi talli.

that-one after wards he-sees-them otherwise hither those-who-climb-onto-land-from-the-water, still seven they-are-so-many cows those-who-are-really-ugly those-who-are-lean, near they-stand first those-who-(first)-climbed-onto-land-from-the-water where-they-are on-the-shore there.

Die sieben magern Kühe fraßen die fetten, und man konnte es ihnen nicht ansehen, sondeern sie blieben heßlich wie vorhin.

Nek netami [?wendachquiechink] gachpatschik allogitschik wequamawawall netami gachpatpannil wewulsitpaninga, metschi wequamachtite, ihiabtschi ngutteli linaxowak, elinaxichtitup gepachtite, tacu untschi wisiwunewo.

Those first [?second] those-who-climb-onto-land-from-the-water-(first) [?(second)] those-who-are-lean they-devour-them first those-who-(first)-climbed-onto-land-from-the-water the-late-ones-who-were-really-good-looking, already when-they-devour-them, still the-same they-appear, as-they-appeared when-they-climbed-onto-land-from-the-water, not therefrom they-are-not-fat.

Bald darauf sahe er sieben volle und dicke Aehren auf einem Halm,

Nane Pharao togihhillanep. Nane schai lappi gewite, [77] ikalli wendachquiechink talli laschimop, wnemen chasquem nipachtek nane nischasch tchennol saquem amangigenol, untschi ngutti simaquonink [L., saquemink],

Then Pharao he-woke-up. Then immediately again when-he-sleeps, [77] further a-second-one there he-dreamed, he-sees-it corn that-which-stands then seven they-are-so-many ears-of-corn they-grow-large, from one cornstalk-from,

und darnach sieben dünne Aehren; und die sieben dünnen Aehren verschlungen die sieben dicken Aehren.

woak pili unemen, giechgi nipachteu lappi nischasch tchennol saquemall amatsisowall, linaquot taat aptachachtewall, nel mamachtitsikil wequitamenewawall nel wewulikpaninga saquemall.

and elsewhere he-sees-it, near it-stands again seven they-are-so-many ears-of-corn they-are-ugly, it-appears as-if {they-are-parched-to-death}, those those-which-are-really-ugly they-devour-them those late-ones-who-are-really-good-looking ears-of-corn.

Sobald es Morgen ward, so ließ Pharao alle Wahrsager in Egypten zusammen rufen:

Nane elachpajeke, husca penauwelendamen jul elaschimuitschi [?-muit], nane wuntschi allogemuin, wentschiman wemi nenbigetschik, woak netai medhik nostangik woakai pemachpitschik talli wtagijumink,

Then when-it-is-early-in-the-morning, exceedingly he-reflects-on-them these what-he-dreams, that from he-sends-people, he-calls-them all magicians, and skillfully that-which-is-evil those-who-understand-it all-around those-who-are-present in in-his-land,

Aber sie konnten ihm die Träume nicht ausllegen. Da trat der Oberschenke vor den König,

schuk matta ngutti auwen achpiwi geschiechi wundank kaski eleek. Nane gintsch peki meschatamen, Pharao mechmenachgukil.

JOSEPH DELIVERED FROM IMPRISONMENT.

but not one person he-is-not-there clearly he-who-shows-it can what-it-(can)-be. That until by-chance he-calls-it-to-mind, Pharao his-cup-bearer.

und sprach: Ich gedenke heute an meine Sünde;

Nane wdan Nihillalgukil epilid, schiwelendamowi gutschillachton wemi elekgup enda wundamauwatup Josephall endchi laschimuitup, talli kpahotink

Then he-goes his-lord where-he-is, sorrowfully he-makes-it-known all as-it-was when he-declared-it-to-him Joseph as-much-as he-dreamed, in prison

und erzehlte dem Könige, daß ein hebräischer Jüngling im Gefängnisse säße, der die Kunst, Träume zu deuten, gelernet hätte.

woak luep: ika achpo wuskileno Israelit tschepsit nutschquehind wtelli kpahasin, won wtelli hittaton wundamen lunquamowoaganall eluejuwikil.

and he-said: there he-is-there a-young-man an-Israelite stranger one-who-is-innocent he-thus is-imprisoned, this-one he-thus {speaks-skillfully} he-shows-it dreams what-they-say.

Sobald Joseph vor den König kam, und ihm der König die Träume erzehlet hatte, so sprach er gleich:

Nane schai nalan Josephall untschi enda kpahotink woak nipalan elinquechink Sakima. Nane gischi atschimolchate Josephall, Pharao elaschimuitup, nane necama nachgutemelid lue:

Then immediately he-is-fetched Joseph from where people-are-imprisoned and he-stands-him-up in-his-presence the-king. Then done when-he-is-(done)-telling-the-story-for-him Joseph, Pharao what-he-dreamed, then he he-answers he-says:

[Luckenbach only]

Tacu ni, schuk Gettanittowit nihillatschi wtelli woatellan Pharaoall untschi nhakenk weliechguk enda wulapendank woak lue:

Not I, but the-Great-Spirit Himself He-thus makes-him-aware-of-it Pharao from from-myself He-does-him-good when He-finds-it-useful and he-says:

Die sieben fetten Kühe, und die sieben dicken Aehren, das wären sieben fruchtbare Jahre;

Nek nischasch endchitschik wewulsitschik weuchschumuisak, woak nel nischasch tchenol welikinkil saquemall luejujuwall nischasch tchi gachtinewi enda wemi koecu wulikink wentschitsch wujakhak wemi koecu;

Those seven those-who-are-as-many-as those-who-are-really-good-looking cows, and those seven they-are-so-many those-which-grow-well ears-of-corn they-say seven so-many of-years when every thing it-grows-well so-that-will there-be-plenty (of) every thing;

und hingegen die sieben magre Kühe und die sieben dürren Aehren bedeuten sieben dürre Jahre.

schuk ikalli undachqui aschitte nek nischasch endchitschik wechschumuisak alogitschik woak nel nischasch tchenol saquemall aptachachteki aschitte [78] luejujuwall nischasch tchi gachtinewi mawottaganutsch, enda matta koecu gischigeno'k.

but further on-the-other-side then those seven those-who-are-as-many-as cows those-who-are-lean and those seven they-are-so-many ears-of-corn {those-which-are-parched-to-death} then **[78]** they-say seven so-many of-years there-will-be-famine, when not a-thing it-does-not-finish-growing.

Dabey rieth er dem Könige, daß er sich nach einem klugen Manne umsehen sollte,

JOSEPH DELIVERED FROM IMPRISONMENT.

Nane Joseph Sakimawall wtellan eneninktsch, laptoneu: Juke Pharao ndonawotsch lelpoatschil wewoatakil lennowall,

Then Joseph the-king he-says-to-him let-him-do-it, he-speaks-thusly: Now Pharaoh he-will-seek-him one-who-is-clever one-who-really-knows-things a-man,

der in den furchtbaren Jahren das überflüßige Getreide zu rathe hielte.

wentschitsch gischimat wtelli natschiton, woak wtelli nihillatamen elemamek haki Egypten, wentschi genachgitak wujaki gischiginkil hegihenki neli wujagiechink wemi koecu nel nischasch tchi gachtinall shaki.

so-that-will he-appoint-him that-he takes-care-of-it, and that-he he-owns-it all-over the-land Egypt, so-that he-takes-care-of-them abundantly those-which-grow-up the-plants while it-is-abundant every thing those seven so-many they-are-years so-long.

Diesen Vorschlag ließ sich der König gefallen, und sezte Joseph alsobald über ganz Egypten, daß er der nächste nach dem Könige seyn sollte.

Jun pendanke aptonaganall Sakima wtelli wingsittamenall, woak schai gischimap Josephall wentschitsch mechi gegeyjumhet talli Egyptenink woak wtellapanil: Ni knipalel ktellitsch nihillatamen wikia, woak knihillatellen wemi elemamek ndagijum, ni schuk ktallowilissitolen kitakimaii lehellemattachpink.

This when-he-hears-them the-words the-king he-thus likes-to-listen-to-them, and immediately he-appoints-him Joseph so-that-will greatly he-govern in in-Egypt and he-says-to-him: I I-stand-you-up that-you-will be-master-of-it my-house, and {I-make-you-master-of-it} all all-over my-land, I only I-outdo-you (on) of-the-great-king the-seat.

Darnach zog Pharao seinen Ring vom Finger und gab ihn Joseph an seine Hand, und ließ ihm ein Kleid von weißer Seide anlagen, und hieng ihm eine güldene Kette um seinen Hals.

Nane guttenumen wunachkink untschi, schapulinschewon, Joseph wunachkink wdatawon woak wdakunawall wapelechen silkii equink Sakima ehachquink, woak loquenawawall nguldii sosogahellasall,

Then he-takes-it-off from-his-hand from, a-finger-ring, Joseph on-his-hand he-places-it and he-clothes-him it-is-very-white of-silk clothing a-king the-clothing, and {he-put-it-around-his-neck} of-gold a-chain,

Ja er ließ ihn gar auf seinem andern Wagen fahren, und vor ihm ausrufen: Dies ist des Landes Vater!

woak allegemo wentschitsch allumtschehellalind tacquakil tetuptschehellasumall, abtschi niganin auwen ganschalamuit; lueu: Ne migito, won pejat, Gochuwa ju epijeek hakink!

and he-sends-people so-that-will he-be-driven-away-with-it-(anim.) other his-(other)-chariot, always being-ahead a-person one-who-cries-out; he-says: That bow-down-to-him, this-one he-who-comes, your-father here you-who-are-here in-the-land!

Nützliche Lehren.
WELAPEMQUO ACHGEGINGEWOAGAN.
PRACTICAL APPLICATION.

1. Die guten und bösen Zeiten kommen nicht von ohngefehr, sondern es gehet alles nach der göttlichen Vorsehung.

1. Wemi endchink gachtinall tpisquihillake enda wuli leek, enda wemi koecu wuli gischigink; woak lappi, endchink gachtinall machtschi leek, woak matta koecu gischigeno'k, matta nutschque pejejujuwall, wemi koecu leu Patamawos elitehat, necama elelemukquonk.

1. All so-many-as-they-are they-are-years when-the-time-is-at-hand when good it-is-so, then every thing well it-matures; and again, so-

JOSEPH DELIVERED FROM IMPRISONMENT.

many-as-they-are they-are-years bad they-are-so, and not a-thing it-does-not-mature, not for-nothing they-do-not-come, every thing it-is-so God as-He-thinks, He what-He-allows-us.

Denn Gott ließ es ja dem Könige in Egypten zuvor sagen, daß sieben fette, und sieben magre Jahre nach einander kommen würden.

Patamawos Sakima Pharao wotelan, elitsch leek, nischasch tchi gachtin shaki wulikenoltsch [79] **wemi hegihengi gischiginki woak lappi nischasch tchi gachtinall shaki, nanitsch leu matta koecu gischigenowiwall.**

God King Pharaoh He-makes-him-aware, how-will it-be-so, seven so-many it-is-year(s) so-long they-will-grow-well **[79]** all plants those-which-mature and again seven so-many they-are-years so-long, then-will it-be-so not a-thing they-(will)-not-mature.

2. Wenn weise Leute in einem Lande besordert werden, so wird oftmals groß Unglück abgewendet.

2. Schachachgapewitangik wewoatangik lennowak a gischimgussichtite wentschi gegeyjumhechtit talli hakink, nane woak leu talli cheli sakquilewall achpitschindasuwall, wentschitsch matta mawottaganok.

2. Those-who-are-righteous those-who-really-know-things the-men would if-they-(would)-be-appointed so-that they-govern in in-the-Earth, then also it-is-so there many {troubles} they-are-pushed-from-there, so-that-will not there-(will)-not-be-a-famine.

Wie viel tausend Menschen würden Hungers gestorben seyn, wenn Joseph nicht die Aufsicht über das Getreide bekommen hätte.

Cheli kitapachsowak ju endalauchsitschik schauwalamopannik a Joseph matta gegeyjumhekpanne talli Egyptenink wentschitsch genachgitak gischigenaminkil.

Many they-are-(many)-thousands here those-who-live-here they-(would)-have-fainted-from-hunger would Joseph not if-he-had-not-governed in in-Egypt so-that-will he-take-care-of-them those-things-which-produce-fruit.

3. Bey guten Zeiten soll man sparen, damit man in den bösen Zeiten nicht darben muß.

3. Enda cheli wulatasik eli wujakhak wemi koecu michmitschink, tacu wulittowi ajamachkitasike ulaha wulatasutsch, wentschitsch matta nundehellak endatsch mawotaganik.

3. When much it-is-saved because it-is-abundant every thing that-which-one-eats-repeatedly, not it-is-not-good {if-it-is-wasted} better it-will-be-saved, so-that-will not there-(will)-not-be-need when-in-the-future there-is-a-famine.

Denn es kommen nicht immer fette sondern auch bisweilen dürre und magere Jahre.

Matta abtschi eheschi gachtin wemi koecu wulikenowi, tamse hank pallihillewall hegihenki woak nane aschitte mawottagano.

Not always every it-is-(every)-year every thing it-does-not-grow-well, sometimes as-said they-miss-the-time the-plants and that then it-is-a-famine.

Gottselige Gedanken.
WELAPENDASIK PENAUWELENDAMOAGAN.
PIOUS REFLECTION.

Dem Joseph ist es wohl recht wunderlich ergangen! Es war derselbe bald des Vaters liebster Sohn; bald ein verkaufter Knecht; bald auf den Hals gefangen;

JOSEPH DELIVERED FROM IMPRISONMENT.

Joseph wulelemi missii wtellelemuxinep segauchsit. Nhittami wdellelemuxin Ochwall ehoalatschi Quisall; pibela wtahunnap woak mhallasop hokey wentschitsch wachtschangussit,

Joseph wonderfully here-and-there he-is-allowed-(to-be-somebody) so-long-as-he-lives. First he-is-allowed-(to-be-him) his-father him-whom-he-loves his-son; {off-and-on} he-was-seized and he-was-sold his-body so-that-will he-be-enslaved,

und endlich gieng er doch bis an des Königs Thron.

ajaskami wtenk untschi ihiabtschi wtelli aspenuxin woak mehelemuxin wentschitsch lemattachpit sakimai lehellematta-chpinkink talli.

finally after wards still he-thus is-raised-up and is-honored so-that-will he-sit kingly in-a-(kingly)-seat in.

Mein Gott ich will mich dich auch lassen ganz regieren; du wirst mich wunderlich, doch aber selig, führen.

Woh! N'Patamawos, nolelendamtsch, nolhattenamitsch, ki a wingi gegeyjumhaijanne talli ndehenk, quonna a tatamse leke achwi linamane ta undachqui li elochwalijann, ihiabtschitsch gulochwali, kpeschuwattsch nhakey ntschitschank enda wulatenamit.

O! My-God, I-will-be-glad, I-will-be-happy, You would willingly if-You-(would)-(willingly)-govern-me in in-my-heart, even-if would often if-it-(would)-be-so deeply if-I-observe-it definitely this-way toward as-You-bring-me, still-will You-bring-me, You-will-bring-him myself my-soul where one-is-happy.

Die 19ten Historie.

[80] 19 ELEGUP.—2297.

---

19 AS-IT-WAS.—1415 B.C.

Wie Josephs Brüder zur Zeit der Theurung nach Egypten verreifet sind. 1 Mose, 42sten und 43sten Capitel.

Joseph wimachtineyall enda peltichtit Egyptenink li eli mawottaganik ne talli haki. 1 Mos. 42, &c.

Joseph his-brothers when all-of-them-come to-Egypt to because there-is-a-famine there in the-land. Genesis 42, etc.

Die große Theurung erstreckte sich auch über das Land Canaan, darinnen Jacob wohnte.

Nane talli leep hakink Canaan elewundasik Jacob enda pominit, nane talli woak schai leu, achwi mawottaganowak nek epitschik.

Even there it-was-so in-the-land Canaan that-which-is-called Jacob where {he-moves-about}, even there also immediately it-is-so, very-much they-suffer-famine those those-who-are-there.

Wie derselbe hörte, daß in Egypten Getreide genug wäre, so schickte er seine Söhne dahin, daß sie Getreide kaufen sollten.

Nane Jacob pendanke Egyptenink talli li hatteu enda mhallamawachtink chasquem, nane guntschitamawall Quisineyall wentschi schai ika achtit, woak mhallamenewo mitschewoagan tepi wendauchsichtit.

That Jacob when-he-hears-it in-Egypt there toward it-is-there where many-people-are-buying-it-from-them corn, then he-exhorts-them his-sons so-that immediately there they-go, and they-buy-it food enough they-live-from.

Den einzigen jüngsten Sohn Benjamin ließ er nicht mit reisen, aus Beysorge, daß ihm nicht etwan unterwegens ein Unfall begegenen möchte.

Schuk ne tenksisitschi ehoalatschi Quisall Benjamin matta wtellelemawiwall wentschi witet, eli litehat: koecutsch a medhik meschigagun nawotschi li, achwi koecu linamichtite.

But that little-one him-whom-he-loves his-son Benjamin not he-does-not-allow-him so-that he-goes-with-(them), for he-thinks: a-thing-in-the-future could evil it-(could)-draw-near-them {along-the-way} to, hard a-(hard)-thing if-they-be-treated-so.

Es war aber in Egypten Joseph über das Getreide gesezt, und wenn jemand was haben wollte, so gab der König allemal zur Antwort: Gehe hin zu Joseph, und was er euch saget, das thut.

Schuk Joseph gischimgussop wentschitsch genachgitak [81] talli Egyptenink wemi achgolsowigawanall, nane auwen gatta m'hallank koecu michmitschink, nane Sakima schai wtellawall: Ika all Josephink necama endchi koecu lukquon nanitsch leu.

But Joseph he-was-appointed so-that-will he-take-care-of-them **[81]** in in-Egypt all storehouses, that a-person wants-to he-(wants-to)-buy-it what what-people-repeatedly-eat, then the-king immediately he-says-to-him: There go to-Joseph he as-much-as what he-tells-you that-will it-be-so.

Da nun Jacobs Söhne auch an ihn gewiesen wurden, so fielen sie vor demselben nieder auf ihr Antlitz zur Erde.

Nane ika pejachtite Jacob quisineyall metellen endchitschik weimachtintitschik nane schai peschuwawak Joseph epit. Nane newochtite nel ikalli wendachquiechingil Sakimawall, enda

JOSEPH'S BRETHREN GO TO EGYPT TO BUY CORN.

allowilissilid woak nemhittite opawallessowoagan nane schai pagachtehhellewak hakink li petschi wuschginkuwawink.

Then there when-they-come Jacob his-sons ten they-who-are-as-many-as those-who-are-brothers-to-one-another then immediately they-bring-them Joseph where-he-is. Then when-they-see-him that-one thither (is) one-who-is-a-second king, where he-does-more and when-they-see-it his-wealth then immediately they-prostrate-themselves on-the-ground toward up-to-here on-their-faces.

Joseph kannte sie gleich; sie wusten nicht, daß das ihr Bruder wäre, den sie verkauft hatten. Sie konnten ihn auch an der Sprache nicht erkennen, weil er allemal einen Dollmetscher brauchte, wen er mit ihnen reden wollte.

Necama schai wunennawawall, schuk necamawa matta kaski litehewiwak, won eet kimachtena (L., kimachtenanak). Woak matta kaski woahawiwawall eli ewegelid ahanhuctonhetschi endchi koecu li ajaptonalat, woak eli wilawinaxit Egyptenitschik elachquichtit.

He immediately he-recognizes-them, but they not able-to they-are-not-(able-to)-think, this-one perhaps (is) our-brother. And not able-to they-are-not-(able-to)-know-him because he-uses an-interpreter as-much-as a-thing to he-speaks-to-them, and because he-is-dressed-fancily Egyptians as-they-are-clothed.

Indem sie nun solchergestallt auf den Knien vor ihm lagen, so gedachte Joseph an seinen Traum, daß sich seine Brüder vor ihm neigen sollten.

Neli nek wemi nimigitaguk Joseph, nane wtenda meschatamen elaschimuitup, wimachtineyall elitsch wemi nimigitaguk.

While those all they-bow-down-to-him Josesph, then then-he remembers-it what-he-dreamed, his-brothers how-will all they-(will)-bow-down-to-him.

Er gab sich aber nicht zu erkennen, sondern ließ sie als Kundschafter in Arrest nehmen.

Schuk Joseph matta mhittachganiechtowon hokey, schuk allogemuin wentschitsch wemi kpahasichtit talli, woak wtellelemawall taat kimi gigauchwetschik, medhik undochwetschik, woak wtellawall: Kiluwa eet gundochwenewo gatta woatonewo enda tauwiechink haki.

But Joseph not he-does-not-make-it-manifest his-body, but he-sends-someone so-that-will all they-(will)-be-imprisoned there, and he-considers-them-to-be as-if secret {scouts}, evil those-who-travel-for, and he-says-to-them: You perhaps you-travel-for you-want-to you-(want-to)-know-it where it-is-open the-land.

Sie entschuldigten sich zwar, sie wären ehrliche Leute, zusammen zwölf Brüder. Aber Joseph fragte gleich, wo die andern zwey Brüder wären? Sie gaben zur Antwort: Der jüngste Bruder wäre zu Hause beym Vater und der andere wäre nicht mehr vorhanden.

Schuk necamawa schai luewak: Nihillalijenk nschachach-gapewihhena, tacu kaski ndellsiwuneen, elijenk, niluna ktalogaganak attach nischa ndentchimachtintihhena, wemi mauchsu nochena. Nimachtena tenksisit quajaqui achpo nochenanink, woak mauchsit, tawongela.

But they immediately they-say: Our-lord we-are-upright, not able-to we-are-not-(able-to)-do-so, as-you-say-to-us, we your-servants ten-plus two we-are-so-many-brothers-to-one-another, all he-is-one our-father. Our-brother the-little-one still he-is-there by-our-father, and one, he-is-lost-and-gone.

Darauf sagte Joseph, es sollte einer aus ihrer Mitte nach Hause reisen, und den jüngste Bruder auch herholen;

Nane Joseph apatschi late, wtellawall: Wulit endchi lijeek, nane wuntschi schai gatta wulamoenewo endchi luejeek, mauchsit

JOSEPH'S BRETHREN GO TO EGYPT TO BUY CORN.

kiluwa schai ika atetsch, nalatetsch kimachtowawall eluejeek, nochenanink [82] **achpo,**

Then Joseph coming-back when-he-says-to-them, he-says-to-them: It-is-good as-much-as you-say-to-me, that for immediately you-want-to you-(want-to)-tell-the-truth as-much-as you-say, one (of) you immediately there let-him-go, let-him-fetch-him your-brother as-you-say, by-our-father **[82]** he-is-there,

daran wollte er sehen, ob sie Kundschafter wären oder nicht. Wie sie das hörten, so sagten sie auf ihre Sprache unter einander:

nanitsch a woachquot ktelli matta kimi gigauchwewunewo, schuk schachachgapewitschik kakeyjuwa. Na jun pendamichtite nane wunutschi koecu littowak nihillatschi eliechsichtit, luewak:

that-in-the-future would it-(would)-be-made-known that-you not secretly you-are-not-scouting, but those-who-are-upright (are) yourselves. Then this when-they-hear-it then they-begin-to a-thing they-(begin-to)-say-to-one-another themselves the-way-they-speak, they-say:

Das haben wir an unserm Bruder Joseph verschuldet. Ueber diesen und dergleichen Worten giengen Joseph die Augen über, daß er sich von ihnen wegwenden mußte. Endlich mußte Simeon im Arreste bleiben, und die andern neune mochten ihre Straße ziehen. Wie sie das Korn ausschüteten, so fand ein jeder das Geld in seinem Sack, welches sie für das Korn bezahlet hatten. Denn Joseph hatte einen jedweden das Geld wieder in seinen Kornsack flecken laften. Darüber erschracken sowohl die Söhne als der alte Vater.

[Once again, here, Luckenbach adds many details to the shorter German passage, rather than translating it directly.]

Schachachki juke enda ahiliechgussijank, nane kpatatoneen, eli machtschihankgup kimachtena. Eli mchinqui pallalogasijank, schachachgi na guntschi angeleneen, eli ndochtasik omocum.

Joseph ika nipop enda littichtite, woak nenostawapanil, schuk necamawa tacu owoatowunewo.

Surely now when we-are-roughly-spoken-to, that we-earn-it, for we-did-bad-to-him our-brother. For greatly we-transgress, surely then we-thereby we-die, because it-is-sought his-blood. Joseph there he-stood when when-they-talk-to-one-another, and he-understood-them, but they not they-do-not-know-it.

Nane pendawate wimachtall, nane machtechen wdehink wentschitsch achgettemagelemat, schechihillellowall wdehall eli wdaxilid, achschauochwep wentschi sogahhellak supinkquall. Nane Joseph ihiabtschi mochgamen li wuliechen, wtelli matta schai tgauchsittawawon.

Then when-he-hears-them his-brothers, then it-lands in-his-heart so-that-will he-be-merciful-to-them, {it-(anim.)-is-slipping} his-heart for it-(anim.)-is-tender, he-walked-slowly so-that it-spills-out the-tears. Then Joseph still he-finds-it here it-is-good, that-he not immediately {not-be-kind-to-them}.

Nane lappi tschitanappilide wdehall, nane lappi paan epichtit, nane wunatenan Simonall, eli gatta achgenat, woak allogemo gachpilan elinquechinhittit talli.

Then again {when-it-(anim.)-stays-strong} his-heart, then again he-comes where-they-are, then he-takes-him Simeon, because wants-to {he-(wants-to)-restrain-him}, and he-sends-someone to-bind-him in-their-presence in.

Won Simon eet schachachki kwigeyinep enda mhukqui atschimolsichtit, enda gendelemachtit Josephall, allowi eet necama gattamenep wentschitsch nhillind.

This Simeon perhaps surely he-was-the-older when bloodily they-consult, when they-condemn-him Joseph, more perhaps he desired-it so-that-will he-be-killed.

JOSEPH'S BRETHREN GO TO EGYPT TO BUY CORN.

Nane Simon metschi kpahasite; nane wtelleleman nel peschgunk endchitschik weimachtinditschik wentschi allumsgalid. Joseph wtelli wulelendamenep, wentschi menutesuwawall wemi wtschuhattonk chasquem eteek.

Then Simeon already when-he-is-imprisoned; then he-allows-them those nine those-who-are-as-many-as those-who-are-brothers-to-one-another so-that they-go-away. Joseph he-thus was-glad-about-it, so-that their-sacks all people-make-them-full the-corn where-it-is.

Metschi matschichtite peachtite wikichtit, nane talli enda sokhamhittit chasquem, nane wtenda mochgamenewo memajauchsitschi mekup omonijum hattasu menutesuwawink.

Already when-they-go-home when-they-come where-they-dwell, then there when-they-pour-it-out the-corn, that they-then they-find-it each-one he-gave-it-to-him his-money it-is-placed in-their-sacks.

Nane ganschelendamenewo, salachgihhillanewo, [83] woak tacu kaski woatowunewo koecu eluwejuwik, woak wischasuwi littowak: Schachachgi guntschi allowi meschigaguneen winhattakuwoagan. Gettanittowit ktelliechguneen kpallalogewoaganena untschi eli patatawonk.

Then they-are-amazed, they-are-frightened, [83] and not able-to they-are-not-(able-to)-know-it what what-it-says, and fearfully they-say-to-one-another: Surely us-hereby more it-draws-near-us danger. The-Great-Spirit He-does-it-to-us (for)-our-transgression for because we-earn-it.

Wie dieses Getreide verzehret war, so mußte Jacob seine Söhne zum andernmal nach Egypten senden.

Nane metschi wequitasike tchihhillake petasikpanni mitschewoagan woak eli allumsgejuwik mawottagan, nane quilalissu, na sacquelendank mihillusis Jacob wentschi lappi alike luet: Nane leketsch ika aak mauwi mhallamook mitschewoagan.

Then already when-it-is-eaten-up when-it-is-all-gone that-which-was-brought the-food and as it-goes-on the-famine, then he-is-at-a-loss-what-to-do, that-one he-is-troubled-in-mind-about-it the-aged-man Jacob so-that again reluctantly he-says: That let-it-be there go go-and buy-it food.

Sie wollten aber nicht eher fort, bis ihr jüngster Bruder Benjamin mit ihnen zog. Denn Joseph hatte ausdrücklich gesagt, sie sollten sein Angesicht nicht sehen, wenn sie ihren jüngsten Bruder nicht mit sich brächten.

Schuk matta l'hilchpiwiwak, schwilawewak wentschi ika achtit Egyptenink, gintsch witscheuchquichtite chessemussowawall tenksisit Benjaminall, Josephall eli lukhittit: Katschi lappi pawek, ta a knemowunewo neschgink matta peschuwaweque kimachtowa.

But not they-are-not-willing, they-are-faint-hearted so-that there they-go to-Egypt, unless if-he-goes-with-them their-younger-sibling the-little-one Benjamin, Joseph as he-says-to-them: Don't again do-not-come, not would I-(would)-not-see-you in-my-eyes not if-you-do-not-bring-him your-brother.

[Luckenbach only]

Nane alike Jacob nachgoman wentschitsch witet Benjamin; woak Jacob enda mamtschitsch wawangomat Quisineyall wtellawall:

Then reluctantly Jacob answers-them so-that-will he-go-along Benjamin; and Jacob when lastly he-is-greeting-him his-son he-says-to-him:

[Luckenbach only]

Na Tegauwontowit Eluwantowit kmilguwa wentschitsch gettemagelemuxijeek elinquechink talli na lenno. Schuk sekhagejeek nin ndellsin elsit auwen wemi wunitschanall enkhillat.

JOSEPH'S BRETHREN GO TO EGYPT TO BUY CORN.

That Gentle-Spirit He-Who-is-most-divine He-(will)-give-it-to-you so-that-will you-be-shown-mercy in-his-presence in that man. But so-long-as-you-are-gone that I-act-thusly as-he-does a-person all his-children he-who-loses-them.

Wie sie in Egypten angekommen waren, so stellten sie Josephs Haushalter vor allen Dingen das Geld wieder zu, welches sie in ihren Säcken gefunden hatten.

Nane ika peachitite talli Egyptenink nane wtellsinewo, nesquo mettemigechtik Joseph wikit, gatta schai lappi milanewo genachgitagil na money lappi petochtit,

Then there when-they-come there to-Egypt then they-do-so, not-yet they-do-not-enter Joseph his-house, want-to immediately again they-(want-to)-give-it-to-him the-overseer that money again they-brought,

Er nahms aber nicht an, sondern sagte, ihres Vaters Gott möchte ihnen vielleicht einen Schatz in ihre Säcke gegeben haben. Hierauf empfieng sie Joseph gar freundlich,

schuk necama matta wnatenumowon, schuk wtellawall: Kpatamawossuwa, woak Gooch OPatamawossall gemilgunewo lappi wentschi hattek gemenutesuwawunk. Nane Joseph wulangundowi wawangomawall,

but he not he-does-not-accept-it, but he-says-to-them: Your-God, and your-father His-God He-gives-it-to-you again so-that it-is-there in-your-sacks. Then Joseph peacefully he-greets-them,

[Luckenbach only]

wunatochtawawall lueu: Ta wtellamallsin Gochuwa mihillusis? Nane nundajelensuwi nachpi lappi tamachgitawawall, wtellawawall: Ktallogagan Nochena, anischik quajaqui wulamallsu.

he-inquires-of-them he-says: How does-he-feel your-father the-aged-man? Then (with)-humility with again they-bow-down-toward-him, they-say-to-him: Your-servant our-father, thank-you still he-feels-well.

und wie er unter ihnen seinen leiblichen Bruder Benjamin zu gesichte bekam. So sprach er zu ihm: Gott sey dir gnädig, mein Sohn!

Bischi Joseph majawi nuktinquamawall [84] **chessemussall Benjaminall, nel wawangomawall untschi wdehenk eli lat: Patamawos tgauchsittaqui Nquis!**

To-be-sure Joseph rightly {he-looks-at-one-person} **[84]** his-younger-sibling Benjamin, that-one he-greets-him-warmly from from-his-heart as he-says-to-him: God let-Him-be-kind-to-you my-son!

Es entbrannte aber sein Herz gegen seine Bruder dergestalt, daß er sich der Thränen nicht enthalten konnte, und deswegen in seine Kammer gehen mußte.

Tacu kaski allowi li aptonewi eli wdaksilid wdehall; nane schai palli wdan ehachpit, enda nalai lupakik. Nane lappi paan epilid, lappi gulinatschinaxu, tacu techi neichgussii elamandank talli wdehenk, woak eli lubakgup.

Not able-to more toward he-is-not-(able-to)-speak for it-(anim.)-is-soft his-heart; then immediately elsewhere he-goes where-he-stays, where safely he-weeps. Then again he-comes where-they-are, again {?he-appears-composed}, not utterly he-is-not-seen what-he-feels in in-his-heart, and how he-was-weeping.

Mittlerweile ward der Tisch gedeckt und Josephs Brüder mußten zur Tafel bleiben.

Neli na ju lekgup, nane gischitasuwall mitschewoagan woak endalipuinkall wulitasuall, nane talli lemattachpoltowak.

While that-one here he-wept, then they-are-prepared the-food and the-tables they-are-made-well, then there all-of-them-sit-down.

JOSEPH'S BRETHREN GO TO EGYPT TO BUY CORN.

[Luckenbach only]

Joseph nechoha mizu, ngutti ehendalipuinkgink; nek mechelemuxitschik mikindama'kgil woak pili ehendalipuink talli mizachtowak, woak wimachtall lappi pili ehendalipuink talli nihillatschi wipundowak,

Joseph alone he-eats, one table-at; those those-who-are-honored those-who-serve-him also another table there all-of-them-eat, and his-brothers again another table there themselves they-dine-with-one-another,

[Luckenbach only]

eli juk nechnutemalatschik awessissall, Israelitschik nan wdelikinewo, machtelemawak talli elinquechinhittit Egyptenitschik, wentschi niskelemachtit wipomanewo ngutti ehendalipuinkgink talli.

because these these-who-watch-them animals, the-Israelites that they-thus-raise, they-despise-them in in-their-presence the-Egyptians, so-that they-think-they-are-dirty (if) they-dine-with-them one table-at there.

Er sezte sie aber mit Fleiß, wie sie waren geboren worden, welches ihnen recht wunderlich vorkam.

Nane Joseph wimachtall wulelemelendamook, kikeyit ika lappo, nane wuntschi giechgi elhiga'kil, nane wuntschi ahanhucqui elhigawachtitschik elgiquejeitschik, teek petschi tenksisit wtenk achpo.

Then Joseph his-brothers they-wonder-about-it, the-elder there he-thus-sits, that from close {his-subordinates}, then from over-and-over-again {those-who-are-near-to} those-who-are-like-as, {there} unto the-little-one lastly he-is-there.

Sie faßen aber an einem Tische besonders, weil die Egypter mit den Hebräern nicht zu speisen pflegten.

[Not translated into Delaware, here, but mentioned in Luckenbach's account previously.]

Das essen aber ward ihnen von Josephs Tische vorgetragen, und Benjamin ward fünfmal mehr vorgelegt, als den andern. Sie saßen auch so lange beysammen, bis sie alle mit einander waren trunken worden; und des andern Tages, (wie sie den Rausch ausgeschlaffen hatten,) so zogen sie mit großen Freuden wieder nach Hause.

Woak chamawak Joseph wdehendalipuingemink untschi, schuk Benjamin allowi palenachtchen lappi petawon, elgiqui lihind takanil, woak wulelendamowi mizachtowak. Nane wtenk woak menhawall welhiki besonhasikil mechmenenkil. Nane pili gischquike wulelendamowi tpittawe matscholtowak.

And they-are-fed Joseph from-his-table from, but Benjamin more five-times again he-is-brought-it, like-as they-are-done-to the-others, and gladly all-of-them-eat. Then after also they-are-given-drinks those-which-are-good {those-which-are-spiced} {drinks}. Then another when-it-is-(another)-day gladly together all-of-them-go-home.

Nützliche Lehren.
WELAPEMQUO ACHGEGINGEWOAGAN.
PRACTICAL APPLICATION.

1. Es ist gewiß, daß Gott alle Dinge zuvor weiß, ehe sie geschehen. Die Brüder Josephs fielen vor ihm nieder; und das hatte etliche Jahre vorher im Traume offenbahret.

1. Nane kitschiwi leu Patmawos nigani wtelli woaton wemi koecu eleki nesquo pejewik. Joseph wimachtineyall nundajelensuwi [85] nimigitagol. Na jun elek, Patamawossall metschi cheli gachtin talli lunquamoaganink woatelukgunep Joseph.

JOSEPH'S BRETHREN GO TO EGYPT TO BUY CORN.

1. That truly it-is-so God beforehand He-thus knows-it every thing as-they-are not-yet it-does-not-(yet)-come. Joseph his-brothers humbly **[85]** they-bowed-down-toward-him. That here as-it-is, God already many it-is-year(s) in in-dreams He-made-him-aware-of-it Joseph.

2. Das Gewissen schläft zwar eine Weile, aber zu rechter Zeit machete es auf.

2. Tamse auwen koecu pallalogasite quonna matta schai guschamandamoque talli wdehenk, ihiabtschi leu ngutten tpisquihhillaque quilalissu, wentschitsch amandank wemi koecu li elauchsitup.

2. Sometimes a-person a-thing when-he-transgresses even-if not immediately if-he-does-not-have-his-feelings-hurt in in-his-heart, still it-is-so one-time when-the-time-is-at-hand he-is-at-a-loss-what-to-do, so-that-will he-feel-it every thing toward how-he-lived.

Wie Josephs Brüder in große Roth gerathen waren, so sagten sie unter einander: Das haben wir an unserm Bruder Joseph verschulder.

Nane leep talli Joseph wimachtineyall eli wischassichtit woak littowak: Wemi jun kpatatoneen eli pallalogasijank li Chesemussenanink, eli matta ktemagelemawonk enda winuwamquongup enda mhallamagejankgup wentschitsch wachtschangussit.

That it-was-so in Joseph his-brothers as they-are-frightened and they-say-to-one-another: All this we-earn-it because we-transgress toward toward-our-younger-sibling, for not we-do-not-show-him-mercy when he-beseeched-us when we-sold-him so-that-will he-be-enslaved.

3. Die besten Complimenten sind wohl, wenn man einander aus treuem Herzen was Gutes wünschet.

3. Nall nan eet majawi allowi welhiki wawangundowoagan, wulapensohalate auwenil untschi mesitschewi wtscheyjunque wdehenk talli enda wawangomate auwenil.

3. That one perhaps rightly (is) (the) more good greeting, if-he-blesses-him who from wholly inwardly in-his-heart in when when-he-greets-him-warmly a-person.

Joseph empfieng seinen Bruder Benjamin mit diesen Worten: Gott sey dir gnädig, mein Sohn!

Nane wtellsin Joseph eli peihakquenat [?-enaxit] woak wawangomat chessemussall Benjaminall, wtenda lanep: Patamawos tgauchsittaqui N'quis!

That he-does-so Joseph as he-is-glad-to-see-him and he-greets-him-warmly his-younger-sibling Benjamin, when-he said-to-him: God let-Him-be-kind-to-you my-son!

Gottselige Gedanken.
**WELAPENDASIK PENAUWELENDAMOAGAN.
PIOUS REFLECTION.**

Es fängt bey Joseph an, sein Bruderherz zu brennen, als er mit Benjamin zum erstenmale spricht.

Nane Joseph wtallemi amandamenep wingellek wimachtintiwi ahoaltowoagan woak lingihhillelowall wdehall enda netami wawangomat woak aptonalat chessemussall Benjamin.

That Joseph he-began-to feel-it that-which-burns brotherly love and it-(anim.)-melts his-heart when first he-greets-him-warmly and he-speaks-to-him his-younger-sibling Benjamin.

Herr Jesu! dich darf ich auch meinen Bruder nennen; allein ich kenne dich noch nicht von Angesicht. Hilf Gott! wie wohl wird mir zur selben Zeit geschehen wenn ich dich sichtbarlich im Himmel werde sehen.

Wo ki nihillalijan NJesus! nepe woak ndelliechge wentschi wimachtangomellan, quonna ta nesquo neschginkunk untschi

knanewulowunep. Wo! Nihillalijan N'Patamawos, tatsch hatsch ne ndellamallessi, ta likhikqui wuschginqui newulanne Awossagame talli.

O you my-Lord Jesus! I-likewise also I-am-done-to so-that {I-am-a-friendly-brother-to-(you)}, even-if definitely not-yet by-my-eyes by I-did-not-really-see-you. O! My-Lord my-God, how-will it-will-be-asked that (will)-I-feel, definitely at-that-time face-to-face when-I-see-you Heaven in.

Die 20ste Historie.

[86] 20 ELEGUP.—2298.

---

20 AS-IT-WAS.—1414 B.C.

Wie sich Joseph seinen Brüdern zu erkennen gegeben hat. 1 Mose, 44ste und 45ste Capitel.

Joseph enda woatelat hokey [?hokeyall] necama majawi wtelli wimachtin. 1 Mos. 44, &c.

Joseph when he-makes-them-aware-of-it himself he rightly that-he is-a-brother. Genesis 44, etc.

Wie Josephs Brüder zum andernmal nach Hause ziehen wollten, so befahl Joseph seinem Haushalter, daß er ihnen die Säcke mit Speise füllen, und einem jeglichen sein Geld oben in seinen Sack frecken sollte.

Nane Joseph wimachtall lappi gatta matscholtinewo nane wtenda lan genchgitakil, lappi hattol memajauchsit monijum menutesink gischi wtschuhattasike chasquem,

Then Joseph his-brothers again want-to all-of-them-(want-to)-go-home that then-he says-to-him the-caretaker, again place-it each-one-of-them his-money in-his-sack done when-they-are-(done)-being-filled (with) corn,

Darnach sollte er Josephs silbernen Tafelbecher oben in des Jüngsten Sack legen; und das that der Haushalter den Abend vorher.

schuk ni sillebelii mechmenetawa happi hattol Benjamin menutesink. Nane schai wulagunii wtelli mikindamenep Josephall endchi lukgup; matta koecu woatowiwak.

but my of-silver my-cup in-the-bargain place-it Benjamin in-his-sack. Then immediately in-the-evening he-thus worked-it Joseph as-much-as he-told-him; not a-thing they-did-not-know-it.

Als sie nun des Morgens nur zur Stadt hinaus waren, so befahl er seinem Haushalter, daß er ihnen nachjagen sollte.

Nane elachpajeke allumsgewak, medchi pewak wikuteneyik, nane Joseph wtellawall genachgitagil, schai pachsukquil, nawall; nane allowi wundamauwan eneninktsch machtalate.

Then when-it-is-early-morning they-go-away, as-soon-as they-come (to) the-end-of-the-city, then Joseph he-says-to-him the-caretaker, immediately rise-up, pursue-them; then more he-declares-it-to-him that-which-he-will-do when-he-overtakes-them.

Wie er sie nun eingeholt hatte so sezte er sie zur Rede, warum sie das Gute mit Bösem vergotten und Joseph seinen silbernen Tafelbecher mitgenommen hätten?

Nane metalate schai guschaptonalawall wtellawall: Kiluwa quatsch medhik lissijeek [87] **enda wulatschachgussijeek, gemotgehhimo? Koecu ktelelendamenewo kakeyjuwa, wentschi ajumeek nihillalid mechmenetak?**

Then when-he-overtakes-them immediately he-chastises-them he-says-to-them: You why evil do-you-do-so [87] when you-are-treated-well, are-you-thieves? What are-you-thinking yourselves, so-that you-take-it my-lord his-cup?

[Luckenbach only]

Ta temiki wuntschi meneen, na wuntschi apui mochgamen li matta hattewi, gahena kpallawewihhimo.

Not anything from-he drinks, that-one from-he easily he-finds-it toward not it-is-not-here, surely you-transgress.

JOSEPH MAKETH HIMSELF KNOWN TO HIS BRETHREN.

Die Söhne Jacobs mußten sich gewiß, und sagten gleich: bey wem der Becher gefunden wurde, der sollte des Todes sterben, und die andern alle sollten Josephs Knechte seyn.

Nek gettemaxitschik pelachpitschik wunagatamenewo wtelli wulamoenewo, wentschitsch nechgutemichtit luewak: Sche junitsch leu, auwentsch mochgamund juk ktallogaganak, welatak mechmenetunk, nanetsch angel, woak niluna endchijenk otalogaganintsch nhakeyina, nan nihillalquon.

Those those-who-are-poor those-who-are-innocent they-trust-it that-they they-tell-the-truth, so-that-will they-answer they-say: See! this-will it-be-so, who-will he-who-(will)-be-found (of) these your-servants, he-who-has-it the-cup, then-will he-die, and we as-many-as-we-are he-will-have-as-servants ourselves, that-one your-lord.

Aber als der Haushalter alles durchfuchte, so fand sich zu allem Unglücke der Becher in Benjamins Kornsäcke.

[Luckenbach's version provides much more detail.]

Na genachgitak nechgomate wtellawall: Gohan leketsch elowejeek. Nane schai wuliechwalenanewo wdallemunsowawall woak wdaschchumui wulachenumenewawall omenutesuwawall, nane nutschi ndonasu nhittami gegeyit nane teek petschi tenksisitink.

That caretaker when-he-answers he-says-to-them: Yes let-it-be-so as-you-say. Then immediately {they-make-them-lay-down} their-animals and hastily-they they-unbind-them their-sacks, then begins-to he-(begins-to)-search at-first the-older then {there} unto unto-the-little-one.

↓↓↓

Metellen tchenol metschi latonasike woak nesquo mochgasiwi, nane wunutschi nutschque wulelendamenewo, eli litehachtit:

Metschi quilasu, npallachpuaganena mhittschiechen; nane wiechgawotschi mochgasu mechmenetak Benjamin menutesink!

Ten they-are-so-many already when-they-are-searched-thusly and not-yet it-is-not-found, then they-begin-to for-nothing they-(begin-to)-be-glad, as they-say-to-one-another: Already {it-is-looked-for}, our-innocence it-is-evident; then unexpectedly it-is-found his-cup Benjamin in-his-sack!

Die Söhne Jacobs wußsten nicht, wie das zugienge, daher zerrissen sie vor Schrecken ihre Kleider, und zogen wieder in die Stadt.

Quila likhikqui sallachgihhillewak, nane tatochgillachtonewo equichtit eli nachpi amangeuchtumichtit [L.,-amangiechummichtit], woak lappi wemi wdukiwak utenink li Joseph wikit.

At-a-loss at-that-time they-are-terrified, {they-tear-them-to-shreds} their-clothes as with-it {they-weep-greatly}, and again all they-turn-back to-the-city to Joseph his-house.

Wie sie zurück kamen, und auf ihren Knien lagen, so redete sie Joseph an und sprach: Wie habt ihr das thun dürfen? Wisset ihr nicht, daß ein solcher Mann wie ich bin auch verborgene Dinge errathen könne?

Nane wtenda pehuwen, woak schai neli nischitquitaguk elinquechink talli, necama ahi guschaptonalawall; wtellawall: Quatsch jun lissijeek? Matta ksi gowoatuwunewo, elsit lenno ni elsija, eli wemi koecu nitai mochgama?

Then there-he waits, and immediately while they-kneel-down-to-him in-his-presence in, he extremely he-upbraids-them; he-says-to-them: Why this do-you-do-so? Not pray do-you-not-know-it, as-he-acts a-man I as-I-act, how every thing skillfully I-find-it?

Seine Brüder konnten nichts darauf sagen, sondern Juda sprach im Namen aller: Gott hat die Missethat deiner Knechte funden, siehe, wir und bey dem der Becher funden ist, sind meines Herren Knechte.

JOSEPH MAKETH HIMSELF KNOWN TO HIS BRETHREN.

[Once again, Luckenbach gives a more detailed version of Hübner's German, here, rather than a direct translation.]

Nane angellowi ganschamallsowinaxinewo wimachtall, tacu koecu kaski lueiwak, nane Juda schuk nechoha wdaptonelchawall wimachtall lue: Koecu a ntellaptonalawuna nihillalquenk? Ta hatsch a [88] nuntschi geschiechachgenimaneen nhakeyena?

Then deathly they-appear-astonished his-brothers, not a-thing able-to they-are-not-(able-to)-say, then Judah only alone he-speaks-for-them his-brothers he-says: What could we-speak-to-him our-lord? How it-will-be-asked could **[88]** we-thereby (could)-we-clearly-relate-it ourselves?

↓↓↓

Noli woatoneen koecu wentschi meschigaquenk jun juke enda sacquauchsijenk. Gettanittowit guschaptonalawall ktallogaganall, ngutti mchinqui pallawewoagan mikindamenkgup! Penna niluna woak na mechgamund mechmenetunk wemi wachtschanihhena ki Nihillalijenk.

Well-we we-know-it a-thing so-that it-draws-near-to-us this now where we-have-a-troublesome-life. The-Great-Spirit He-chastises-them your-servants, one great transgression we-worked-it! Behold we and that one-who-is-found (with) the-cup all we-are-slaves (to) you our-lord.

Joseph sagte darauf: Das sey ferne von mir: der Mann, bey dem der Becher funden ist, der soll mein Knecht seyn: ihr aber zieht hin mit Frieden zu eurem Vater.

Joseph lue: Ta a kaski ne lewi, tacu pechowatei ntelli a lissin, na lenno eli mogamund mechmenetunk, nanitsch eli wachtschanak, schuk kiluwa nalai matschik gochuwawink li.

Joseph he-says: Not could able-to that it-(could)-not-be-(able-to)-be-so, not {it-is-not-near} that-I could do-so, that man as he-is-found (with) the-cup, that-one-will for I-enslave-him, but you safely go-home to-your-father to.

Darüber erschrack nun niemand so sehr als Juda, weil er für Benjamin gut gesagt hatte. Er bat deswegen gar sehr, Joseph möchte doch ihn anstatt des jungsten Bruders zum Knechte behalten: Denn sonsten, wo sie nach Hause kamen, und Benjamin nicht mitbrächten so würden sie die grauen Haare ihres Vaters mit Herzeleid in die Grube bringen.

[Luckenbach gives his own expanded version of these events.]

Jun aptonagan ganschhittaquot talli Juda whittawakink, eli ochunk talli nachpekhamat hokey nachpi chessemusall wtellitsch lappi peschuwan,

This word it-makes-a-terrible-noise in Judah in-his-ears, because to-his-father there he-pledges-to-him his-body with his-younger-sibling that-he-will again bring-him,

↓↓↓

nane ika wteligapawin awulaptoneu lue: Nihillalijan lelemil n'nukaptonen [?n'nukt-] ki petschi kittawakink, woak katschi ktahimguwon ktallogagan, eli ki tpisqui lissian Pharao elsit.

then there he-stands-thusly he-speaks-well he-says: My-lord allow-me {?I-speak-once} you hither in-your-ear, and don't {?do-not-let-him-exasperate-you} your-servant, for you exactly you-do-so Pharaoh as-he-does.

↓↓↓

Nihillalit sche wunatochtawapannil wtallogaganall luep: Quajaqui eet gutochwihhimo, woak eet quajaqui gowimachtihhimo pili?

He-who-is-my-lord see! he-asked-them his-servants he-said: Still perhaps do-you-have-a-father, and perhaps still do-you-have-a-brother elsewhere?

↓↓↓

Nane ndelluwehhena: Ihiabtschi notochwihhena woak metschi kekeyju, ngutti woak nowimachtihhena wuskileno, gischigop metschi mihillusilide, woak chansinga matta tschitsch achpiwi, woak necama nachoha piineu ngutti gachhoesowawink untschi, woak wetochwink wtallowelemawall.

Then we-say: Still we-have-a-father and already he-is-old, one also we-have-a-brother a-young-man, he-was-born already when-he-was-very-old, and his-late-older-brother not once-more he-is-not-here, and he alone he-has-him-left-over of-their-mother of, and the-father he-values-him-more-than-others.

↓↓↓

Nane ki ktellanep ktallogaganak: Undach pescho nolilawehantsch; schuk niluna ndellawuna Nihillalit: Na wuskino, ta kaski ngallawiwall ochwall, ngallate a, angellelowalltsch ochwall; aschitte ktellanep ktalloguganak:

Then you you-said-to-them your-servants: This-way bring-him I-will-comfort-him; but we we-say-to-him my-lord: That young-man, not able-to he-is-not-(able-to)-leave-him his-father, if-he-(would)-leave-him (would), he-will-die his-father; then you-said-to-them your-servants:

↓↓↓

Matta peschuwaeque kchessemusowa, ta tschitsch knemowunewo neschkink. Nane ndallemusganenap li ktallogaganink nochenanink woak ndatschimolchawunap [89] nihillalid endchi pendamenk.

Not if-you-do-not-bring-him your-younger-sibling, not once-more you-do-not-see-it my-face. Then we-went-away to to-your-servant to-our-father and we-related-to-him **[89]** my-lord as-much-as we-hear.

↓↓↓

Nane tamse ngutten nochena ntelguna: Lappi ika loltik, woak mhallamoo'k kechitti mitschewoagan. Schuk ntellawuna: Ta kaski ne lewi, gintsch n'chessmussena witscheuchquenque, eli matta a kaski nemowenk na lenno wuschgink, matta witscheuchguwenkque chessemusena.

Then sometime once our-father he-says-to-us: Again there all-of-you-go, and buy a-little food. But we-say-to-him: Not able-to that it-is-not-(able-to)-be-so, unless our-younger-sibling if-he-goes-with us, because not would able-to we-(would)-not-be-(able-to)-see-it that man his-face, not if-he-does-not-go-with-us our-younger-sibling.

↓↓↓

Nan ktallogagan Noch, ntellguna: Gowoatonewo naga wikimakpana, wtelli schuk nischa gischigopanil nquisall. Mauchsu nhakenk untschi allumsgep woak luen: mehoapanna, woak juke shaki matta tschitsch newoawi.

That-one your-servant my-father, he-says-to-us: You-know-it that-late-one my-late-deceased-wife, that-she only two they-were-born my-sons. He-is-one from-myself from he-went-away and it-is-said: he-was-eaten, and now until not once-more I-do-not-see-him.

↓↓↓

Na piinet juke nhakenk untschi allumochwaleque, woak winhattaguwoagan pemishigak, allamhakinktsch kpetonewo newoaphoquawunall machtschigamikunk nachpi schiwelendamoagan.

That-one who-is-left-over now from-myself from if-he-is-taken-away, and danger {it-meets-him}, under-the-earth-will you-bring-it my-gray-hairs to-the-graveyard with sorrow.

JOSEPH MAKETH HIMSELF KNOWN TO HIS BRETHREN.

↓↓↓

Nane wuntschi juke lappi ika pajane ktallogagan nooch epit, woak matta ika peschuwawachge wuskileno, eli wtschitschank li glitat won wtschitschangunk,

That from now again there if-I-go your-servant my-father where-he-is, and not there if-I-do-not-bring-him the-young-man, as his-soul to he-clings-to-him this-one to-his-soul,

↓↓↓

natsch ne leu, nenke wtelli matta achpiwon ehoalatschi, wuntschitsch angellen, woak niluna ktallogaganak npetonentsch woaphocquawunall ktallogagan nochena li alamhakie.

then-will that it-(will)-be-so, when-he-sees-it that-he not he-is-not-there him-whom-he-loves, thereby-will-he die, and we your-servants we-will-bring-them the-gray-hairs (of) your-servant our-father to under-the-earth.

↓↓↓

Nane ntellsin ni, nachpekhama nhakey talli nochunk, ntellitsch lappi peschuwan n'chessemus, woak ndellap: matta lappi petolowane wuskino, ni nhakenk hatteketsch mandundowoagan, sekitsch lehellecheja.

That I-do-so I, I-pledge-to-him myself there to-my-father, that-I-will again bring-him my-younger-sibling, and I-said-to-him: not again if-I-do-not-bring-him-to-you the-young-man, I in-myself let-it-be-there the-blame, so-long-as-will I-live.

↓↓↓

Ulaha lelem ktallogagan, jun ndappin, wulapachpinall nchessemusall, wentschi wedallogaganid nihillalid, woak lelem won wuskino nalai witschewotetsch wimachtall.

Better allow-him your-servant, here I-stay, he-replaces-him my-younger-sibling, so-that he-is-his-servant my-lord, and allow-him this young-man safely let-him-go-with his-brothers.

↓↓↓

Ta hatsch ndennumen matschieane li nochunk woak ehoalatschil quisall matta witscheuchguwenque? Ta a nkaski litehai, ni nemen a Nooch enda aptelendank. Nane [90] **pachkantschi tepelendamen Joseph endchi pendanke.**

How it-will-be-asked do-I-do-it if-I-go-home to to-my-father and him-whom-he-loves his-son not if-he-does-not-go-with-us? Not could I-(be)-able-to I-(could)-not-(be-able-to)-think, I I-(would)-see-it would my-father when he-grieves-to-death. Then [**90**] entirely (he)-is-satisfied-by-it Joseph as-much-as as-he-hears.

Endlich konnte sich Joseph nicht länger halten, soondern ließ jedermann hinaus gehen, und sagte darnach zu seinen Brüdern, wie sie ganz alleine bey ihm waren: Ich bin Joseph, eure Bruder; lebet mein Vater noch?

[Luckenbach's expanded version]

Wtelli newoan wimachtall elgiqui wdehii schielendamowitehachtit, eli pallalogasichtitup li hokenk; woak lappi pili wtellinawawall juke, elgiqui allowi gachta wulilawehachtit ochuwawall, lamoe elihachtitup.

He-thus sees-them his-brothers like-as heartily they-repent, how they-transgressed toward toward-himself; and again otherwise he-observes-them now, like-as more want-to they-(want-to)-comfort-him-(more) their-father, long-ago than-they-did-to-him.

↓↓↓

Nane poquihillalin wdehall, hokewawink li, nane alai tschitanitehe allowi li. Nane wiechgawotschi ganschalamo lue: Schai ktschik endchijeek Egyptenijeek;

That it-(anim.)-is-broken his-heart, toward-themselves toward, then in-vain does-he-stand-firm-in-mind more towards. Then unexpectedly he-cries-out he-says: Immediately go-out as-many-as-you-are you-who-are-Egyptians;

↓↓↓

nane wunutschi amangeuchtumen, wdallogakanall kotschemink untschi tepi pendagol, lue: Ni Joseph nhakey, lalamo, ni Joseph! Quajaqui eet lehellecheu Nooch?

then he-begins-to weep-greatly, his-servants outside from enough they-hear-him, he-says: I (am) Joseph myself, he-cries-out-thusly, I (am) Joseph! Still perhaps does-he-draw-breath my-father?

Seine Brüder konnten ihm kein Wort darauf antworten, so sehr waren sie vor hieß sie näher zu sich treten,

Schuk wimachtall tacu kaski nachgomguwiwall, eli sallachgihillachtit endchi ganschipendawachtit, tacu kaski nguttaptonewiwak. Nane ahoaltuwi quihimawall, wdellawall: Undach ligapawik! nhakenk paak! Woak ika petschigapawinewo;

But his-brothers not able-to they-are-not-(able-to)-answer, because they-are-terrified so-much-as they-hear-him-in-amazement, not able-to they-are-not-(able-to)-speak-one-word. Then lovingly he-encourages-them, he-says-to-them: This-way stand-towards! To-myself come! And there they-stand-hither;

und sagte zu innen: Sie sollten sich darum nicht bekümmern, daß sie ihn verkaufet hätten: den um ihres Lebens willen hätte ihn Gott vor ihnen hergesandt. Es wären noch fünf theure Jahre vor der Thüre, also sollten sie nach Hause reisen, und mit ihrem Vater ohne Verzug nach Egypten kommen, da sollten sie im Lande Gosen wohnen, und reichlich von ihm versorget werden.

[Luckenbach's more detailed version]

woak wtellapanil: Ni Joseph nhakey kimachtowa, nall won eli mhallamagejekgup li Egyptenink, katschi sacquelendankhek, katschi awisachki litehaheek: nemanunkgitaguna, eli mhallamagejeekgup nhakey.

and he-said-to-them: I (am) Joseph myself your-brother, that this-one as you-sold to to-Egypt, don't do-not-be-troubled-in-mind, don't seek-cause-to do-not-(seek-cause-to)-think: he-is-angry-with-us, because you-sold myself.

↓↓↓

Ni ntelli penamen Gettanittowit elelemit, wentschi jun paja, kiluwa wentschi lehellechejeek, elitsch quajaqui tschitsch palenchtchi gachtinewitsch matta koecu gischikenowi, woak mawottagan allumsgejuju.

I I-thus look-at-it the-Great-Spirit how-He-allows-me, so-that here I-come, you so-that you-live, for-will still once-more five-so-many of-years-will not a-thing it-will-not-mature, and famine it-goes-on.

↓↓↓

Tacu kiluwa ktellihiwunewo, ni nowoaton Patamawos megungi nigani npetalogalgun na ju talli, wentschitsch putameek untschi mchinqui winhattaguwoaganink, woak wentschitsch tachpalak Pharao nahelii wemi Egyptenitschik, woak ntelli allowelemuxin, wemi talli elemamek haki Egypten.

Not you you-do-not-do-it-to-me, I I-know-it God purely beforehand he-sends-me-hither there here in, so-that-will you-escape from great danger-from, and so-that-will I-maintain-him Pharaoh together-with all Egyptians, and that-I am-more-esteemed, all there all-over the-land Egypt.

↓↓↓

JOSEPH MAKETH HIMSELF KNOWN TO HIS BRETHREN.

Nane gihimawall wtellawall. Schauwelendamook, [91] **ika aak nochunk, mawi lo wulelendamowaptonamik: Quis Joseph quajaqui lehellecheu,**

Then he-encourages-them he-says-to-them: Hurry, [91] there go to-my-father, go-and tell-him the-glad-tidings: Your-son Joseph still he-lives,

↓↓↓

undach all ni epia, nahelii wemi epitschik wikian, endchangundijank, woak petschi nachpochwel, wemi endchi nihillalatt woak nihillataman, katschi wauchtamsihan.

this-way go I where-I-am, together-with all those-who-are-there where-you-dwell, as-many-as-are-related-to-us, and hither take-them-along-also, all as-many-as those-whom-you-own and those-which-you-own, don't do-not-tarry.

↓↓↓

Haki enda luwunsik Goshen kdappintsch pechotschi epia, ki woak knitschanak woak gochwissak, wuskchummook woak kikechumook. Nitsch nihillatschi ktenda tachpalellen, eli tschitsch palenachtchi gachtinewi mawottakanik, wentschitsch matta wiqualamoiwun, woak wemi epitschik wikian.

The-land where it-is-called Goshen you-will-be-there close-by where-I-am, you and your-children and your-grandchildren, young-animals and old-animals. I-will myself you-there I-(will)-maintain-(you), as once-more five-so-many of-years there-is-famine, so-that-will not you-(will)-not-suffer-hunger, and all those-who-are-there where-you-dwell.

Darauf fiel er seinem Bruder Benjamin um den Hals, und Benjamin weinte auch an seinem Halse.

Nane wdehii okikochquenawall majawi chessemusall Benjaminall woak lupakgup, woak ma aschundei lupakgopannik.

Then heartily he-hugs-him-around-the-neck proper his-(proper)-younger-sibling Benjamin and he-wept, there-it-lies! alternating they-wept.

[Luckenbach only]

Nane takquakil wimachtall mosktonamawall, woak maimawall, nek gulenatschihillewak wentschi aptonalachtit, woak tacu kaski mochgamoiwak aptonagan enda tepilawemachtit, eli bischi gachta penundelachtit, elgiqui schiwelendamoitehachtitup, woak juke elgiqui genamachtit woak ahoalachtit.

Then the-others his-brothers he-kisses-them, and he-reconciles-them, those {they-are-refreshed} so-that they-speak-to-him, and not able-to they-are-not-(able-to)-find-it a-word where they-satisfy-him, for to-be-sure want-to they-(want-to)-show-him, like-as they-repented, and now like-as they-thank-him and they-love-him.

Er beschenkte darnach seine Brüder einen jedweden mit einem Feyerkleide. Benjamin aber gab er fünf Feyerkleider, und noch darzu dreyhundert Silberlinge.

Nane Joseph milan wemi memajauchsitschi ngutti welhik ehachquink, schuk Benjaminall milawall nachapachki tchi phakei sillebelall woak palenachtcheleneyachgattol welhiki ehachquinki.

Then Joseph he-gives-it-to-them all each-one one good garment, but Benjamin he-gives-it-to-him three-hundred so-many pieces (of) silver and there-are-five-different-sorts (of) those-which-are-good garments.

Seinem alten Vater schickte Joseph zugleich zehn Esel mit Getreide.

Woak milawall Ochwall; metellen tchoak kwechquoanitawakatschik endchi najundamichtit, wewulikil latschessowoaganall Egyptenink

wentschijeyikil; woak lappi pili metellen tchoak kwechquoanitawakatschik nejundankgik mitschewoagan.

And he-gives-it-to-him his-father; ten they-are-so-many donkeys as-many-as they-carry-on-their-backs, those-which-are-really-good possessions of-Egypt those-which-are-of; and again another ten they-are-so-many donkeys those-who-carry-it-on-their-backs food.

Zulezt gab er ihnen eine gute Regel mit auf die Reise, und sagte zum Abschiede: Zanket nicht auf dem Wege.

Nane mamtschitsch enda wangomat wimachtall, nan wtellawall, quitelawall: Katschi gageloltihek nawotschi li elemiechink, woak katschi koecu achgenindihek, ochpenindihek, ninutschi elsijeekgup [92] **medhik, woak nalai paak Gochena epit.**

Then lastly when he-salutes-them his-brothers, that-one he-says-to-them, he-warns-them: Don't do-not-quarrel-with-one-another {along-the-way} towards by-the-way, and don't a-thing do-not-blame-one-another, {do-not-take-revenge-on-one-another} before-now as-you-did **[92]** that-which-is-evil, and safely come (to) our-father where-he-is.

Wie sie nach Hause kamen, so sagten sie zu ihrem alten Vater: Dem Sohn Joseph lebet noch und ist ein Herr über ganz Egyptenland.

Nane wulelendamowi matscholtowak, woak ika peachtite ochuwawall epit wiquahemink, amangiechsowak, wtellawall ochuwawall: Quis Joseph quajaqui pommauchsu, woak wtelli kigeyjumhen wemi elemamek haki Egypten!

Then joyfully all-of-them-go-home, and there when-they-come their-father where-he-is in-the-house, they-shout, one-says-to-him their-father: Your-son Joseph still he-is-alive, and he-governs all all-over-the-land Egypt!

Jacob aber glaubte es nicht eher, bis er die Wagen sahe, die ihm sein Sohn Joseph zugesendet hatte. Darauf ward sein Geist ganz lebendig, und sagte: Ich habe genug, daß mein Sohn Joseph noch lebet: ich will hin, und will ihn sehen.

[Luckenbach's expanded version]

Schuk ehoalgussit hilusis Jacob jun pendanke, ta a kaski wulistamowun eli wsami ganschelendank, woak wulelendank, eli wdehall miqui ta palliliechenelitup,

But he-who-is-loved the-old-man Jacob this when-he-hears-it, not could able-to he-(could)-not-be-(able-to)-believe-it for excessively he-is-amazed, and he-is-glad-about-it, as his-heart often definitely {it-(anim.)-fainted-away},

↓↓↓

tacu olsittawawiwall, liteheu: gelunewoaganall npendamenall, tacu woawelendamowi, woak wemi elsittank wtellelendamen taat lunquamoagan, gintsch newote nel tetuptschehellasall,

not he-does-not-believe-it, he-thinks: lies I-hear-them, not he-is-not-sure, and all as-he-listens-to-it he-thinks-of-it as-if a-dream, until when-he-sees-them those wagons,

↓↓↓

woak nenke nel miltowoaganall Joseph elogemuitschil, eluetschil: matschachtook nooch, nane wdallemi gulenatschihhellan, wtellsin elsit auwen wtallumi wuski lehellechet woak luen:

and when-he-sees-them those gifts Joseph those-which-he-sends, as-he-says: Carry-them-home (to) my-father, then he-begins-to {be-refreshed}, he-does-so as-he-does a-person he-begins-to anew he-(begins-to)-live-(anew) and says:

↓↓↓

JOSEPH MAKETH HIMSELF KNOWN TO HIS BRETHREN.

Juke ntepelendam, gahane ntepelendam, nquis Joseph eli quajaqui pommauchsit, schai ika nda, gohan nan ndellsin schai nemauwi newoan, nesquo angellowa.

Now I-am-satisfied, surely I-am-satisfied, my-son Joseph how still he-lives, immediately there I-go, yes that-one I-do-so immediately I-go-to see-him, not-yet I-do-not-(yet)-die.

↓↓↓

Nane schai wetschpo Jacob nahelii wemi wikit epitschik woak wemi endchi nehellatank, wentschi allumsgat, untschi enda Mamre enda luwundasik, woak pejate Bersabaink, pemamek kikhigan schawanewunk undachqui haki Canaan, nane wdenda nagihhillan, wihomawall naga ochuwawunga Isaaca OPatamawossall,

Then immediately he-dresses Jacob together-with all his-house those-who-are-there and all as-much-as that-which-he-owns, so-that he-goes-away, from where Mamre where it-is-called, and when-he-comes to-Beer-Sheba, that-which-is-in-a-line (with) the-border on-the-south on-this-side (of) the-land Canaan, then there-he stops, he-sacrifices-to-Him his-deceased-father the-late-Isaac his-God,

↓↓↓

woak winuwamawall wentschi penundeluxit petschi wdehenk Patamawos elitehat, wentschitsch a schachachgelendank tatsch elsit, nesquo nekachtumo'k jun haki, eli nigani wundamundup nek hokenk untschi ahanhucqui gischigitschik, wtelli nihillatamenewotsch.

and he-beseeches-Him so-that he-is-shown hither in-his-heart God what-He-thinks, so-that-in-the-future could he-be-sure-of-it definitely-in-the-future how-he-(will)-act, not-yet he-does-not-(yet)-leave-it this land, because beforehand he-was-shown those from-himself from over-and-over-again those-who-are-born, that-they they-will-own-it.

↓↓↓

Nane Patamawos pendawawall, eli achgettemagelid, wuneichquitawan [93] nipaii, nischen wentschiman, lan: Jacob! Jacob!

Then God He-hears-him, because He-is-merciful, {He-is-seen-with-him} **[93]** by-night, twice he-is-called, he-is-told: Jacob! Jacob!

↓↓↓

Nane nechgutinke lue: Jun ndappin: Woak wtellgol: Ni Gettanittowit nhakey, naga Gochuwa OPatamawosin nhakey! Katschi quitankhan, ejajan Egypten, natsch ne ktenda lihellen wikijan, wdendatsch ahanhucqui gischigintsch, wentschitsch allumikichtit mechinqui Elhakewitink.

Then when-he-answers he-says: Here I-am-here: And He-says-to-him: I (am) the-Great-Spirit Myself, that-late-one your-father is-his-God Myself! Don't do-not-dread-it, where-you-go Egypt, then-will that you-then I-do-it-to-(you) your-house, there-will-he over-and-over-again will-be-born, so-that-will they-grow great in-his-tribe.

↓↓↓

Nitsch nihillatschi kwitschewul Egyptenink li; Joseph metachquinquenuktsch ika talli, woaktsch nan kakey allalehellechejuwike, nalltsch jun npeton, woak nektsch kakenk wentschijeyitschik npeschuwawak lappi jun hakink.

I-will Myself I-(will)-go-with-you to-Egypt to; Joseph he-will-cover-your-eyes there in, and-will that-one your-body when-it-expires, then-will here I-bring-it, and those-will from-yourself those-who-are-from I-(will)-bring-them again this to-(this)-land.

↓↓↓

Nane wemchomsink metschi mischeninke jul elinaquo majawelendamoagan, nalai pachsucquin, wtallemusgan. Nane

JOSEPH MAKETH HIMSELF KNOWN TO HIS BRETHREN.

metschi pechotschi pachtite nane lan Juda: Ki niganihhilla, mauwi amaman Joseph, ktelli metschi pechotschi paneen.

Then the-grandfather already when-he-receives-it these those-which-look-like a-certainty, safely he-rises-up, he-goes-away. Then already close-by when-they-come that he-is-told Judah: You go-before, go-and notify-him Joseph, that-we already close-by we-come.

Er machte sich auch mit seinem ganzen Hause auf den Weg, welches in zwey und siebzig Seelen bestand.

Neke likhicqui nischaschtchinachge tchoak hokenk wentschije-yitschik wikit epitschik, gathagetschik Egyptenink li.

Lately at-this-time seventy they-are-so-many of-himself those-who-are-of his-house those-who-are-there, those-who-depart to-Egypt to.

Als ihm Joseph entgegen kam, sagte der Vater zu ihm: Ich will nun gerne sterben, nachdem ich dem Angesicht gesehen habe, daß du noch lebest.

[Luckenbach's version]

Nane Joseph amaminde, schai wdapishigawawall li Goschenink, tetuptschehellasink achpop eli schauwelendank. Newote ochwall okikochquenawall eli wangomat, woak quin lubak.

Then Josesph when-he-is-notified, immediately he-goes-to-meet-them to to-Goshen, in-the-wagon he-was-there because he-is-in-a-hurry. When-he-sees-him his-father he-hugs-him-around-the-neck as he-greets-him, and a-long-time he-weeps.

↓↓↓

Na hilusis Jacob, eli metschi nischinachgetchi gachtinewi allowiwi wimbenemat jul husca ehoalatschi Quisall, eli abtschi nachpi quieseuchtinkgup,

That old-man Jacob, as already twenty-so-many of-years more he-has-sympathy-for-him this-one exceedingly him-whom-he-loves his-son, because always in-addition he-wept-for-his-son,

↓↓↓

juke enda neuchtichtit, wtellawall Josephall eli wachtschuwiechinelid wdehall wulelendamoagan: Nquis juke nuwingi angel, eli nema geschgink, ktelli quajaqui pommauchsin.

now when they-see-each-other, he-says-to-him Joseph because it-(anim.)-is-filled his-heart (with) joy: My-son now I-willingly die, for I-see in-your-eyes, that-you still live.

Der König Pharao befahl, daß Joseph seinen Vater und seine Brüder in dem besten Orte des Landes sollte wohnen lassen. Das that Joseph, und gab ihnen das Land Gosen ein, darinnen sie in der langwierigen Theurung gar wohl versorget werden.

[Luckenbach's much expanded version]

Nane Joseph schai lue: Nitsch koecu ntellan Pharaoh wentschitsch milgejeek haki enda nalai achpijeek. Alod kiluwa ktellanewotsch Pharaoh, lukqueque: Koecu eet wendauchsijeek?

Then Joseph immediately he-says: I-will a-thing I-(will)-say-to-him Pharaoh so-that-will you-be-given-it a-land where safely you-are-there. Yet you you-(will)-say-to-him Pharaoh, when-he-says-to-you: What perhaps do-you-live-from?

↓↓↓

Ktellawatsch: [94] **Ktallogaganak nane schuk wdihili nutemalanewo awessisall, nane nachpikineen. Jun lissijeque natsch nalai knihillatamenewo nechoha achpijeek schigi haki talli Goschenink.**

You-will-say-to-him: [94] Your-servants that only they-still-continually they-watch-them animals, that we-are-by-nature. This if-you-do-so then-will safely you-(will)-own-it alone where-you-are fine land in in-Goshen.

JOSEPH MAKETH HIMSELF KNOWN TO HIS BRETHREN.

↓↓↓

Woak nane leep endchi koecu winuwamachtit Pharaohall, wemi ktemaksittawat, apatschi luete wtellawall Josephall: Koecu wentschi a boahit gooch schitta kimachtak koecu getatamichtit?

And that it-was-so as-much-as what they-ask-him Pharaoh, all {he-hears-them-poorly}, coming-back as-he-says he-says-to-him Joseph: What so-that could {?He-be-unable-to-hit-me} your-father or your-brothers what do-they-desire?

↓↓↓

Elemamek haki Egypten ndaichtauwan, lelem enda winginamichtit enda wulik haki achpichtitetsch, nalai wikichtitetsch Goschenink talli enda gachtatamichtit.

All-over the-land Egypt {I-open-it-to-them}, allow-them where they-are-pleased-with-it where it-is-good land let-them-be-there, safely they-will-dwell in-Goshen there where they-desire.

↓↓↓

Nane wtenk untschi Joseph peschuwan Ochwall Pharao elinquechink talli. Nane welilissit mihillusis machelemuwi wawangomawall Pharaoall nachpi wulapensowoagan; Nane Sakima natutemawawall Jacoball: Kecha eet gachtinami?

Then after wards Joseph he-brings-him his-father Pharaoh in-his-presence in. Then he-does-well the-aged-one honorably he-warmly-greets-him Pharaoh with a-blessing; then the-king he-asks-him Jacob: How-many perhaps are-you-years-old?

↓↓↓

Nane Jacob wtellenummen elgiqui langomguk wemchomsink, eli laat Pharaoall: Seki pominija jun talli Pemhagamikgek metschi nguttapachki woak nachinachgetchi gachtin;

Then Jacob he-acts like-as he-is-his-friend a-grandfather, as he-says-to-him Pharaoh: So-long I-sojourn here in the-world-round-about already one-hundred and thirty-so-many it-is-year(s);

↓↓↓

nagei woak sacquelendamowi n'lehellechen juke petschi gischquik, woak tacu n'shaki lehellechewun nemechomseninga elgiqui gunauchsichtitup nekachge tschepsitpannik ju talli Pemhagamikgek, ni elsija.

for-a-while also troubled I-live now until (to)day, and not so-long-I do-not-live my-late-grandfathers like-as they-lived-a-long-time those-deceased-ones those-who-were-strangers here in the-world-round-about, I as-I-am.

↓↓↓

Nane Jacob wulapensohenall Pharaoall nane gutschin, woak wikin woak wemi wikit epitschil talli Goschenink. Jun enda leke michmetschi nischinachge woak nischa tchapachki gachtin, peschgunktchinachge woak peschgunk, likhikqui nutschi gischelendasop haki.

Then Jacob he-blesses-him Pharaoh then he-goes-out, and he-dwells and all his-house those-who-are-there in in-Goshen. This when it-is-so {already} twenty and two so-many-hundred it-is-year(s), ninety and nine, at-that-time began-to it-(began-to)-be-created-by-thought the-Earth.

↓↓↓

Woak Joseph wuliechtauwanep ochwall woak wimachtall wemi endchichtitup, nahelii wemi wunitschanowawall. Nane wunihill-atamenewo epichtit, [95] woak nallauwi achpinewo talli Goschenink enda wulatschachgussichtit sekitsch lowihhillak mawottagan.

And Joseph he-makes-it-good-for-them his-father and his-brothers all as-many-as-they-were, together-with all their-children. That theyown-it where-they-are, **[95]** and safely they-are-there in in-Goshen where they-are-treated-well until-will it-pass-by the-famine.

Er rächete sich auch weiter an seinen Brüdern nicht, sondern sagte zu ihnen: Ihr gedachtet es böse mit mir zu machen, aber Gott gedachte es gut zu machen.

Woak Joseph tacu techi ochpenemawiwall Wimachtall eliechgukgup schuk wtellawall: Kiluwa bischi nane likhikqui enda mhallamagejeek nhakey machtschilitehenemoalihhimo schuk Patamawos gulupp-atschi husca welhik npenauwelemukgun.

And Joseph not utterly {he-does-not-take-revenge-against-them} his-brothers (for) what-they-did-to-him but he-says-to-them: You to-be-sure then at-that-time when you-sell myself you-design-evil-against-me but God {also} exceedingly that-which-is-good he-thinks-about-me.

Nützliche Lehren.
WELAPEMQUO ACHGEGINGEWOAGAN.
PRACTICAL APPLICATION.
1. Womit einer gesündiget, damit wird er gemeiniglich wieder gestraft.

1. Nane hilleu nen medhik auwen eweget wentschi gatta pallihat auwenil, nal ne medhik ta likhikqui guluppatschi meschigagun, wentschitsch nihillatschi emandank pelihatschi elihatup.

1. That commonly that evil a-person who-uses so-that wants-to he-(wants-to)-harm-him a-person, that-one that evil definitely at-that-time {also} it-draws-near, so-that-will himself he-(will)-feel-it him-whom-he-harms as-he-did-it-to-him.

Joseph war in grossen Aengsten, als er in die Grube geworfen ward; jetzo wußten hingegen seine Brüder nicht, wo sie vor Angst bleiben sollten, als sie eines Diebstahls beschuldiget wurden.

Jun knemeneen elihindup Joseph enda hakialachgunk lanechwingup husca wischasop woak anankhapasu eli wischalind. Nane wtenk untschi tpisqui wtellamallsinenewop, wipachsowak wimachtineyall enda achquimquichtit wtelli gemotgenewo nguldii mechmenetonk.

This we-see-it what-he-was-done-to Joseph when in-the-hole-in-the-ground he-was-cast exceedingly he-was-afraid and he-is-shaking-with-fear because he-is-frightened. Then after wards exactly they-felt-it-thusly, they-fear their-brother when he-blames-them that-they they-steal of-gold the-cup.

2. Gott sorget für die Frommen, auch in den größten Landplagen. Da aller Orten Hungersnoth war, so war Jacob mit seinem ganzen Hause im Lande Gosen wohl versorget.

2. Patamawos wtelli genachgihan welsittankgil enda gantschi achwi linamichtit, woak enda sakqui lek. Bischi wemi ta talli elgigunk wiwuni haki mawottaganop, nane ihiabtschi Jacob nachpi wemi nihillalatschil wikit epitschik wulitachpalgussowak talli haki Goshen elewundasik.

2. God He-thus takes-care-of-them the-believers when terribly difficult they-are-treated-so, and when troublingly it-is-so. To-be-sure all definitely there as-wide-as all-around the-Earth there-was-famine, then still Jacob with all those-whom-he-owns where-he-dwells those-who-are-there they-are-well-maintained in-the-land Goshen that-which-is-called.

3. Gott der Herr kann alles zum Besten wenden, wenn es gleich noch so böse gemeynet ist. So sagte Joseph zu seinen Brüdern, die ihn verkauft hatten: Ihr gedachtet es böse mit mir zu machen, aber Gott gedachte es gut zu machen.

3. Patamawos Tepanittowit wtellenumen wentschitsch gulupp-iechtak medhik, wentschitsch welhik untschijeyjutsch.

3. God the-Spirit-of-Sufficiency He-does-it-thusly so-that-will He-turn-it-about evil, so-that-will good it-will-be-of.

Quonna ju endalauchsit medhik penauwelendank woak medhik gotta [L., gotta] mikindamen, ihiabtschi Patamawos hitta guluppiechton machtschilitehewoagan welhikink li.

Even-if here one-who-lives-here evil he-considers-it and evil he-wants-to work-it, still God skillfully He-turns-it-about the-evil-thinking to-good to.

Nane wtellowen Joseph elatup wimachtineyall: Kiluwa bischi kmatschilitehhenemoallihhimop enda mahellamagejeekgup nhakey, alod Patamawos welhik penauwelemukguna.

That he-says Joseph as-he-says-to-them his-brothers: You to-be-sure you-designed-evil-against-me when you-sold myself, yet God that-which-is-good he-thinks-about-us.

Gottselige Gedanken.
[96] **WELAPENDASIK PENAUWELENDAMOAGAN.**
PIOUS REFLECTION.

Zwölf Kinder können sonst kaum einen Vater speisen, da doch ein Vater oft zwölf Kinder speist und tränkt;

Illi achtschingi leu tellen attach nischa Amemensak wentschitsch tachpalachtit mauchsitschi wetochwingi; ihiabtschi tepi leu ngutti wetochwink tachpalawall attach nischa unitschanall.

Still scarcely is-it-so ten plus two children so-that-will they-maintain-him he-is-one father; still enough it-is-so one father he-maintains-them ten-plus two his-children.

deswegen muß man dich, mein Joseph, glücklich preisen, der du den Vater hast mit Haus und Hof beschenkt.

Nane wentschi mchelemuxit Joseph eli nechoha tepi lissit wentschitsch milat Ochwall wemi koecu nundehellalid enda wikilid, woak uteney enda hakihelid.

That therefore he-is-honored Joseph because alone enough he-does-so so-that-will he-give-it-to-him his-father every thing he-lacks where he-dwells, and a-town where he-plants.

Wie selig will ich mich auch meines Ortes schätzen, wenn ich die Eltern einst im Alter kann ergötzen!

Welsittank amemens nechgutink lue: Nane ni ndellsin, nolhatte-namitsch tepi a hitta lennemane wentschitsch tapalak woak wuligenachgihak ngegeyjujumak petauchsichtite enda ktemakhak.

A-believer a-child who-answers he-says: That I I-do-so, I-will-store-it enough could skillfully when-I-do-so so-that-will I-maintain-them and I-take-good-care-of-them my-parents if-they-live-so-long where {it-is-pitiful}.

APPENDIX

gelelendelelenewo = {I present it to you} [1]

neckachtingil = those things which are left behind [1; 2]

ktitehalelohumo = I cause you to think [2]

patamoei = godly [5]

witapensohalgussijek = you are made to have a benefit with [7]

gulutagenewo = {?you use it well} [7]

tauwunemagejek = {you are opened to it} [9]

litasik = {it is established thusly} [10]

schigalek = it is thin [10]

elemagechink = {as the way goes through} [10]

ktemakhak = {that which is pitiful; it is pitiful} [11; 232]

aptahoalquek = {he who loves you to death} [11]

equauchsija = {I depart this life} [13]

achquispe = {comes over the water} [21]

endcheleneyachgissitschil = {as many kinds as they are} [22]

endchagewichtit = {as many tribes as they are} [22]

endchelenawachgissitschil = {as many kinds as they are} [23]

neuchgatatschil = those which are four-legged [23]

eluwelemuxit = he who is thought greatest [26]

wsamuiton = he shuts it [28]

tachquapohaltowoagan = marriage [29]

niganiechinkgi = {first ones} [29]

tequachpohalendtschi = those who are married [29]

metenumhittitup = {they finished doing it} [36]

macheleneyachi = {manifold ways} [38]

nsacquilissi = I act distressed [38]

nachgowi = {?every} [38]

ntellachwelitsch = {I will wish thusly for} [38]

laehasop = he acted thusly [42]

pemaksitschik = {those trees which are round about} [42]

wundachquaptoneu = {he speaks that way} [43]

tachgehhellewall = {they suddenly awaken} [45]

kpomsgeton = {you go on it} [48]

kmantowintsch = you will be a spirit-being [53]

nelachpichtitup = while they were there [53]

sopochwenesa = {they have walked naked} [53]

medauweget = he uses badly [54]

mchelensitak = {?it is resplendent} [54]

guluppenummauwil - {turn it around for me} [54]

luphittehan = {beats him to death} [57]

manunkhittaksu = he sounds angry [57]

nosamiechge = {it is too much for me} [59]

samileu = excessively it is so [59]

wentamemensemuxitschik = those who are children of [59;59]

guluppatschi {also} [59; 102; 229; 229]

APPENDIX

wulatagano = {?it lies well} [61]

pachsowamate = if he denies it to him [61]

petalamo = it cries out unto; it cries hither [58; 62]

ponilischimuintsch = {?will run away from} [62]

kitalteuhetup = he built a big boat [63]

gamolachgat = {it is the width} [64]

mengachtingi = of the great mountains [65]

achpamilachtan = it sails around [66]

medhikteu = {?it is a bad fire} [71]

espikhetschil = those who build up the structure [74]

dowalachtit [?ndonalachtit] = {?they seek him} [84]

nuntschen = is with child [85]

wunumikitawawall = {he bows to them} [87]

elgikuteneyik = as wide as the city is [88]

schaschgunemawak = {they are squeezing} [89]

gelchgiechgook = {he makes them laugh} [90]

tchitonall = destroys them [92]

pemhattekil = those which are thereabout [92]

sikewiachsin = a stone of salt [92]

antschi = anew [101]

gutschillachtiganehenep = {he made a trial} [101]

sogate'hemok = {he does not shed it} [102]

sesachquoak = {that which is troubling} [103]

n'chumi = my daughter-in-law [105]

ktasisguwakhakunk = in your earthen bottle [107]

wtellochwewoagan = his trip [107]

quisak = your sons; sons [68; 111]

wdanisak = daughters [111]

nischigopannil = he raised those two [113]

clami = quietly [113]

elitehenemoalat = {as he wishes to tell him} [115]

ndonamail = seek it for me [115]

wulitail = make it well for me [115]

chettitall = little hides [117]

pintschigete = when he comes inside [117]

ahimaquo = {it has a strong odor} [119]

koecuniki = those which are real [122]

wtelitehenemoalguwunep = {he did not wish it to be him} [122]

schiman = flees him [129]

machtangoman = to be mean to him [129]

allumamehhelleu = {she swiftly goes away} [135]

machtangundawoagan = {bad relations} [139]

cheluntschet = {she is pregnant many times} [141]

achquepenalguk = {he wrestles with him} [xiii; 143; 152]

nguttgi = {I am moving} [143]

niganoochachtasuall = {they are taken ahead} [145]

pachsinan = {halves-them} [146]

pachganechwin = {break him away} [147]

nanquepenaltowak = {they wrestle with each other} [147]

tschipoame = {the-hollow-of-the-thigh} [147]

tschilihillan = he has a sprain [147]

gulah = {oh that} [11; 18; 44; 148; 173]

APPENDIX

nachanaquo = {there is danger} [151]

witschgenemowon = {he does not go along with it} [154]

nguttigischquackat = {it is one day's journey} [156]

pemuteneyahetschik = those who made the towns round about [156]

atschimolchime {relate it to me in the future} (fut. imp.) [157]

quilalikhikqui = {at a loss at that time} [160]

mhukhoatonewo = {they put blood on them} [160]

liwilawemawawall [?**wulilawemawawall**] = they comfort him [161]

wsamelendank = {he feels it excessively} [161]

woalhalgeja = I am buried [161]

gagelutasuall = {?they are done repeatedly} [163]

linawot = he observes him [154; 166]

achgenenawall = {she holds fast to him} [168]

gechkpahotink = {the prison} [170]

ehachpoanha'kgil = he bakes bread for him [175; 176]

schiwelendamuwinaxinewo = they look sorrowful [176]

nischenawachki = two of the same kind [180]

mechachenneu = it is a great stream [180]

schapulinschewon = a finger-ring [186]

loquenawawall = {he put it around his neck} [186]

allumtschehellalind = he is driven away with it [186]

sakquilewall = {troubles} [187]

pibela = {off and on} [189]

tgauchsittawawon = {he is not kind to them} [196]

achgenat = {he restrains him} [196]

tschitanappilide = {when it stays strong} [196]

tgauchsittaqui = let him be kind to you [200; 204]

elhigawachtitschik = {those who are near to} [201]

otalogaganintsch = {he will have as servants} [209]

quilasu = {it is looked for} [210]

n'nukaptonen [?n'nukt-] = {?I speak once} [212]

ktahimguwon = {?do not let him exasperate you} [212]

pemishigak = {it meets him} [214]

ochpenindihek = {do not take revenge on one another} [221]

wuneichquitawan = {he is seen with him} [224]

ktemaksittawat = {he hears them poorly} [227]

boahit = {?he is unable to hit me} [227]

ndaichtauwan = {I open it to them} [227]

ochpenemawiwall = {he does not take revenge on them} [229]

www.ingramcontent.com/pod-product-compliance
Lightning Source LLC
Chambersburg PA
CBHW022120080426
42734CB00006B/196